ALL ABOARD!

Published by Times Books
An imprint of HarperCollins Publishers
Westerhill Road, Bishopbriggs, Glasgow G64 2QT
www.harpercollins.co.uk

HarperCollins Publishers
1st Floor, Watermarque Building, Ringsend Road, Dublin 4, Ireland

First edition 2021
© HarperCollins Publishers 2021
Text © Julian Holland

The majority of the text first appeared in
Amazing and Extraordinary Railway Facts (2007),
More Amazing and Extraordinary Railway Facts (2010) and
Amazing & Extraordinary Facts: Trains & Railways (2011),
all published by David & Charles.

The Times® is a registered trademark of Times Newspapers Ltd

A catalogue record for this book is available from the British Library

ISBN 978-0-00-846795-1

10 9 8 7 6 5 4 3 2 1

Printed by GPS Group, Slovenia

If you would like to comment on any aspect of this book,
please contact us at the above address or online.
e-mail: times.books@harpercollins.co.uk

www.timesbooks.co.uk

THE TIMES

ALL ABOARD!

Remembering Britain's Railways

JULIAN HOLLAND

Contents

Ex-GWR 'Manor' Class 4-6-0 No 7827 Lydham Manor skirts the beach huts at Goodrington Sands with a Kingswear to Paignton train on the Dartmouth Steam Railway in Devon.

Introduction

Randomly dip in and out of this collection of railway stories, many of them personal, which I have collected over the years. In doing so, you will find out how I came to fall in love with railways at an early age, a love which continues today. For starters here is a personal story of mine recalling one of the blackest days in the history of Britain's railways.

Crypt School, Gloucester. Wednesday 27 March 1963 was not a good day for me. As far as I can recall it was double physics followed by PE before disappearing off down to the art room for a bit of skiving – my art master, Bernie Jones, didn't seem to mind as I was probably helping out with the scenery for the school's next Shakespearean blockbuster. Out of the corner of my eye I kept a lookout for the daily train of coal empties that used to struggle up from Gloucester's Bristol Road gasworks to Tuffley Junction – the regular loco was usually Fowler '4F' 0-6-0 No 44123 and if the track was wet then we were treated to some wheel spin, stalling and sanding. With O-Levels looming my trainspotting had been somewhat limited to a few local trips, on the previous weekend hanging around Gloucester on the Saturday – two 'Jubilees' Nos 45739 *Ulster* and 45575 *Madras* – and visiting Horton Road and Barnwood sheds on the Sunday. Even by this

BELOW: *My 'Local Hero' (see pages 18–19), ex-GWR 'Castle' Class 4-6-0 No 5017* The Gloucestershire Regiment 28th 61st, *departs from Gloucester Central with an express for Paddington, c.1960.*

date it was still virtually all steam with the highlight on the Sunday being Class '9F' 2-10-0 No 92000 in ex-works condition. Little did I know that within a few years this wondrous railway scene would be swept away forever!

On the same day a hundred or so miles away to the east, the Chairman of the British Railways Board, Dr Richard Beeching, was giving a news conference in the Charing Cross Hotel on the publication that day of his report on the future of Britain's railways – entitled 'The Reshaping of British Railways' it was available from Her Majesty's Stationery Office for the princely sum of one shilling (5p). The rest is history. R.I.P. British Railways.

RIGHT: *My trainspotting notebook page for March 1963. Locomotives spotted in Gloucester and Cheltenham at the time of the Beeching Report's publication.*

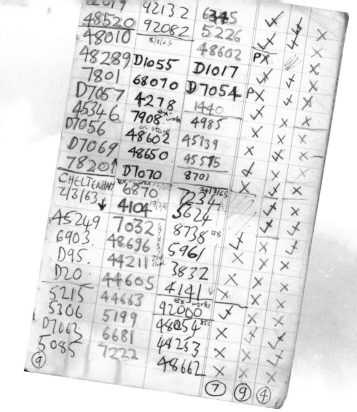

Behind the scenes

British Railways' motley collection of departmental and service locomotives

By 1961 the writing was on the wall for British Railways' large fleet of steam locomotives. The diesel invasion was underway and mass withdrawals of steam locos were taking place – however, there were a few hidden corners of this vast empire where veteran steam, diesel and electric locomotives were still hard at work. Never seen in regular service, they trundled around railway works, engineers' departments, sleeper depots or railway-owned quarries and were classed as Departmental or Service Locomotives – what a motley crew they were!

Of all the British Railways (BR) regions the Western was the most up-to-date, making use of pretty standard fare such as pannier tanks around Swindon Works and a small collection of 1950s diesel service locos – the total tally was four-coupled No 20, 0-6-0s PWM650–PWM654 and two petrol locomotives Nos 24 and 27.

The Southern Region had a more mixed bag including two 0-4-0 diesel loco No DS600 and four-wheeled Ruston & Hornsby DS1169 (Broad Clyst) and 0-6-0 No DS1173 (Engineers' Dept). There were two electric locos – DS74 (Durnsford Road power station) and DS75 (Waterloo & City line). The steam bag consisted of ex-LB&SCR/SE&CR 'A1' Class 0-6-0s DS680 and DS681 and ex-LB&SCR 'A1X' Class 0-6-0 DS681 (all three at Lancing Carriage Works) and ex-L&SWR 'G6' Class 0-6-0s DS682 (30238) and DS3152 (30272) – the last two working at Meldon Quarry.

The London Midland Region had seven 0-4-0 standard-gauge service diesels (ED1–ED7) all built by John Fowler in 1936 except ED7 which was built in 1955. ED10 was a 3ft-gauge diesel built by Ruston & Hornsby in 1955 for working at Beeston (Notts) Sleeper Depot – the loco is preserved at the Irchester Narrow Gauge Railway

Museum. The ex-L&YR works at Horwich still had an 18in-gauge system in 1961 that was operated by 1887-vintage 0-4-0 saddle tank 'Wren' (now part of the National Collection) and four-wheeled Ruston & Hornsby ZM32 (built by Ruston & Hornsby in 1957 and now preserved at the Steeple Grange Light Railway). Still carrying their LMS numbers were ex-L&YR standard-gauge 0-6-0 '2F' saddle tanks Nos 11304, 11305, 11324 and 11368. Other LMR steam locos carrying their BR numbering including 'Jinty' '3F' 0-6-0T, ex-L&YR '2F' 0-6-0ST and '3F' 0-6-0T were used as service locos at Horwich, Crewe and Wolverton Works.

The Eastern and North Eastern Regions probably had the most interesting collection of departmental locomotives. Apart from 1950s-built diesel shunters (four-wheeled Nos 52, 56, 81 and 85 and 0-6-0 Nos 88, 91 and 92) and Bo-Bo electric loco No 100, the rest were a very mixed bag of steam locos – Nos 2 and 9 were ex-GNR Class 'J52/2' 0-6-0 saddle tanks, Nos 7, 40 and 41 were Class 'Y3' four-wheeled geared Sentinel tanks, No 32 was an ex-GER Class 'J66' 0-6-0 tank, Nos 44 and 45 were ex-GER Class 'J69' 0-6-0 tanks, Nos 39 and 54 were Class 'Y1' four-wheeled geared Sentinel tanks and No 33 was an ex-GER Class 'Y4' 0-4-0 tank.

LEFT: *Southern Region Departmental Service locos at Eastleigh on 10 March 1963. On the left SR Class 'G6' 0-6-0T DS 682 (No 30238) formerly from Meldon Quarry and on the right SR Class 'A1' 0-6-0T DS 680 formerly from Lancing Carriage Works.*

BELOW: *Western Region Departmental Service Class 97 0-6-0 diesel loco PWM 650 is seen at Taunton on 22 March 1981.*

A steep climb

The Lickey Incline

Located between Barnt Green and Bromsgrove stations in Worcestershire, the Lickey Incline (named after the nearby Lickey Hills) is the steepest and most continuous standard-gauge mainline railway incline in Britain. It is 2 miles long with a gradient of just under 1-in-38 and was opened in 1840 as part of the Birmingham & Gloucester Railway. Ever since then trains have required banking assistance from locomotives (often in multiple) based at Bromsgrove. Probably the most famous of these was the Midland Railway's unique 0-10-0, nicknamed 'Big Bertha', that carried a large headlight at the top of its smokebox door. The loco served as a banker on the Lickey from 1919 to 1956. Also tried out as a banker in the 1950s was the unique LNER Class 'U1' Garratt 2-8-0+0-8-2 articulated locomotive. When the Lickey became part of the Western Region in 1958 it became commonplace for '9400' Class pannier tanks and a solitary BR Standard '9F' 2-10-0 to provide banking assistance. Class 35 diesel-hydraulics D7021–D7025 from Worcester shed replaced steam in 1965, followed by English Electric Type 3s (Class 37). By then many diesel-hauled trains could ascend the incline under their own power although very heavy freight trains still need assistance from the rear today, provided by a Class 66 diesel.

BELOW: *Banked in the rear by two WR 0-6-0PTs ex-LMS 'Jubilee' Class 4-6-0, No 45585* Hyderabad *powers its way up the Lickey Incline with a train full of holidaymakers from the West Country on 28 July 1962.*

Narrow-gauge adventure

Welsh narrow-gauge railways

Since the successful rescue of the Talyllyn Railway by a group of railway enthusiasts in 1951 (see pages 148–9), many other Welsh narrow-gauge preservation schemes have seen the light of day and are now some of the most popular tourist attractions in the principality.

Corris Railway

Opened in 1859 to transport slate from the quarries around Corris to the Cambrian mainline at Machynlleth, this 2ft-3in.-gauge line was originally worked as a horse tramway. Steam locomotives were introduced in 1879 and passenger services in 1883. In 1930 the railway was taken over by the Great Western Railway (GWR) and passenger traffic ceased a year later. Nationalised on 1 January 1948, the line ceased operating on 20 August of that year when the Afon Dyfi flooded and severely damaged the southern section. Two of the railway's steam locomotives and some goods wagons were purchased by the Talyllyn Railway in 1951 and can still be seen in operation on that railway today. Formed in 1966, the Corris Railway Society has reopened a section of line and passenger services, hauled by a new steam locomotive based on an original Corris engine, now operating from Corris to Maespoeth. The Society hopes to extend the line southwards towards Machynlleth.

Ffestiniog Railway

Opened in 1836 as a horse-drawn and gravity tramway to carry slate from the quarries at Blaenau Ffestiniog down to the harbour at Porthmadog, the 1ft-11½in.-gauge Ffestiniog Railway (see also pages 202–5) was converted to steam power in 1865. Passenger services on this independent railway were withdrawn in 1939 but goods traffic continued through to 1946 when the line closed. A preservation group was formed in 1951 and the first section of line from Porthmadog to Boston Lodge was reopened to passengers in 1955. The 13½-mile line was

BELOW: *Stored out of use at Machynlleth on 4 November 1949 are Corris Railway 0-4-2STs No 3 (built 1878) and No 4 (built 1921). They were bought by the fledgling Tallylyn Railway Preservation Society from British Railways in 1951 and can be seen at work on that line today.*

then reopened in stages to Tan-y-Bwlch, Dduallt (where a spiral was built to take the railway at a higher level past the new hydro-electric reservoir), finally reaching Blaenau Ffestiniog in 1982. Passengers are carried in Victorian rolling stock hauled by steam locomotives, including the unique double Fairlies, all of which have been beautifully restored in the company's Boston Lodge Works. Trains run on this scenic line throughout the year with a full service operating between the end of March and early November.

Vale of Rheidol Railway

Opened in 1902, this 1ft-11¾in.-gauge line was originally built to serve lead mines, the timber industry and tourism. In 1913 the Vale of Rheidol Railway was taken over by the Cambrian Railways, which in turn was absorbed by the Great Western Railway in 1922. While goods traffic had ceased by 1920, the GWR virtually rebuilt the line as a tourist attraction and modernised the locomotives and rolling stock. Temporarily closed during World War II, the railway was nationalised in 1948 and, after the end of mainline steam in 1968, became the only steam-operated line owned by British Railways. It was finally sold by BR in 1989 and the three original steam locomotives converted to oil burning. The company now operates steam-hauled trains along the scenic 11¾-mile line between the months of April and October.

Welsh Highland Railway

The Welsh Highland Railway originated as the North Wales Narrow Gauge Railway Company in 1877 and was acquired by the Welsh Highland Railway in 1923. The 22-mile line, the longest narrow-gauge line in Wales, ran through the heart of Snowdonia from Dinas Junction, south of Caernarfon, to Porthmadog via Beddgelert and the Pass of Aberglaslyn. It was not a commercial success and finally closed in 1937. In 1964 a preservation group was formed to reopen the line and, after much legal argument, the neighbouring Ffestiniog Railway was finally allowed to take on the rebuilding and operation of the line in 1995. Aided by major lottery funding and EU grants, this superb railway was completely reopened between Caernarfon and Porthmadog in 2011 – a total distance of 25 miles! Trains, mainly steam-hauled, operate throughout the year with a full service between March and end-October.

Welshpool & Llanfair Railway

One of the first railways built under the 1896 Light Railways Act, the 2ft-6in.-gauge Welshpool & Llanfair Light Railway opened in 1903 to link farming communities in the Banwy Valley with the market town of Welshpool. It has some of the steepest gradients (1-in-24) on any adhesion railway in Britain and, until closure, the last section of the line ran through the back streets of Welshpool to connect with the town's standard-gauge station. From its opening the line was operated by Cambrian Railways until absorbed into the GWR in 1923. Passenger traffic ceased in 1931 but goods traffic continued through Nationalisation in 1948 until closure by BR in 1956. A preservation group re-opened part of the line to passengers in 1963. The line was later reopened as far as Welshpool (Raven Square) where a new terminus was built on the western outskirts of the town. Steam trains are operated by a mixed bag of locomotives, including the line's two original Beyer, Peacock engines, and rolling stock from many countries around the world. Services operate from the end of March through to October.

Also see page 78 for the Snowdon Mountain Railway and pages 148–9 for the Talyllyn Railway.

There are also two other narrow-gauge railways in Wales that have been built on the trackbed of closed standard-gauge lines and one on the trackbed of a 4ft-gauge line:

Bala Lake Railway

This 1ft-11½in.-gauge railway runs along the trackbed of the former standard-gauge Bala & Dolgelly Railway, which opened in 1868. The line was finally closed by BR in 1965 and the present line was opened between 1972 and 1976. Steam and diesel passenger trains operate between April and October along 4½ miles on the eastern shore of Lake Bala between Bala and the original standard-gauge station at Llanuwchllyn.

RIGHT: *W&LR 0-6-0T No 822 (The Earl) hauls a trainload of coal and an empty cattle wagon through overgrown track in the Banwy Valley on 17 May 1956 shortly before British Railways closed the line on 5 November.*

Brecon Mountain Railway

This 1ft-11¾in.-gauge railway runs for 5 miles along part of the trackbed of the former Brecon & Merthyr Tydfil Junction Railway which opened in 1868 and was closed by BR in 1964. Construction of the present line started in 1978 and the first trains ran from Pant to Pontiscill in 1980. The line has since been extended alongside Taf Fechan Reservoir to a terminus at Torpantau just short of the site of the former B&MTJR station and beyond it the dank and dripping 666-yd Torpantau Tunnel, 1,313ft above sea level. Steam-operated passenger trains, hauled by former German and American narrow-gauge locomotives, operate between the end of March and the end of October.

Llanberis Lake Railway

The 4ft-gauge Padarn Railway was opened in 1843 to transport slate from the quarries at Llanberis to Port Dinorwic. Originally a horse-drawn tramway, the line was converted to steam haulage in 1848 and continued in use until 1961. The present 1ft-11½in.-gauge line was opened along 2 miles of the trackbed of the old Padarn Railway between Llanberis (Gilfach Ddu) and Penllyn in 1972. Since extended to Llanberis Village, passenger services, which operate between the end of March and early November, are hauled by diminutive steam locomotives that formerly worked in the nearby Dinorwic slate quarries.

Warships and Westerns

The Western Region's short-lived love affair
with diesel-hydraulic transmission

The British Railways Modernisation Programme of 1955 spelt the end of steam locomotive haulage in this country. Before prototype testing could be properly evaluated nearly 3,000 mainline diesel locomotives of many different non-standard types had been ordered by the British Transport Commission (BTC) from manufacturers, including British Railways themselves, up and down the country. Most of these locomotives were of the diesel-electric type but the Western Region, still retaining some autonomy left over from the days of Churchward and Collett, decided to favour diesel-hydraulic transmission.

Briefly, diesel-electrics are locomotives that have a diesel engine which drives a generator. The electric power produced from the generator is then used to power the wheels via electric motors. In a diesel-hydraulic locomotive the power from the diesel engine is transmitted to the wheels via hydraulic transmission through a torque converter. Following the American example, all of the regions of British Railways, apart from the Western Region, opted for diesel-electric locomotives. The Western Region, however, were favourably impressed with the reliability and performance of the German lightweight diesel-hydraulic locomotives that had been operating successfully on the Deutsche Bundesbahn since 1953. The decision to go hydraulic was made and orders were placed in 1956 to build a British version of the German V200 locomotive using German engines and transmission made under licence.

BELOW: *Built by the North British Locomotive Company of Glasgow, pioneering WR 'Warship' Class A1A-A1A diesel-hydraulic D600* Active *heads the down 'Royal Duchy' express at Exeter St David's station on 22 July 1958.*

The first to be ordered were the five Type 4 A1A-A1A 'Warships', numbered D600–D604 (later Class 41), built by the North British Locomotive Company at their Queen's Park Works in Glasgow. These entered service between January 1958 and January 1959. They were soon employed on mainline express services between Paddington and the West Country but poor reliability, high maintenance costs and incompatibility due to a non-standard design soon led to their demise. Based for most of their short lives at Plymouth Laira depot, they were soon relegated to hauling china clay trains in Cornwall. All five locomotives were withdrawn in December 1967 and subsequently scrapped. None of this type was preserved.

There then followed two batches of Type 4 B-B 'Warship' locomotives numbered D800–D870. The first batch, later known as Class 42, numbered D800–D832 and D866–D870, were built at Swindon with deliveries commencing in 1958. The second batch, D833–D865, later known as Class 43, were built by the North British Locomotive Company in Glasgow with deliveries commencing in 1960. Although much more successful than their Class 41 predecessors, both classes also suffered from poor reliability and high running costs. For some years both classes were the mainstay of motive power on mainline trains from Paddington to the West Country. The first withdrawals of Class 42 locomotives began in August 1968 and the first Class 43 was withdrawn in March 1969. The final withdrawals took place in December 1972. Two Class 42s have been preserved.

The next batch of diesel-hydraulics ordered were the 58 Type 2 B-B D6300 class (later Class 22), otherwise known as 'Baby Warships'. Designed for use on branch lines, they were built by the North British Locomotive Company but any weight savings that should have been gained by using diesel-hydraulic transmission were completely outweighed by the heavyweight chassis which was built to carry a diesel-electric setup as used in the NBR's Class 21 locos. First introduced in January 1959, the class was never popular and suffered from engine, transmission and train heating faults. Spares became difficult to obtain as the North British Locomotive Company went out of business and members of the class were cannibalised to keep the others running. The first withdrawals began in December 1967 with the last three finally retiring in January 1972. None of this type was preserved.

Introduced in 1961, the Type 3 B-B D7000 'Hymeks' (later Class 35) were certainly a vast improvement on the disastrous D6300 class. A total of 101 were built by Beyer, Peacock at their Gorton Works in Manchester. Characterised by their stylish body, colour scheme and raised cast aluminium running numbers, they were soon in use on passenger and freight trains across the region. After initially suffering from coolant and transmission problems the class eventually became the most reliable type of diesel-hydraulic used by the Western Region. Withdrawals began in September 1971 with the final members lasting until March 1975. Four members of the class have been preserved.

The final batch of mainline diesel-hydraulics to be delivered to the Western Region were the 74 elegant and stylish members of the Type 4 C-C 'Western' class. Later reclassified as Class 52, they were first introduced at the end of 1961, D1000–D1036 were built at Swindon and D1037–D1073 at Crewe. More powerful than the 'Warship' class, they were soon in charge of the Western Region's mainline expresses. Fitted with two Maybach diesel engines the class suffered from inherent design, transmission and train-heating faults and, more importantly, were, as with the other types of WR diesel-hydraulics, of a non-standard design compared to the rest of the BR network. Due for replacement by the Inter-City 125 sets, the first members of the class were withdrawn in May 1973 with the final withdrawals taking place in February 1977. Seven members of the class were purchased privately for restoration.

The final, and least well-known, type of diesel-hydraulic locomotives to be ordered were the 56 Type 1 0-6-0 D9500 class shunting and short-trip engines. Later classified as Class 14, they were built at Swindon between 1964 and 1965 and had a relatively short working life with BR. First withdrawals began in March 1968 but many members found their way to industrial railways, such as those run by British Steel and the National Coal Board. Three members of the class were later re-gauged and exported to Spain. Eight members of the class have been preserved.

So ended the Western Region's love affair with diesel-hydraulics! Taxpayers' money that was spent on this short-sighted, short-lived and selfish exercise would have been better directed towards the electrification of the mainlines to the West Country and South Wales. So much for autonomy!

Happy birthday, GWR

Celebrating the centenary of the Great Western Railway

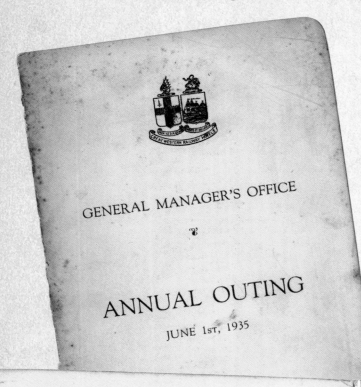

GENERAL MANAGER'S OFFICE

❧

ANNUAL OUTING

JUNE 1st, 1935

1935 was an important year for the Great Western Railway as it was exactly 100 years since the company had received its enabling Act of Parliament to build a railway between London and Bristol. Engineered by Isambard Kingdom Brunel the railway transformed communications between the two cities, providing what was then a fast and comfortable service unheard of in the days of the stage coach.

Over the next 100 years the GWR spread its tentacles to nearly every part of the southwest, south, west and mid-Wales and the Midlands. Divesting itself of Brunel's broad-gauge by 1892, the company had gone on to build world-beating steam locomotives at Swindon under the regimes of successive brilliant chief mechanical engineers – William Dean, George Jackson Churchward and Charles Collet. Joined by almost 50 more companies in the 'Big Four Grouping' of 1923 the company by then owned nearly 4,000 route miles of railway, operated a fleet of

Paddington	dep.	9.10 a.m.
Ruabon	arr.	12.58 p.m.

❧

LUNCHEON ON TRAIN

Hot Roast Lamb, Mint Sauce
Cold Ham
Cold Ox Tongue
Cold Roast Beef
Salad   Vegetables

—

Fruit Tart and Cream
Bavaroise Chocolat

—

Cheese and Biscuits

—

Coffee

❧

Leave Ruabon at 1.10 by Coach for Tour of the Vale of Llangollen. The route will be via Llangollen, Berwyn (Chain Bridge and Horseshoe Falls), Corwen and Bryn Eglwys to Dafarndywyrch at the top of the Horseshoe Pass, returning by way of Valle Crucis Abbey to Llangollen (4 p.m.)

Tea at Llangollen, leaving at 5 p.m. for
Ruabon via Fr... ...

Ruabon	dep.	5.43 p.m.
Paddington	arr.	10.5 p.m

❧

DINNER ON TRAIN

Hors d'Œuvre

—

Potage Crecy

—

Salmon Poche
Sauce Crevette

—

Roast Chicken and Bacon
Cold Meats
Vegetables

—

Pears Melba
Meringue Chantilly

—

Cheese and Biscuits

—

Salad

—

Dessert

ships, numerous commercial docks and a chain of luxury hotels and had pioneered road motor transport and airline services. By 1935 the company had become a household name and along with its loyal workforce well-deserved its title of 'God's Wonderful Railway'!

The GWR chose to celebrate its centenary in a grand fashion, befitting the status of the company, but more about this later. However, before the actual day arrived, many departments of the GWR set about organising special events for their staff.

The General Manager of the GWR Hotels department organised a cracker for his staff on 1 June. His Annual Outing consisted of a special train leaving Paddington at 9.10 a.m. and arriving at Ruabon at 12.58 p.m. En route the party were served luncheon while at Ruabon they detrained for a coach tour of the Vale of Llangollen, visiting Chain Bridge, Horseshoe Falls, Horseshoe Pass and Valle Crucis Abbey. On their return they stopped at Llangollen for tea before boarding their train at Ruabon for the return journey to Paddington. After departing at 5.43 p.m. the party was served a splendid dinner before arriving back in London at 10.05 p.m.

The big day, 31 August, arrived and the GWR had spared no expense in celebrating this milestone. A grand commemorative luncheon was held in the Great Hall of Bristol University. The 400 or so invited guests were treated to a no-expenses-spared slap-up lunch complemented by a 1929 Liebfraumilch, 1926 Perrier Jouet, Crofts 1917 Bristol Milk and Augier Frères 8 Star brandy. After the luncheon there were toasts to 'The King', 'The Great Western Railway' and 'The Guests'.

Guests of honour at the top table included the GWR Chairman and politician Sir Robert Horne, Harold Macmillan MP, Lord Portal, Lord Dulverton, the Marquess of Bath, the Lord Mayor of Bristol, Sir James Milne (GWR General Manager), Lord Apsley and Lord Mildmay. Seated on Table 8, just in front of the top table, was Mr C. B. Collett (Chief Mechanical Engineer of the GWR) and over on Table 25 was a certain Mr F. W. Hawksworth. In addition to politicians and other GWR luminaries other guests included representatives of the national newspapers and *The Engineer* magazine and the cartoonist Mr W. Heath Robinson. The latter had just published his famous and eccentric 'Railway Ribaldry' at the request of the GWR.

LEFT: *The mouthwatering menu of the GWR's General Manager's Annual Outing from Paddington to the Vale of Llangollen on 1 June 1935.*

BELOW: *A host of dignitaries, politicians and celebrities attended the Commemorative Luncheon in Bristol on 31 August 1935 to celebrate the centenary of the Great Western Railway.*

GREAT WESTERN RAILWAY CENTENARY
1835——1935

COMMEMORATIVE LUNCHEON

In the Great Hall Bristol University August 31st, 1935

My local hero

No 5017

As a small lad growing up in Gloucester I wasn't really aware of a major conflict going on nearly halfway round the world. Back in the early 1950s when I was knee-high to a grasshopper our local boys in the Gloucestershire Regiment were part of the United Nations (mainly US) forces that were grappling with the Communist Chinese-backed North Korean invasion of South Korea. The savage fighting swung back and forth up the Asian peninsula until there was a stalemate, followed by protracted peace talks and an armistice, which was signed on 27 July 1953.

However, one action in Korea has since passed into legend and was soon to be recognised by the management of the Western Region of British Railways. In April 1951 the A, B, C and D Companies of the 1st Battalion, Gloucestershire Regiment, along with the Royal Northumberland Fusiliers, the Royal Ulster Rifles and a Belgian battalion were strategically positioned on hilltops overlooking the Imjin River, north of Seoul – their task was to hold back the massed hordes of Chinese soldiers who were threatening to take the South Korean capital for the second time in a year.

Led by their Commanding Officer, Colonel Fred Carne, the Glosters held out on their hilltop (appropriately named Gloucester Hill) against waves of thousands of Chinese soldiers, inflicting enormous casualties on them. Finally surrounded by the enemy, withdrawal was well-nigh impossible for the Glosters so they courageously fought on until their ammunition ran out. In their hundreds the survivors were finally rounded up by the Chinese and sent off to spend more than two years in appalling prisoner-of-war camps in the North. The Glosters' heroic stand on Gloucester Hill has since gone down in the annals of military history.

Eventually released from their prison camps in North Korea, the survivors of the Gloucestershire Regiment – including Colonel Carne, who had spent most of the time in solitary confinement – arrived back home to a rapturous welcome from the people of Gloucester. As a young lad I can well remember watching the 'Glorious Glosters' marching through the streets of the city, the indomitable Colonel Carne at their head, for a service of thanksgiving in the cathedral. The regimental colours along with a wooden cross carved by Colonel Carne while in prison camp can still be seen in the cathedral today.

Flash back to July 1932 when the GWR's latest 'Castle' Class 4-6-0 No 5017 St Donat's Castle emerged sparkling new from Swindon Works. The loco spent the next 22 years working express trains out of Paddington until the Western Region of British Railways decided to honour the heroic Glosters' stand at the Imjin River by renaming the locomotive. Fitted with one of the largest brass nameplates on any ex-GWR loco, No 5017 was renamed *The Gloucestershire Regiment 28th 61st* at a ceremony in April 1954 and appropriately spent the rest of its working life allocated to Horton Road shed in Gloucester.

I have many happy memories of this locomotive, which I saw on a regular basis on the way to and from school each day, often working the 8.19 a.m. 'Cheltenham Spa Express' from Gloucester Central to Paddington and return. Displaced by 'Warship' diesel hydraulics, No 5017 was finally withdrawn in September 1962 after covering nearly 600,000 miles in its lifetime and was ingloriously cut-up at Cashmore's scrapyard in Newport. One of the two enormous brass nameplates along with the Sphinx badge and a cabside numberplate can be seen in the Soldiers of Gloucestershire Museum in the old Custom House in Gloucester Docks. I wish I owned the other one!

LEFT: *My 'Local Hero' ex-GWR 'Castle' Class 4-6-0 No 5017 is seen here at Old Oak Common shed c.1953 when it was still named St Donat's Castle. It was renamed* The Gloucestershire Regiment 28th 61st *in April 1954.*

BELOW: *The nameplate of No 5017 also features the Egyptian Sphinx battle honour to commemorate the 28th and 61st Regiments of Foot holding the line against the French at the Battle of Alexandria on 21 March 1801. One of the nameplates can be seen today at the Soldiers of Gloucestershire Museum in the Old Custom House in Gloucester Docks.*

Reservoir dogs

Two corporation-owned water works railways

Towards the end of the 19th century the need for dependable and clean water supplies for the growing industrialised cities of Britain led several city corporations to look further afield. The building of reservoirs by damming remote rural valleys was a triumph of Victorian engineering which has stood the test of time. The construction of these dams, reservoirs and aqueducts required vast amounts of raw material and construction workers. The sites of the reservoirs were often in remote regions that had poor roads so the building of a railway to carry workers and construction materials was the only answer. Here are the stories of two of these railways.

The Elan Valley Railway

Owned and operated by the Birmingham Corporation Water Department, the standard-gauge Elan Valley Railway was opened in 1896. From a junction with the Cambrian Railways' Mid-Wales line just south of Rhayader the 'mainline' extended for 9 miles up the remote Elan Valley to the site of the furthest dam at Craig-Coch. At its maximum extent, including branch lines and sidings, the railway extended to 33 miles, serving construction sites for dams at Craig-Coch, Penygarreg, Carreg-ddu and Caban-Coch reservoirs. The single-track line, with gradients as steep as 1-in-33, also served Elan village, where navvies lived in an alcohol-free shanty town and had exchange sidings with the Cambrian Railways at Neuadd. From here the Elan Valley Railway's own locomotives, built by Manning Wardle and Hunslet and named after the streams that fed the reservoirs, worked the goods, workmen's and schoolchildren's trains. The Elan Valley reservoirs were linked to Birmingham via a 73-mile aqueduct, its gradient of 1-in-2,300 meant that water took 36 hours to reach Frankley reservoir on the outskirts of the city and the building of the dams and the subsequent flooding of the Elan Valley had several side effects, including the submergence of farms and also the loss of the former home of the Victorian romantic poet, Percy Shelley.

By 1904 the reservoirs were nearing completion and the Elan Valley Railway was preparing for a right royal visit. On 21 July the royal train, carrying King Edward VII and Queen Alexandra, which had travelled from Swansea via the Central Wales line and the connecting spur at Builth Road reached Rhayader station. From here the royal visitors were carried in ancient four-wheeled Cambrian Railways' coaches headed by Manning Wardle 0-6-0T Calettwr for an inspection of what was then still a giant building site. Despite the royal visit construction of the dams and reservoirs was not completed until 1906 by which time the Elan Valley Railway had served its purpose. The branch lines to the various dams had been closed by 1912 and the 'mainline' to Craig-Coch was closed in 1916.

Despite the long passage of time since closure, much of the route of the Elan Valley Railway can be followed today. Known as the Elan Valley Trail, an 8-mile footpath and cycleway from Cwmdauddwr (south of Rhayader) to Craig-Coch dam, follows the route of the old railway line around four of the Elan Valley reservoirs and their dams. A visitor centre has been converted from the old railway workshops and the adjacent car park was once the site of the locomotive shed and sidings.

RIGHT: *The second-hand steam railcar bought from the GWR is seen at Lofthouse-in-Nidderdale station, c.1921. Passenger services ended on the Nidd Valley Light Railway in 1929.*

BELOW: *On 21 July 1904 King Edward VII and Queen Alexandra visited the nearly completed Elan Valley reservoirs of the Birmingham Waterworks by Royal Train. An Elan Valley Railway special train conveyed them up the valley.*

With its thriving textile industry the 'boom town' and the 'wool capital of the world' of Bradford was at bursting point by the last decade of the 19th century. At the beginning of the 19th century Bradford was just a small market town with a population of 16,000 – by 1850 this had reached 182,000 and by 1891 it was over 200,000 souls. Clean drinking water was in short supply, a situation that created ideal conditions for cholera and typhoid leading to a very low life expectancy.

Looking further afield for a supply of clean water Bradford Corporation's Water Works Committee built a reservoir in the Nidd Valley at Gouthwaite, 40 miles to the north of the city between Pateley Bridge and Ramsgill. An aqueduct and underground pipeline linked Gouthwaite Reservoir to Chellow Heights Reservoir on the outskirts of Bradford. Unlike the Elan Valley scheme no large scale railway was built to serve the site as most of the raw materials needed for building the dam were obtained locally.

By the end of the century the people of Nidderdale were clamouring for their own railway. A 14-mile branch line had already been opened by the North Eastern Railway in 1862 from Harrogate to Pateley Bridge. Authorised in 1901 as a narrow-gauge railway, the Nidd Valley Light Railway opened for traffic as a standard-gauge line between Pateley Bidge and Lofthouse-in-Nidderdale in 1907. Even before the line was built it had been taken over by Bradford Corporation Waterworks Committee who had plans to build two further reservoirs in the Nidd Valley. There was, however, one problem and that was that the Light Railway Order stipulated that a passenger service also had to be run over the line as far as Lofthouse – in buying the line Bradford Corporation became the first local authority in the country to own a public railway. Another problem was that the Nidd Valley terminus at Pateley Bridge was a quarter of a mile away from the NER terminus – passengers who had arrived by NER train were often perplexed by the total lack of signage and Nidderdale's brave new integrated transport system often failed at the first hurdle!

The two new reservoirs at Angram and Scar House were completed in 1904 and 1921 respectively. Beyond Lofthouse there was a further 6 miles of goods-only line to Scar House and Angram Reservoirs, so steeply graded that even short goods trains often required four locomotives (two at the front and two at the rear). Workmen's trains also travelled along this route serving the navvies' temporary villages (complete with hospital, school, mission hall, bank and social hall) built at the dam construction sites. The passenger service consisted of four return trains each weekday but this was reduced to three each way in 1918 and in order to reduce running costs a second-hand steam railcar was bought from the Great Western Railway in 1920. Soon, competition from road transport up the valley was having a negative effect on the railway's finances and closure to passengers came on 31 December 1929.

Despite the loss of passenger services the line lived on until the completion of Scar House Reservoir in September 1936. After this the fate of the railway was sealed and it was all sold, lock, stock and barrel, in a mega auction in June 1937.

Today much of the trackbed between Pateley Bridge and Lofthouse is a footpath. A display about the railway can be seen in the Nidderdale Museum in Pateley Bridge.

The Slow, Miserable & Jolty

The Stratford-upon-Avon & Midland Junction Railway

Once grandly titled 'The Shakespeare Route', the east-west Stratford-upon-Avon & Midland Junction Railway (SMJR) was formed in 1909–10 by the amalgamation of four existing but bankrupt railways.

First on the scene was the Northampton & Banbury Junction Railway (N&BJR) which opened from Blisworth, on the LNWR mainline, to Towcester in 1866 and from Towcester to Cockley Brake Junction, on the LNWR's branch from Verney Junction to Banbury, in 1872. Built to serve ironstone mines around Blisworth, the company briefly changed its name to the Midland Counties & South Wales Railway but the proposed lengthy extension to Ross-on-Wye in Gloucestershire was soon forgotten and the company reverted to its original name. Cheaper imported ironstone from Spain soon put an end to the railway's brief period of profitability.

The second of the SMJR's constituent railways was the East & West Junction Railway (E&WJR) which was authorised in 1864 to build a 38¼-mile line from Stratford-upon-Avon to Towcester. Following years of financial problems the line eventually opened in 1872 but it was continually beset by problems, being run by an Official Receiver for many years with its passenger service suspended.

Next on the scene was the Evesham, Redditch & Stratford-upon-Avon Railway which was authorised to build a 7¾-mile line from Broom Junction, on the Evesham & Redditch Railway, to Stratford-upon-Avon where it would meet the aforementioned E&WJR. It opened in 1879 but was also soon in trouble with an Official Receiver being appointed in 1886.

The final SMJR constituent company was the Stratford-upon-Avon, Towcester & Midland Junction Railway which was authorised to build a line from Ravenstone Wood Junction, on the Midland Railway's Bedford to Northampton branch, to Towcester, crossing above the LNWR's mainline at Roade. Opened in 1891 it, too, was soon in financial trouble and passenger services were hurriedly withdrawn with an Official Receiver being appointed in 1898.

Despite together offering an east-west cross-country route with numerous mainline connections, these four motley and financially bankrupt railways were in dire straits by the end of the 19th century. None of the major neighbouring railway companies were interested in purchasing them so the SMJR was formed by the amalgamation of three of these companies in 1909. The fourth, the N&BJR, joined in 1910.

The opening of the Great Central Railway's London Extension in 1899, with a connecting spur to the E&WJR at Woodford & Hinton (later Woodford Halse), saw through carriages running between Marylebone and Stratford-upon-Avon, hence its marketing name as 'The Shakespeare Route'. The SMJR also became an important through route for Midland Railway freight traffic, in particular bananas, between Bristol and St Pancras, via Ashchurch and Broom Junction. Local passenger traffic was sparse with three return journeys between Blisworth and Stratford sufficing on weekdays and its worn out and decrepit track soon earned the railway the nickname of the 'Slow, Miserable & Jolty'!

The SMJR became part of the LMS in 1923 and not only grew as an important east-west route for freight traffic bypassing Birmingham but also for excursion traffic until World War II. A Karrier Ro-Railer converted single-decker bus was also tried out by the LMS but this service was unsuccessful and was withdrawn after a short time in 1932. Following the war passenger services were withdrawn between Broom Junction and Stratford in 1947 and between Blisworth and Stratford-upon-Avon in 1952. Blisworth to Cockley Brake closed completely in 1951 and Blisworth to Ravenstone Junction similarly in 1952. Now under the control of the Western Region of British Railways, freight continued to use the SMJR for some more years, including a growing number of iron ore trains (usually hauled by '9F' 2-10-0s or 'WD' 2-8-0s) from Northamptonshire to South Wales which ran via a new connection with the Honeybourne line at Stratford which had opened in 1960. From that date the section west to Broom Junction closed completely. By 1965 the ironstone traffic to South Wales had declined and the remaining SMJR route was closed completely on 5 July with the exception of the section from Fenny Compton that still serves the MOD depot near Kineton.

FOOTNOTE: The author well remembers a lengthy railtour organised by the Gloucestershire Railway Society in 1960 which travelled to Derby Works via Ashchurch, Evesham, Redditch and Birmingham then back on a lengthy and convoluted journey to Blisworth where it joined the SMJR route to Stratford-upon-Avon. The engine, preserved MR Compound 4-4-0 No 1000, stalled on the climb out of Blisworth, coming to a complete halt until copious amounts of sand had been sprinkled on the rails and progress very slowly resumed. Happy days!

LEFT: *Built in 1890 ex-Midland Railway '3F' 0-6-0 No 43222 is seen here at the S&MJR station at Stratford-upon-Avon while hauling an SLS enthusiasts' railtour on 29 April 1956.*

BELOW: *Ex-GWR '9000' Class No 9015 pauses at Fenny Compton with the South Midlander railtour on 24 April 1955.*

Diesel and gas turbine locomotive prototypes

Private enterprise prototypes built in the 1950s and 1960s

In the race to gain lucrative contracts for building British Railways' new fleet of mainline diesels in the 1950s and '60s, several leading locomotive manufacturers produced designs for evaluation by their potential client. Some had a very short life and one even disappeared without trace behind the Iron Curtain.

'Deltic' (DP1)

Forerunner of the Class 55 diesels, the 'Deltic' prototype, was a familiar sight on both the ECML and WCML. Also known as DP1 it was built by English Electric at their Vulcan Foundry in 1955 and was finished in a striking powder-blue livery with cream side stripes and speed whiskers. The twin-'Deltic' marine engines had a combined power output of 3,300 hp. It was withdrawn in 1961 and has since been preserved as part of the National Collection.

Falcon (D0280)

Built in 1961 by Brush Traction as a second-generation lightweight diesel-electric loco, the one-off experimental D0280 Falcon was fitted with twin Maybach diesel engines. Finished in a striking lime green and brown livery Falcon saw trials on the ER and LMR before being repainted in two-tone green and allocated for a time to Bath Road diesel depot, Bristol, and operated mainline services to Paddington. It was eventually sold to BR in 1970 for its scrap value and was subsequently rebuilt at Swindon as No 1200. Due to its non-standard design it was withdrawn in 1975 and subsequently scrapped.

BELOW: *In its striking lime green and brown livery diesel-electric prototype D0280 Falcon hauls a down express through Greenwood north of Hadley Wood Tunnels on the East Coast Main Line in July 1962.*

GT3

This strange-looking 4-6-0 gas turbine locomotive was built by English Electric in 1961. Resembling a slab-sided steam locomotive, GT3 also had a tender and required turning at the end of each journey. Finished in red livery the loco was tested on the Great Central Main Line and on the WCML before being returned to its manufacturer the following year. It was finally scrapped in 1966.

Lion (D0260)

Resplendent in gleaming white livery, prototype mainline diesel D0260 *Lion* took part in trials for a new BR Type 4 diesel fleet. Built in 1962 by the Birmingham Railway Carriage & Wagon Company at Smethwick, the loco was withdrawn at the end of 1963 when BR ordered a fleet of Type 4 (Class 47) diesels from Brush Traction.

DP2

Similar in outline to the 'Deltic' Class 55 diesels, English Electric prototype DP2 was the test-bed for the company's Type 4 diesels (later Class 50) introduced in 1967. Built at Vulcan Foundry in 1962 the loco saw service on the ECML and WCML until it was withdrawn following a serious accident at Thirsk in July 1967.

Kestrel (HS4000)

Prototype Co-Co diesel HS4000 *Kestrel* was built by Brush Traction in 1968. It was powered by a 4000 hp Sulzer engine and finished in a yellow ochre and dark brown livery. Following trials the loco was refitted with lighter bogies and went into service on the ECML. The loco was withdrawn in 1971 and sent to Russia as a research vehicle and has not been seen since!

Spotted by the author while on a trainspotting trip to Swindon on 11 July 1962 was the brand new white-liveried (with gold stripes) D0260 Lion prototype diesel-electric locomotive. Built by the Birmingham Railway Carriage & Wagon Company this handsome loco had a very short life and was withdrawn at the end of 1963.

Steam dreams

Reliving steam-hauled journeys of the 1960s

Carlisle to Glasgow Central

Passengers on the down 'Royal Scot' on 1 August 1964 were none too pleased when their English Electric Type 4 diesel failed as the train arrived at Carlisle. They probably didn't notice two excited teenage boys boarding the train as the diesel was taken off and replaced by a rather grimy BR Standard Class '7' 4-6-2 No 70002 *Geoffrey Chaucer*.

As it was a Saturday the express should have left Carlisle at 4.07 p.m. but eventually left for its journey north at 4.32 p.m. Poor old *Geoffrey Chaucer* really wasn't up to the task but our two trainspotters faithfully recorded every bit of the journey in their notebooks, spending most of the journey with their heads out of the window!

The first part of the journey up Annandale was excruciatingly slow: Quintinshill, Kirtlebridge and Ecclefechan all being passed at a measly 36 mph; Lockerbie was passed at 63 mph before we made an unscheduled stop at Beattock at 5.34 p.m. to attach a banking engine. So far we had covered 39½ miles in 62 minutes – some express! After a 3½-minute stop at Beattock we were off again, breasting the summit at 6.01 p.m. at a speed of 30 mph. From then on it was all downhill and *Geoffrey Chaucer* did his best to speed things up a bit along the Clyde Valley: Elvanfoot was passed at 69 mph; Crawford and Abington at 72, Lamington at 70 before slowing for Carstairs (6.25 p.m.) which we passed at 35 mph. Speed slowly picked up again with a maximum of 65 mph recorded at Carluke (6.36 p.m.) and 63 at Shieldmuir Junction. Glasgow Central was reached at 7 p.m. – exactly 1 hour late. The passengers were pretty fed up but the two trainspotters were ecstatic. Obviously in poor condition, *Geoffrey Chaucer* and his crew had done their best, covering the 102¼ miles in 2 hrs 28 min at an average speed of 41.39 mph. Now the Pendolinos only take around 1 hr 15 min at an average speed of nearly 82 mph, progress indeed, but I would rather arrive 1 hour late behind a steam loco.

FOOTNOTE: *Geoffrey Chaucer* was finally withdrawn from Carlisle Kingmoor shed in January 1967 and sent to the great steam scrapheap in the sky.

RIGHT: *Ex-LNER 'A4' Class 4-6-2 No 60019* Bittern *streaks along near Gleneagles with a Glasgow to Aberdeen express in April 1966. This steam swansong ended in just over four months' time. Fortunately* Bittern *has been preserved.*

BELOW: *Replacing a failed diesel BR Standard Class '7' 4-6-2 No 70002* Geoffrey Chaucer *is seen departing from Carlisle with the down 'Royal Scot' on 1 August 1964. Somewhere on this train, with his head out the window, was the author logging the journey to Glasgow Central for posterity.*

Aberdeen to Glasgow Buchanan Street

Our intrepid trainspotters had caught the 8.25 a.m. 3-hour express (aka 'The Grampian') from Glasgow Buchanan Street to Aberdeen on 31 July 1964. Sadly the hoped-for 'A4' didn't materialise and we had to be content with Birmingham Railway Carriage & Wagon Co. Type 2 D5368. After a trawl around Ferryhill (all steam including seven 'A4s') and Kittybrewster (all diesels apart from stored No 60007) we returned on the 1.30 p.m. to Glasgow Buchanan Street, supposedly the up 'The Grampian' express but in reality a stopping train taking 4 hours for the 153-mile journey via Forfar.

At the head of our train was 'A4' 4-6-2 No 60019 *Bittern* which, despite the numerous stops along the way, managed to achieve some reasonable speeds: 72 mph between Aberdeen and Stonehaven; 70 between Stonehaven and Laurencekirk; 66 between Laurencekirk and Bridge of Dun; 65 between Bridge of Dun and Forfar; 73 between Forfar and Coupar Angus; 73 between Coupar Angus and Perth; 64 between Perth and Gleneagles; 66 between Gleneagles and Dunblane; 78 between Dunblane and Stirling; 78 between Stirling and Larbert.

FOOTNOTE: Our trainspotters were also lucky to have a ride behind No 60024 *Kingfisher* between Stirling and Buchanan Street on 23 August 1966, just before the end of the 'A4s' swansong on this route. Happy days!

Banbury to Oxford

The York to Bournemouth through train was an interesting working, travelling via the Great Central line through Woodford Halse and Banbury. At the latter station, on a sunny 9 September 1965, our two trainspotters boarded the train for the journey down to Oxford. They were lucky indeed as, although the reign of steam on the Western Region was due to end in just under four months, our train engine which came on at Banbury was 'Hall' Class 4-6-0 No 4920 (formerly *Dumbleton Hall* but by then minus its valuable nameplates) of Bristol (Barrow Road) shed.

Our train left Banbury at 2.42 p.m., passing King's Sutton at 2.50, Aynho at 2.53 and reaching 60 mph at Fritwell, which was passed at 2.56 p.m. Unfortunately the train was halted by signals at Heyford for 9 minutes but put on a good spurt of speed reaching 64 mph between Bletchington and Kidlington, which was passed at 3.18 p.m. Wolvercote Junction was passed at 59 mph and we came to a screeching halt at Oxford station at 3.25 p.m. where the Bournemouth to York train was seen heading northbound behind 'Modified Hall' 4-6-0 No 7912 *Little Linford Hall*.

FOOTNOTE: This was the author's last journey behind an ex-GWR loco before the end of steam on BR. Luckily, *Dumbleton Hall* survived withdrawal at the end of 1965 and was saved for preservation after having spent over 10 years at Woodham's scrapyard in Barry.

Blue streak

The short-lived 'Blue Pullman' trains of the 1960s

In 1954 the British Transport Commission became the proud owners of the British Pullman Car Company. A year later the British Railways Modernisation Programme was published – one of its main objectives was the replacement of steam by diesel power. A committee was soon set up to look into the introduction of diesel-hauled express passenger trains and in 1957 it was announced that the Metropolitan-Cammell Carriage & Wagon Company of Birmingham would build five high-speed diesel multiple-unit sets to be introduced in 1958 on the London Midland Region between London St Pancras and Manchester Central and on the Western Region between London Paddington and Bristol/Birmingham.

At that time the design of these luxurious trains was fairly ground-breaking – the classic Pullman livery of brown and cream was replaced by blue (known as Nanking blue) and white with a grey roof, the passenger coaches were fitted with double-glazing, air conditioning and sumptuous seating and passengers were served at their tables by staff dressed in matching blue uniforms. Sporting the Pullman Car Company's crest on the nose, the streamlined power cars at each end of the train were each fitted with a 1,000 hp NBL/MAN diesel engine driving electric transmission with a top speed of 90 mph. The two LMR sets were six-car formation (this included the two non-accommodating power cars) providing 132 first-class seats and the three WR sets were eight-car formation providing 108 first-class and 120 second-class seats.

Following delays caused by extended trials and modifications the first 'Blue Pullmans' entered revenue-

Train travel second to none...Western Region blue Pullman

earning service on the LMR between St Pancras and Manchester on 4 July 1960. Designed to cater for businessmen, the up service left Manchester Central during weekdays at 8.50 a.m. and, after calling at Cheadle Heath, completed the 189-mile journey to St Pancras in 193 minutes. Leaving St Pancras at 6.10 p.m. the return journey was completed in 191 minutes. A shorter fill-in turn from St Pancras to Nottingham and back was short-lived. Following the completion of electrification between Euston and Manchester Piccadilly the two LMR sets were transferred to the Western Region in March 1967.

'Blue Pullman' services on the Western Region between Paddington and Bristol and Paddington and Wolverhampton Low Level commenced on 12 September 1960. An additional service was introduced between Paddington and Swansea in the summer of 1961.

A steam-hauled set of traditional brown and cream Pullman cars was always kept in reserve at Old Oak Common. The transfer of the two six-car sets from the LMR in March 1967 saw the introduction of an additional service to Bristol and a new service to Oxford. The introduction of High Speed Trains (HST125) on the WR led to the demise of 'Blue Pullman' services with the last train, an enthusiasts' special, running on 5 May 1973. None have been preserved.

LEFT: *A British Railways poster of 1960 advertising the new Western Region 'Blue Pullman' service between London Paddington and Bristol/Wolverhampton Low Level, seen at speed in Sonning Cutting.*

BELOW: *A British Railways poster of 1960 advertising the new 'Midland Pullman' service between Manchester Central and London St Pancras.*

The New MIDLAND PULLMAN

First Class de luxe travel — Supplementary fares

8.50 am	Manchester Central	9.21 pm	Mondays to Fridays from 4th July	12.45 pm	St. Pancras	4.00 pm
9.04 am	Cheadle Heath	9.07 pm			Leicester	
12.03 pm	St. Pancras	6.10 pm		2.10 pm	London Road	2.33 pm

 The last word in rail comfort. Limited accommodation, book in advance

A Kent railway village

Ashford Locomotive Works

The South Eastern Railway's mainline from London to Dover via the small town of Ashford opened throughout in 1844. Soon, the expanding railway found its original railway works at New Cross too cramped so in 1846 the company set about finding a new, green fields site in Kent. Ashford was the chosen location because of its convenient location on the new mainline. Buying 185 acres of land for £21,000, the SER built a new railway works along with 132 labourers' cottages around a village green, a pub, a Mechanics Institute, gas works, a school and public baths.

The first new mainline locomotive (a 'Hastings' Class 2-4-0 designed by Richard Cudworth) rolled out of the 26½-acre Locomotive Works in 1853. The adjoining Carriage & Wagon Works opened in 1855. The population of Ashford more than doubled between 1841 and 1861, by which time it had reached 7,000 and by 1882 the railway was employing around 1,300 workers. The main workshop of the railway works was by far the biggest building, measuring 400ft long, 90ft wide and 28ft high. Adjacent to this the 640ft-long Carriage & Wagon Workshop also housed its own furnaces and a foundry.

The South Eastern Railway amalgamated with the London, Chatham & Dover Railway in 1899 after which Ashford became the main works for the newly-formed South Eastern & Chatham Railway.

After the 'Big Four Grouping' of 1923 Ashford became one of the three main workshops of the new Southern Railway, the others being at Brighton and Eastleigh. Construction of new coaches was transferred to Eastleigh and carriage repairs to Lancing in 1929. From that date Ashford concentrated mainly on locomotive and wagon construction and repair, both activities continuing into the BR era with the locomotive side ceasing in 1962 (when it was transferred to Eastleigh) and wagon repair and construction continuing until 1981. During the Second World War the works also built Browning machine guns for use on Blenheim fighter-bombers.

During its long history Ashford Locomotive Works built or rebuilt nearly 1,000 locomotives, the majority of them steam but, towards the end, diesel construction as well. New steam locomotives ranged from 239 designed by James Stirling for the SER, 196 designed by Harry Wainwright for the SE&CR and 118 designed by Richard Maunsell for the SE&CR and the Southern Railway. The latter included many famous classes that survived to see service on British Railways including 'N', 'N1' and 'U' Class 2-6-0s and 'W' Class 2-6-4 tanks. Under Southern Railway and later BR management the Works turned out 30 diesel shunters, 20 of Bulleid's 'Q1' Class 0-6-0s, 14 Stanier '8F' 2-8-0s, and the first two of the SR mainline diesel-electrics, Nos 10201 and 10202 – the latter was the last locomotive to be built at Ashford when it was rolled out in the Autumn of 1951.

RIGHT: *This BR leaflet shows a general view of the main locomotive repair building at Ashford Works, c.1960.*

BELOW: *Ashford Works built twenty of the Bulleid's utilitarian 'Q1' Class locos for the Southern Railway in 1942. Here No 33040 is apparently in need of some tender loving care outside the works on 4 June 1960.*

An eccentric railway empire

Colonel H. F. Stephens and his light railways

The son of the Pre-Raphaelite artist Frederic George Stephens, Holman Fred Stephens was born in 1868 and went on to become a leading exponent of the building and managing of light railways in England and Wales. As a student he attended University College, London, where he studied civil engineering before enrolling as an apprentice engineer at the Metropolitan Railway's Neasden Works in 1881. Following his apprenticeship, Stephens went on to hold the post of assistant engineer during the construction of the Cranbrook & Paddock Wood Railway, which opened on 1 October 1892. As an associate member of the Institute of Civil Engineers from 1894, Stephens was allowed to design and construct railways and he wasted no time setting about his first project. In anticipation of the passing of the 1896 Light Railways Act, which allowed the building of low-cost and lightly constructed railways in lightly-populated rural areas, Stephens formed a company, known as the Light Railway Syndicate, with his friend Edward Peterson in 1895. Designed to obtain orders for new light railways, the

company claimed to have potential investors who were willing to invest in such schemes. In reality this was not so and, although seven light railway schemes were proposed by the company, only one light railway, the Sheppey Light Railway which opened in 1901 between Queenborough and Leysdown-on-Sea, was actually built.

Despite his failure to obtain contracts from the Light Railway Syndicate, Stephens was highly successful building and managing railways in his own right. His first, the 2-mile narrow-gauge Rye & Camber Tramway, was opened in 1895 and preceded the Light Railways Act by one year. His first light railway, the Rother Valley between Robertsbridge and Rolvenden in Kent, was opened on 2 April 1900 and was the first railway to be built under the provisions of the 1896 Light Railway Act. In addition to building and managing many lines in England and Wales (see accompanying list), Stephens twice extended his Rother Valley Railway, now known as the Kent & East Sussex Railway, first to Tenterden in 1903 and finally to Headcorn in 1905.

Between 1900 and his sudden death in 1931, Stephens ran his railway empire from a modest office at 23 Salford Terrace in nearby Tonbridge. His second-in-command, William Henry Austen (1878–1956) came

BELOW: *Ex-LB&SCR 'A1X' Class 0-6-0T No 32655 waits for passengers to board its one-coach train for Tenterden at Robertsbridge on 5 September 1953.*

from a much humbler background than the charismatic and forthright Stephens and was referred to by his boss as 'my outdoor assistant'. On Stephens' death Austen took over the far-flung railway empire but the writing was soon on the wall for these, by now, ramshackle rural railways. Increased competition from buses brought about the termination of many passenger services leaving just a skeleton goods service operated by second-hand and antique locos. By 1948 most of these idyllic little lines had closed and only three – the Kent & East Sussex (now a successful heritage railway), the East Kent, and the Shropshire & Montgomeryshire – became part of the nationalised and newly-formed British Railways.

The 'Colonel Stephens' Railways

Cranbrook & Paddock Wood Railway

Route: Paddock Wood – Hawkhurst

Distance: 11½ miles

After completing his apprenticeship with the Metropolitan Railway, Stephens was appointed resident engineer during the line's construction between 1890 and 1894. The railway was taken over by the South Eastern & Chatham Railway in 1900 and closed in 1961.

Rye & Camber Tramway

Route: Rye – Camber Sands

Distance: 2 miles

Opened in 1895, this little narrow-gauge line was the first to be completely designed, built and operated by Stephens. It closed in 1939.

The Hundred of Manhood & Selsey Tramway

Route: Chichester – Selsey

Distance: 8 miles

Built and managed by Stephens, this agricultural light railway was opened to Selsey Town in 1897. It was further extended to Selsey Beach in 1908 but, due to road competition, the line closed in 1935.

Kent & East Sussex Railway

Route: Robertsbridge – Headcorn

Distance: 21 miles

Built, owned and managed by Stephens, this line was opened between Robertsbridge and Rolvenden in 1900, Rolvenden to Tenterden in 1902 and finally to Headcorn in 1905. Although serving a sparsely populated rural area the railway struggled on into Nationalisation in 1948. All passenger traffic ceased in 1953 and the section between Tenterden and Headcorn was closed. The remainder of the railway closed in 1961. The section between Tenterden Town and Bodiam has now been reopened as a heritage railway.

The Sheppey Light Railway

Route: Queenborough – Leysdown-on-Sea

Distance: 8½ miles

Engineered by Stephens, this railway was opened in 1901 and owned and operated by the South Eastern & Chatham Railway from 1905. Struggling through to become part of British Railways in 1948, the railway finally closed in 1950.

Bere Alston & Calstock Railway and East Cornwall Mineral Railway

Route: Bere Alson – Callington

Distance: 19 miles

Working with Messrs Galbraith & Church, Stephens designed and equipped this railway, including converting a former narrow-gauge mineral line and constructing the graceful concrete-block viaduct across the Tamar at Calstock. Opened in 1908, the 5-mile section from Gunnislake to Callington was closed in 1966 but the remainder is still open to passengers as a branch line from Plymouth.

Burry Port & Gwendraeth Valley Railway

Route: Burry Port – Cwm Mawr

Distance: 12 miles

Between 1909 and 1913 Stephens was responsible for upgrading this hitherto mineral line to passenger-carrying standards. The railway became part of the GWR in 1923 and passenger traffic ceased in 1953. Remnants of the line were kept in use for coal traffic until 1996.

Shropshire & Montgomeryshire Light Railway

Route: Shrewsbury Abbey – Llanymynech and a branch from
   Kinnerley Junction to Criggion

Distance: 24 miles

Opened originally in 1866 as the Potteries, Shrewsbury & North Wales Railway this line was closed in 1880 due to financial difficulties. Seeing an opportunity, Stephens took over the dormant railway in 1907 and rebuilt it to light railway standards. Also owned and managed by Stephens, the line, renamed the Shropshire & Montgomeryshire Light Railway, opened for business in 1911. Passenger services ceased in 1933 and the railway lingered on until it was taken over by the military in 1941. Nationalised in 1948, the line remained on lease to the military until closure in 1960.

Weston, Clevedon & Portishead Railway
Route: Weston-super-Mare (Ashcombe Road) – Portishead
Distance: 14 miles
Originally built as a tramway, the line was converted to a light railway in 1907. From 1911 until its closure in 1940, the line was managed by Stephens and his successor, W. H. Austen.

East Kent Light Railway
Route: Shepherdswell – Wingham and a branch from Eastry to Richborough Port
Distance: 18 miles
Designed, built and managed by Stephens, this line opened for coal traffic from the Kent Coalfield in 1911. Passenger services commenced in 1916 and ceased in 1948 when the railway became part of British Railways. By 1951 most of the line had been completely closed with only the section to Tilmanstone Colliery remaining open until 1986. Today, a short section from Shepherdswell to Eythorne is run as a heritage railway.

Edge Hill Light Railway
Route: Burton Dassett Junction – Edge Hill Quarry
Distance: 3½ miles
Designed to carry ironstone, the short-lived freight-only Edge Hill Light Railway was engineered by Stephens in 1919. Opened in 1922 and incorporating a cable-worked incline, the railway was never a success due to the poor quality of the ironstone. The line closed in 1925.

Snailbeach District Railway
Route: Pontesbury – Snailbeach
Distance: 3 miles
Originally opened in 1877, this narrow-gauge line was built to convey lead ore from mines in the Stiperstones Hills in Shropshire. Although initially a successful commercial enterprise, traffic had declined to such a low point that by the 1920s it had almost ceased to operate. Then, in 1923, Stephens purchased the line and set about re-equipping it and bringing it back to life. The opening of a stone quarry and a stone-crushing plant to supply the county council with road-building material brought increased traffic and through the 1930s the line prospered. In 1947 it was leased to Shropshire County Council who continued to operate part of it until final closure in 1959.

Ffestiniog Railway
Route: Porthmadog – Blaenau Ffestiniog
Distance: 13½ miles
This pioneering Welsh narrow-gauge railway, originally opened to convey slate in 1836, had by the end of World War I fallen on hard times. To revive the railway's fortunes Stephens was appointed Manager in 1923 and Chairman in 1925 until his death in 1931. At the same time he automatically became manager of the Welsh Highland Railway which was then under the same ownership as the Ffestiniog. His successor W. H. Austen continued in this role until he resigned in 1936. Their timely intervention almost certainly saved the Ffestiniog Railway from early closure. The railway ceased to operate in 1946 but was brought back to life by a group of dedicated railway enthusiasts and is now one of the premier tourist attractions in North Wales. The Welsh Highland Railway closed in 1936 but has been completely reopened as a tourist line between Caernarfon and Porthmadog.

Ashover Light Railway
Route: Clay Cross – Ashover
Distance: 7 miles
Engineered by Stephens, this narrow-gauge line was opened in 1924 to convey stone for the Clay Cross Company. Passenger services ceased in 1936 and the line closed completely in 1950.

North Devon & Cornwall Junction Light Railway
Route: Great Torrington – Halwill Junction
Distance: 20 miles
Rebuilt partly from an existing china clay narrow-gauge line, this railway was engineered and managed by Stephens until its opening in 1925 when it came under the operational control of the Southern Railway. Becoming part of British Railways in 1948, the line closed to passengers throughout and to goods between Halwill and Meeth in 1965. The northern section from Great Torrington to Meeth remained open for china clay traffic until 1982.

Swansea East Dock

The home of unique short-wheelbase steam locomotives

Swansea East Dock was a good 20-minute walk from Swansea High Street Station or, alternatively, a short ride on a United Welsh bus heading towards Neath. The shed was opened by the GWR in 1893 and provided locos for the extensive rail network serving Swansea Docks and associated heavy freight trains. The shed's allocation of 48 locos in October 1961 were all tank engines and included 28 0-6-0 pannier tanks of various types, four '4200' 2-8-0 tanks, three '7200' 2-8-2 tanks and 10 '5600' 0-6-2 tanks. To traverse the sharp curves around the docks the shed was also home to the two unique ex-Powlseland & Mason 0-4-0 saddle tanks Nos 1151 and 1152 of 1907 vintage and ex-Cardiff Railway 0-4-0 saddle tank No 1338 dating from 1893. No 1152 was soon withdrawn and the shed was allocated two unusual 'foreigners' in the shape of ex-LMS 0-4-0 saddle tank No 47003 and ex-Lancashire & Yorkshire Railway 0-4-0 saddle tank No 51218 of 1891 vintage. Set in a bleak, windswept landscape Swansea East Dock finally closed in June 1964.

Sub-sheds of Swansea East Dock were Gurnos (closed 1962) and Upper Bank (closed 1963).

BELOW: *A wonderfully evocative picture of the back streets around Swansea East Dock. Here Powlseland & Mason 0-4-0ST No 1152 trundles past Tyrell's Ship Store on its way to its next spot of shunting, 22 June 1949. This diminutive loco was built by Peckett in 1912 and withdrawn in 1961.*

All at sea

Railway-owned docks, harbours and ships

As an island nation Britain depends for its survival on foreign trade – the majority of our imports and exports still go by sea. The coming of the industrial age and the building of railways during the 19th century saw a vast expansion of trade and by the beginning of the 20th century the power of Britain's railways had extended over the sea as well as over land. By that time, although no shipping company owned a railway, a great many railway companies owned ships, and an even larger number owned docks and harbours. Many companies had the word 'Docks' in their full titles – Port Talbot Railway & Docks Co., King's Lynn Docks & Railway etc. – signifying the importance to them of this side of their business.

To give an idea of the magnitude of the sea power of Britain's privately owned railways 120 years ago, let us briefly look at the marine undertakings, including docks and steamships, that were owned by some of the leading companies.

London & North Western Railway

Holyhead Harbour, Greenore Harbour (Ireland), Garston Docks near Liverpool, joint owner with Lancashire & Yorkshire Railway of Fleetwood Docks; 16 steamships and joint ownership of 8 other steamships.

Great Western Railway

Harbours at Plymouth, Llanelly, Briton Ferry, Brentford, Bridgwater, Newquay and New Milford and joint ownership (with the Irish company the Great Southern & Western Railway) of Fishguard Harbour and Rosslare Harbour in Ireland; 16 steamships.

North Eastern Railway

Docks at Hull, Hartlepoool, Tyne Dock (exporting 7 million tons of coal per annum), Middlesbrough, Monkwearmouth and coal staithes at Blyth and Dunston-on-the-Tyne.

Midland Railway

Harbour at Heysham; 4 steamships for Isle of Man service.

Great Central Railway

Docks at Grimsby and Immingham; 13 steamships.

Lancashire & Yorkshire Railway

Docks at Fleetwood; 5 steamships and joint owner of 5 other steamships. Also owned Goole Shipping Company.

Great Eastern Railway

Harbour at Parkeston Quay; 12 steamships.

London & South Western Railway

Southampton Docks; 15 steamships.

London Brighton & South Coast Railway

Newhaven Harbour; 2 steamships and joint owner of 14 steamships, Isle of Wight ferries.

South-Eastern & Chatham Railway

Harbours at Folkestone and Whitstable and facilities at Port Victoria, Queenborough, Strood, Gravesend, Rye and Dover; joint owner of 19 steamships.

Taff Vale Railway

Penarth Docks and Harbour, exporting 4 million tons of coal per annum.

Barry Railway

Barry Docks, exporting nearly 9 million tons of coal per annum.

Cardiff Railway

Bute Docks

North British Railway

Docks/harbours at Methil, Burntisland, Bo'ness, Alloa, Charlestown, Kincardine, Tayport, Silloth and Mallaig; 7 steamships.

Glasgow & South Western Railway

Harbours at Troon, Largs and Fairlie; 10 steamships.

In 1903 the total revenue of Britain's railway companies from canals, harbours, docks and steamships was just over £4 million – a staggering amount at that time.

During the period 1923 to 1947 the 'Big Four' railway companies continued with this seagoing tradition. From 1948 the shipping interests of the 'Big Four' were nationalised under the name of British Transport Ships until 1970 when it became known as Sealink. The latter ceased to exist in 1984 when it was privatised and sold to Sea Containers which, in turn, sold it to Stena Line in 1991.

LEFT: *The Sealink ferry* Antrim Princess *waits to load vehicles for Larne at Stranraer Harbour on 27 May 1983. On the right is Stranraer Harbour station with a Class 27 diesel at the head of a train for Glasgow.*

BELOW: *A 1975 poster advertising the delights of travelling by Sealink ferries to the Continent and Ireland.*

The Dockers' Umbrella

The Liverpool Overhead Railway

Liverpool's rapid growth as a major port during the 19th century soon led to serious congestion on the approach roads to the docks. The main artery linking all of these, Dock Road, soon became clogged with horse-drawn vehicles transporting goods to and from the ships and the numerous railway level crossings only added to the delays. Not only were goods delayed but also so were the public. To alleviate this congestion a plan was put forward as early as 1852 to build an elevated passenger-carrying railway along the dock front. However, nothing came of this or a similar proposal put forward in 1877. Finally, in 1888, a group of local businessmen formed the Liverpool Overhead Railway Company and received permission from the Mersey Docks & Harbour Board to construct the railway.

Work started in 1889 and a decision was soon made that the railway should be powered by electric traction which, at that time, was still in its infancy – thus making

the Liverpool Overhead the world's first electric elevated city railway. It was also the first railway in the world to have an automatic electric signalling system. The standard-gauge 6-mile line, running from Seaforth Carriage Sheds in the north to Herculaneum Dock in the south, was officially opened on 4 February 1893 by the Marquis of Salisbury. There were 11 intermediate stations, Brocklebank Dock, Canada Dock, Sandon Dock, Clarence Dock, Princes Dock, Pier Head, James Street, Custom House, Wapping Dock, Brunswick Dock and Toxteth Dock and, initially, services began and ended at Alexandra Dock station in the north. Other stations at Seaforth Sands, Langdon Dock, Huskisson Dock, Nelson Dock and a new southern terminus (underground!) at Dingle were opened in 1896.

LEFT: *Liverpool Overhead Railway driving car No 20 enters James Street station in October 1956. Two months later the 'Dockers' Umbrella' closed for good.*

BELOW: *Liverpool Overhead Railway driving car No 41 arrives at Gladstone Dock station in 1953.*

The Liverpool Overhead Railway soon became affectionately known by its customers and local people as the 'Dockers' Umbrella'. There were no major accidents and, up to the 1950s, it safely carried millions of dock workers along its route. Although the railway suffered severe damage from German bombing raids during World War II, repairs were quickly carried out due to its strategic importance in the running of the overstretched docks. Escaping Nationalisation in 1948, the railway company embarked on a modernisation programme for its ancient rolling stock but, despite this, the writing was soon on the wall for this unique British railway. In 1955, coupled with dwindling dock operations, it was found that the original iron viaducts that supported the line were badly corroded and required replacement. The cost of carrying out this work, estimated to be in the region of £2 million, was far beyond the financial means of the company and the line closed for good on 30 December 1956. Despite public protest and rescue attempts the line had been completely dismantled by early 1959. Today, very little remains of this Liverpool institution apart from the tunnel mouth to the old underground Dingle terminus.

The first Severn Bridge

The Severn Railway Bridge

For centuries the lowest crossing of the River Severn was at Gloucester and until the building of the Severn Railway Bridge further downstream trains between Bristol and South Wales were forced to take a long and circuitous route via the city.

Close to the Welsh border to the west of the River Severn lies the ancient Forest of Dean, an important source of iron ore and coal since medieval times. The opening of the then narrow-gauge Severn & Wye Railway & Canal Company in 1813 linked the Severn at Lydney and the Wye at Lydbrook and provided an outlet for the output of these mines. In reality a horse-drawn tramway, this steeply-graded line was ripe for modernisation by the time the broad-gauge South Wales Railway had opened along the west bank of the Severn in 1851. However, it took another 18 years before the Severn & Wye (S&W) was re-laid to broad-gauge and steam power was introduced. By then Brunel's broad-gauge was in decline and the railway was converted to standard-gauge in 1874.

On the opposite side of the Severn the Midland Railway's 4-mile branch from Berkeley Road, on the Bristol to Gloucester mainline, to docks at Sharpness opened in 1876. By then coal trains from the Forest of Dean to Bristol and the southwest had to travel the long way round via Gloucester. Bridging the gap between the Severn & Wye Railway at Lydney and the Midland Railway at Sharpness seemed the obvious answer and thus was the Severn Bridge Railway born.

Authorised in 1872, the Severn Bridge Railway, financially backed by the S&W and the MR, involved the building of 4 miles of railway from Sharpness to Lydney via a 1,387yd-long bridge over the River Severn. The 22 cast-iron spans were 70ft above the river with one of them operating as a swing bridge where it crossed the Gloucester & Sharpness Canal. Work began in 1875 but the company soon faced financial problems and was jointly bought out by the GWR and the MR, becoming the Severn & Wye & Severn Bridge Joint Railway (S&W&SBJR).

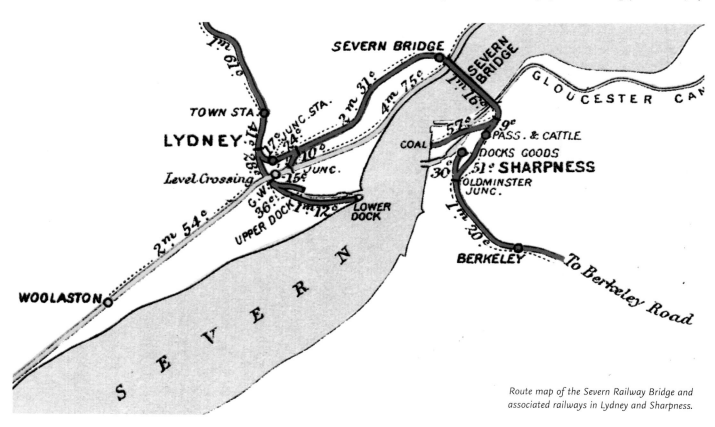

Route map of the Severn Railway Bridge and associated railways in Lydney and Sharpness.

The bridge finally opened on 17 October 1879 but its usefulness soon disappeared when the Severn Tunnel was opened further downstream in 1886. Meanwhile the Severn & Wye Railway & Canal Company was also facing financial problems and in 1894 it merged with the S&W&SBJR to become the Severn & Wye Joint Railway, jointly owned by the GWR and MR.

Passenger services over the bridge consisted of six trains each way on weekdays, the majority taking just over 1½ hours for the 20½-mile journey between Berkeley Road and Lydbrook Junction. A new link was opened in 1908 at Berkeley Road enabling freight trains from the bridge to travel south to Westerleigh, where there was a connection with the GWR's new Badminton cut-off line, and Bristol. This was also used as a diversionary route when the Severn Tunnel was closed, usually on Sundays, for maintenance.

Passenger services north of Lydney ceased as early as 1929 from which date trains from Berkeley Road via the Severn Bridge terminated at Lydney Town. Hauled by GWR 0-6-0 pannier tanks the pattern of six passenger trains each way continued into BR days and provided a useful link for schoolchildren who lived on one side of the Severn but went to school on the opposite side.

The end abruptly came for the Severn Railway Bridge on a foggy 25 October 1960 when two loaded petroleum barges heading up river to Sharpness were swept into one of the support columns, causing two of the spans to collapse. Luckily no train was on the bridge at the time but five people on the boats died in the accident.

Damaged in a further accident in 1961 the bridge was never repaired leaving the remaining 4-mile branch from Berkeley Road to Sharpness served by an autotrain until closure on 31 October 1964. The bridge was later dismantled but the stone circular pier of the swing bridge at Sharpness can still be seen today and the foundations of some of the bridge's piers can be spotted in the mud at times of low tide. The Sharpness branch is still *in situ* and is occasionally used by scrap metal trains to Sharpness Docks. It is also waiting patiently for the Vale of Berkeley Railway to reopen it as a heritage railway.

BELOW: *The steam-powered turning gear for the railway swing bridge across the Gloucester & Sharpness Canal, located at the eastern end of the Severn Railway Bridge. Seen here on 15 August 1959, just over a year before the bridge was terminally damaged in a collision by two loaded petroleum barges.*

This artist's impression of the Severn Railway Bridge was published in 1850, some 29 years before the structure was completed. It appears to have double-track and the final structure was somewhat less impressive.

Hi-de-Hi!

The railway camping coach

By the 1930s the popularity of the great outdoors with the urban masses had made hiking and camping a boom business. Keen to take advantage of this new craze, Britain's 'Big Four' railway companies soon hit on the idea of providing 'camping coaches' parked in a siding at rural or coastal stations. Not only did budding campers travel to their destination by train but they also used local rail services while on holiday – this proved to be a real money spinner for the railway companies.

In 1933 the London & North Eastern Railway became the first to provide camping coaches when they adapted 10 redundant ex-Great Northern Railway six-wheeler carriages and placed them at 10 different beauty spots across their system. Not to be outdone, the GWR and the LMS followed suit the following year with the Southern Railway in 1935. Proving very popular with holidaymakers, larger adapted bogie carriages were later introduced that could sleep up to eight people.

Camping coaches were suspended for the duration of WWII but were reintroduced in 1947. Under British Railways the number of locations increased dramatically with some popular destinations offering a whole row of camping coaches. More luxurious accommodation was also offered in the shape of adapted Pullman coaches and by 1957 there were over 120 locations on offer from Glenfinnan in Scotland to St Erth in Cornwall – the Western Region alone had 44 locations, mainly in Wales and the West Country. Sadly, changing holiday habits and the fairly spartan accommodation on offer led to the demise of camping coaches in 1971. A few entrepreneurs have since offered refurbished coaches at railway stations such as St Germans and Hayle in Cornwall.

L·N·E·R CAMPING COACHES in England and Scotland

Accommodation for six persons from £2·10·0 per week
Ask for details at any L·N·E·R Station or Office

LEFT: *Poster produced by the London & North Eastern Railway in 1939 to promote holidays in camping coaches.*

RIGHT: *Happy holidaymakers relax in front of their Pullman camping coach based at Betws-y-Coed station in North Wales, 1960.*

King of the Castles

Charles Collett

Charles Benjamin Collett was born in London in 1871 and after studying engineering at university went on to work for marine engineers Maudsley, Sons & Field – based in Lambeth, the company had been founded in 1798 and specialised in designing and building marine steam engines. In 1893 Collett moved to Swindon where he worked in the Great Western Railway's drawing office as a draughtsman. He married in 1896 and two years later was promoted to Assistant to the Chief Draughtsman. Inching his way up the GWR's corporate ladder he was then promoted to Technical Inspector at the locomotive works in 1900 followed by a swift appointment to Assistant Manager. He held this position until 1912 when he became Works Manager, an important post that he held until 1919 when he became deputy to the GWR's Chief Mechanical Engineer (CME), George Jackson Churchward.

Churchward retired in 1922 leaving an important legacy of locomotive design and construction – standardisation of parts and his 4-cylinder 'Star' and 2-cylinder 'Saint' Class 4-6-0s were important ingredients that the methodical Collett went on to successfully develop further. Groomed for the job, Collett took over as CME at Swindon and the following year introduced one of his most successful locomotive classes, the 4-cylinder 'Castle' Class. Designed to haul heavy express trains, the 'Castle' was an improvement on Churchward's 'Star' Class which had been introduced in 1907. So successful was the 'Castle' Class that a total of 171 were newly built or converted from the 'Star' Class over the next 27 years with some members remaining in service until 1965. 'Castle' Class locomotives became famous in 1932 when they hauled the 'Cheltenham Flyer', then the world's fastest regular express train.

During his tenure as CME at Swindon Collett introduced no less than 25 new steam locomotive classes, ranging from the humble '1400' Class 0-4-2 tanks, the numerous '5700' 0-6-0 pannier tanks and the powerful '7200' Class 2-8-2 heavy freight tank locos to the 'Hall', 'Grange' and 'Manor' Class 4-6-0s. Without doubt his most famous design was the 'King' Class 4-6-0s that were introduced in 1927 to haul the GWR's crack express trains. A further development of the 'Castle', they were the most powerful 4-6-0 locomotives to be built in Britain, weighing 135 tons with a tractive effort of 40,300 lb. Only 30 were built and because of their weight were restricted to operating on the mainlines from London Paddington to Bristol, Plymouth, Cardiff and Wolverhampton. The first of its class, No 6000 *King George V* crossed the Atlantic in 1927, only three months after being newly outshopped from Swindon, to appear at the Baltimore & Ohio Railroad's centenary celebrations.

An able organiser, Collett was also responsible for carrying out a major programme to re-equip Swindon's locomotive workshops, cutting manufacturing costs and improving locomotive manufacturing quality that itself increased mileages between major overhauls. He also extended the Automatic Train Control fail-safe system over much of the GWR network.

Despite his prolific career as a steam locomotive designer, Collett was amongst the first to see the future of diesel power on railways. In 1934 he successfully introduced the first of 38 streamlined diesel railcars which were widely used not only on branch lines but also as twin-sets with buffet facilities on long-distance expresses such as the Birmingham (Snow Hill) to Cardiff route (see page 130).

Already a widower since 1923, Collett retired in 1941, to be succeeded by Frederick Hawksworth as the last CME at Swindon before Nationalisation, and died in 1952 aged 80.

LEFT: *The pinnacle of Charles Collett's career at Swindon Works were the 30 'King' Class 4-6-0s introduced in 1927. Here No 6003* King George IV *is seen at Old Oak Common engine shed on 28 August 1935.*

BELOW: *At the opposite end of Collett's design spectrum were the 863 members of '5700' Class 0-6-0PTs introduced in 1929. Here No 8753 (of '8750' sub-class) is seen outside Swindon Works in 1938.*

Let us pray

Three famous men of the cloth who loved railways

Bishop Eric Treacy (1907–78)

Born and educated in London, Eric Treacy became a Deacon in the Church of England in 1932 and was Vicar of Edge Hill, Liverpool, from 1936 to 1940. Taking up photography as a hobby in the 1930s he was soon drawn to Lime Street Station and the photogenic qualities of steam railways. His first published photograph was of a 'Royal Scot' leaving Lime Street with an express, which appeared in the *Liverpool Post*. In 1935 he became a member of the Railway Photographic Society and soon gained a reputation for his atmospheric railway shots. By the outbreak of World War II he had become an established railway photographer of the railway scene in north-west England with his photographs taken at Shap still considered to be some of the finest ever taken.

Following World War II when he was a military Chaplain, Eric Treacy moved on to become Rector of Keighley and soon discovered the photogenic qualities of the Settle & Carlisle line – his photographs taken during this period capture the raw beauty of steam locomotives working hard in a wild and desolate landscape at locations such as the 'Long Drag' up to Blea Moor, Ribblehead Viaduct, and Ais Gill Summit. His photographs were soon appearing in a growing number of railway magazines and books – his first major book was *Steam Up*, published in 1949.

Throughout his clerical career Eric Treacy not only pursued his love of railway photography but also got an insight into railway life, meeting footplatemen and taking footplate rides. From 1949 to 1961 he was Archdeacon of Halifax and in 1968 was made Bishop of Wakefield. Despite this high office his love of railways never diminished and with the end of steam in 1968 he turned his attention to the less romantic diesel scene. This passion for railways continued after his retirement in 1976 with his appointment to the Council of the Friends of the National Railway Museum in York. Eric Treacy died suddenly at Appleby station on his beloved Settle & Carlisle line in 1978 while photographing preserved '9F' 2-10-0 No 92220 *Evening Star*. Fittingly, his collection of 12,000 photographs is now part of the NRM's archive.

RIGHT TOP: *A real life 'Thomas the Tank Engine' is seen in action at Bo'ness on the Bo'ness & Kinneil Railway.*

RIGHT BOTTOM: *The Reverend 'Teddy' Boston on the footplate of 0-4-0ST* Pixie *on the Cadeby Light Railway in 1976.*

BELOW: *Famous railway photographer Bishop Eric Treacy of Wakefield poses for the camera in 1974. Fours years later he died while photographing his favourite railway, the Settle & Carlisle.*

Reverend Wilbert V. Awdry (1911–97)

From an early age Wilbert Awdry, son of the Vicar of Ampfield, near Romsey in Hampshire, couldn't fail to have a love of railways. His father, known as 'Railwayman Parson' had been interested in railways all his life and a move to Box in Wiltshire, within sight and sound of the GWR mainline, in 1917, firmly cemented young Wilbert's growing passion for them. Educated at Wycliffe Hall, Oxford, Wilbert Awdry was later a teacher in Jerusalem before becoming an Anglican priest in 1936. In 1940 he became a curate in Kings Norton, Birmingham, and it was here that his famous 'Railway Series' of children's books was born.

In 1942 his son, Christopher, was suffering from measles so to entertain the poor lad his father made a small, wooden model engine which he later named 'Thomas'. At Christopher's suggestion Wilbert made up stories about an imaginary railway on the Island of Sodor – its star was, of course, 'Thomas the Tank Engine'. His first book, 'The Three Railway Engines' was illustrated by Reginald Payne and published in 1945. New titles followed annually until 1972 when 26 had been published. The amazing success of these books never dazzled Wilbert and, in retirement, he enjoyed his time with involvement in the railway preservation movement and by creating model railway layouts and showing them at exhibitions up and down the country, often assisted by his friend Rev 'Teddy' Boston – the latter was immortalised as the 'Fat Clergyman' in Awdry's books!

Although Wilbert Awdry died in 1997 his imaginary railway, characters and locomotives live on – an enormous commercial success, 'Thomas the Tank Engine' has spawned a lucrative worldwide business empire in recent years with TV and film spin-offs, merchandising and 'Days out with Thomas' events on heritage railways.

Reverend 'Teddy' Boston (1924–86)

A close friend of Rev. Wilbert Awdry, 'Teddy' Boston became Rector of Cadeby and Vicar of Sutton Cheney in Leicestershire in 1960. Immortalised in the Rev. Awdry's *Thomas the Tank Engine* series as the 'Fat Clergyman', 'Teddy' Boston filled his rectory with model railways, the grounds with a passenger-carrying steam-operated 2ft-gauge light railway, and founded the annual Market Bosworth Steam Rally. The mainstay of steam motive power on the line was provided by 0-4-0 saddle tank 'Pixie' which Boston bought in 1962 from a local quarry. After his death in 1986 the Cadeby Light Railway was kept open by his widow until 2006 when it finally closed.

The old Slow & Dirty revival

Railway activities along the closed Somerset & Dorset Joint Railway

Its loss greatly mourned by local people and railway enthusiasts alike, the Somerset & Dorset Joint Railway was finally put to sleep after years of deliberate neglect on 7 March 1966 – the line saw its last trains, all enthusiasts' specials, on the previous day. For years the railway disappeared into the landscape, slowly being overtaken by nature. Fear not, however, as all is not lost with many green shoots of recovery now sprouting up along the line. Here are the highlights from north to south:

Bath Green Park station

The restored vaulted glass roof and station building survives next to a supermarket. It provides a covered space for markets and events. The booking office is now a restaurant.

Devonshire Tunnel, Combe Down Tunnel, Tucking Mill Viaduct and Midford Viaduct to Wellow

Trackbed converted by Sustrans for the 'Two Tunnels Greenway' footpath and cycleway which opened in 2012. It forms part of the National Cycle Network Route 24

which also takes in the route of the closed ex-GWR line from Radstock to Frome, known as Colliers' Way.

Midsomer Norton station
Now owned by the Somerset & Dorset Railway Heritage Trust who have restored the station and platforms, built a replica signal box and are currently relaying track southwards towards Masbury. Trains along this short route are run at weekends and are usually hauled by a diesel shunter or Sentinel steam locomotive. Long term plans include relaying the track to Chilcompton.

Charlton Viaduct, Shepton Mallet
This Grade-II-listed 27-arch viaduct now forms the impressive backdrop to Kilver Court Gardens that were originally developed by Showerings, the manufacturer of Babycham. The gardens, also known as the 'Secret Garden of Somerset', are open to the public throughout the year.

Trackbed of original 'mainline' west of Glastonbury
Much of the trackbed is now a 5-mile footpath and cycleway from the western outskirts of Glastonbury to Ashcott (refreshments at the quaint 'Railway Inn') and Shapwick. The route passes through several nature reserves formed from old peat workings, popular with birdwatchers throughout the year.

Yenston, south of Templecombe
The 2ft-gauge Gartell Light Railway now runs southwards from Yenston along about 1 mile of the S&D trackbed. Both steam- and diesel-hauled trains operate on this fully-signalled line on selected Sundays during the summer.

Shillingstone station
The main station building and platform have been restored by the Shillingstone Railway Project and are open to the public at weekends and on Wednesdays. Current plans include relaying a ½-mile of track. A length of trackbed here has been opened as the North Dorset Trailway for walkers, cyclists and horse riders.

LEFT: *Where once the 'Pines Express' stormed uphill from Bath Green Park, cyclists and walkers now enjoy the peace and quiet of the 'Two Tunnels Greenway' near Midford.*

BELOW: *The fully-signalled Gartell Light Railway makes use of 1 mile of Somerset & Dorset Joint Railway trackbed south of Templecombe.*

South Wales – land of plenty

A mega shed bash in South Wales

It was 5 a.m. on Sunday 7 April 1963, only 11 days after the publication of the 'Beeching Report' in which the good doctor had proposed the wholesale slaughter of Britain's railways and the earlier-than-expected retirement of steam locomotives. Humming the latest Bobby Vee hit 'The Night Has a Thousand Eyes', I was standing on the pavement by the A38 in Gloucester – my mission was to visit all of the steam sheds in South Wales in one day thanks to a coach tour organised by the Warwickshire Railway Society. This was probably my last chance before steam (and the associated coal industry) in the South Wales' valleys was confined to the dustbin of history and, as it was a Sunday, there was a good chance that most locomotives would be taking their day of rest inside the sheds.

In the pre-dawn darkness the Society's hired Bedford coach pulled up alongside and my adventure had begun. The other occupants of the steamed-up vehicle just grunted at me as we moved off to our first destination, the Gloucester Horton Road (85B) sub-shed at Lydney.

Here, in the gloomy interior, we spotted eight 0-6-0PTs, the majority '1600' Class employed on the remaining freight duties in the Forest of Dean. Next stop was Severn Tunnel Junction (86E) where we arrived at 7 a.m. Here there was a pretty impressive line-up of 71 locos, all steam except for three diesel shunters and two 'Westerns'. While most of them were naturally tank or freight locos there were a surprising number of named engines: 'Hall' Class Nos 5932, 5979, 5994, 6941, 6950; 'Modified Hall' Class No 6977; Grange' Class Nos 6820, 6873.

Newport was only a few miles down the A48 and here we visited the freight loco sheds at Newport Pill (86B) and Ebbw Junction (86A). By this date diesel shunters were taking over duties around Newport Docks and there were no less than 15 on Pill shed along with 18 steam of which the majority were the '4200' Class 2-8-0Ts. Ebbw Junction was pretty well packed with freight locos and of the 75 locos spotted only four were diesel shunters. Named locos were 'Hall' Nos 4907, 5939; 'Modified Hall' No 6975;

'Grange' No 6813; 'Castle' No 5073. Next on the list was Cardiff East Dock (88L) which by that date had replaced recently dieselised Canton as the main steam shed in Cardiff – it was pretty impressive stuff, albeit the 44 steam locos seen were all rather down at heel, with 19 named locos: 'Hall' Nos 4953, 5937, 5942, 6935, 6939, 6957; 'Castle' Nos 4080, 5014, 5015, 5043, 5051, 5074, 5096; 'Modified Hall' Nos 6987, 6995; 'Grange' Nos 6876, 6877; 'County' Nos 1000, 1028. Cardiff Cathays (88M) was next on the list although I noted that it was a bit of a dump and contained only one steam loco (No 6606), the rest being DMUs and diesel shunters.

This trip was not for the faint-hearted and as the pace quickened our coach driver dropped us off at Radyr (88B), 55 locos of which only four were diesel; Barry (88C), 28 all steam; Dai Woodham's scrapyard, 32 rusting hulks including 'King' Nos 6023, 6024; Llantrisant (88G), 12 all steam; Tondu (88H), 35 all steam; Duffryn Yard (87B), 60 all steam including 'County' No 1001, ex-L&YR 0-4-0ST No 51218, 'Hall' Nos 4919, 6945 and 'Modified Hall' Nos 6989, 6998. Next on this whistle-stop tour was Neath (87A) which had 60 locos, all steam except two diesel shunters. Namers here included 'Hall' Nos 4910, 4961, 4966, 5981; 'Grange' Nos 6844, 6845, 'Castle' No 7003.

Phew! Now it was up the valleys with Neath (N&B), a sub-shed of Neath with 11 steam, followed by Glyn Neath sub-shed with five steam then over the mountains to Class '5600' country: Treherbert (88F), 11 steam; Ferndale sub-shed, six steam; Aberdare (88J), 45 steam; Merthyr (88D), 14 steam; Dowlais Cae Harris sub-shed, five steam; Rhymney sub-shed, 11 steam; Aberbeeg (86F), 30 locos of which only three were diesel shunters. By now it was late evening and pitch dark and the driver unfortunately decided that it was too late to visit Pontypool Road (86G) and in the middle of the day he had also forgotten to visit Aberycnon (88E) – a pity, as I never did manage to get there!

What a day! Worn out, I was dropped off in Gloucester in the late evening with my notebook filled to bursting after visiting 21 sheds and the Barry dump. A total of 619 steam locos were seen although the writing was well and truly on the wall for them and within two years all had been consigned to the scrapyard. RIP.

BELOW: *One of the 21 engine sheds in South Wales that I visited in one day: the inside of the roundhouse at Aberdare engine shed (88J), seen here on 15 September 1963.*

We're all going on a steam summer holiday

My (trainspotting) holiday in Lyme Regis

Saturday 3 August 1963 started as a dull and drizzly day but who cared, we were going on holiday to Lyme Regis and not in a car but by steam train. Hooray!

Suitcases packed, our long and convoluted journey started at my local station, Gloucester Eastgate, where BR Standard Class 5MT 4-6-0 No 73068 headed south with the 7.30 a.m. three-carriage stopping train for Bristol. With less than 18 months to go before this service was withdrawn it was surprising how well patronised this train was and by the time we reached Yate the train was so full there was standing room only. After achieving a top speed of 62 mph between Berkeley Road and Charfield we arrived on time at Mangotsfield where we alighted to wait for our train to Bath Green Park.

Mangotsfield was a pretty dire station to hang around on but during our hour-long sojourn there I did see Stanier 'Black 5' 4-6-0 No 44776 roaring northwards with a Bristol to Newcastle relief express. Finally our long wait was over and our Bournemouth West-bound six-coach train of mixed SR green and BR maroon carriages pulled in from Bristol headed by Ivatt Class 2 2-6-2T No 41249.

BR Standard Class '5' 4-6-0 No 73012 departs from Bath Green Park with a local train to Bournemouth on 9 September 1963.

Heading into Bath Green Park I spotted ex-S&DJR Class '7F' 2-8-0 No 53808, Fowler '4F' 0-6-0 No 44560, a couple of ex-GWR pannier tanks and BR Standard Class 3 2-6-2Ts on 82F engine shed.

The next stage of our journey to Templecombe was behind BR Standard Class 5MT 4-6-0 No 73054 which left Bath Green Park 10 minutes late. Working hard to catch up lost time, we thundered through the single-bore Devonshire and Combe Down tunnels as we began our climb over the Mendips. By this date the poor old S&D had been relegated to secondary status after losing its summer-Saturday trains from the north to Bournemouth the previous year – traffic by now was much reduced and we only passed two northbound trains, one a goods headed by ex-S&DJR 2-8-0 No 53809 and the other a local headed by No 73047, before we reached Templecombe 15 minutes late.

Despite the rain, which by now had increased in intensity, Templecombe was in 1963 still a great place to watch steam trains – not a diesel in sight for miles around. We didn't have long to wait for our train to Axminster which arrived from Waterloo behind 'Merchant Navy' Class 4-6-2 No 35016 *Elders Fyffes*. Accelerating hard out of the station we reached a maximum speed of 87 mph before our next stop at Yeovil Junction where ex-GWR 2-6-2T No 4593 was seen on the autotrain to Yeovil Town. En route I also spotted five Bulleid Light Pacifics, an 'S15' 4-6-0 and a 'U1' 2-6-0 before we arrived at Axminster around 5 minutes late.

Since 1913 the 6-mile picturesque branch line to Lyme Regis had been home to three of the ex-LSWR Adams radial 4-4-2Ts but by 1963 these were just a fading memory. By then traffic on the line was in the charge of Ivatt Class 2 2-6-2Ts and the last part of our long journey from Gloucester was behind No 41307 of Exmouth Junction shed. We arrived at the little hilltop terminus exactly at 1 p.m. – 5½ hours of 100% steam haulage from Gloucester. Steam was soon to disappear from the Lyme Regis branch with the Ivatts being replaced by DMUs in November of that year.

For me the rest of the holiday was spent trainspotting on Axminster station and at Exeter and apart from the diesel invasion at the ex-GWR St David's station I had a very satisfying bag of steam locos by the time I went home. The journey back to Gloucester on 10 August was virtually all steam again: Lyme Regis to Axminster, No 4120; Axminster to Templecombe, No 34054 *Lord Beaverbrook* ('Merchant Navy' No 35020 *Bibby Line* was seen roaring through Templecombe with the down 'ACE'); Templecombe to Bath Green Park, No 73052; Bath to Mangotsfield, No 41208; Mangotsfield to Gloucester Eastgate, D41 – shame about that last one as it spoilt my 100% steam record for the holiday!

My holiday destination of Lyme Regis. Here Ivatt Class '2' 2-6-2T No 41206 is seen on arrival from Axminster on 9 August 1963. The single coach in the siding was a through working to Waterloo with it being attached to an up express at Axminster.

The last mainline

The Great Central Railway

The last mainline to be built into London, the Great Central Railway, had its roots in a much smaller company, the Manchester, Sheffield & Lincolnshire Railway. The MS&LR had existed since 1847 when it was formed by the amalgamation of four railway companies and the Grimsby Docks Company in order to improve communications across the Pennines between the important northern industrial centres of Manchester and Sheffield and the fast-growing port of Grimsby. The MS&LR, under its ambitious General Manager and, later, Chairman, Edward Watkin soon flourished and expanded its territory through takeovers and the arrangement of joint running rights with other railways in the region. Up to that point, despite intense competition from its larger rivals, the MS&LR, a major coal carrier, was a thriving concern. However, Edward Watkins was never a man to sit on his laurels and, as part of his dream to build a railway tunnel under the English Channel, planned further expansion southwards to London.

The new railway, from Annesley in Nottinghamshire to a new London terminus at Marylebone, would transform his company from a regional player into a major north-south strategic route which would compete head on with giants such as the Midland Railway and the Great Northern Railway. One section of the line, southward from Quainton Road in Buckinghamshire to Harrow, was to be jointly run with the Metropolitan Railway, of which Edward Watkin was also Chairman, which had already started operating services on this route in 1892. The MS&LR obtained Parliamentary approval for the London Extension, as it was then known, in 1893 and, the following year, to crown his grand dream, Watkin changed the name of his company to the Great Central Railway. Work started on the construction of the 92-mile line in 1895 and it was opened for passenger traffic on 15 March 1899. The line was designed from the outset for fast traffic with a continental loading gauge and no level crossings. Major towns and cities that were served by the

Great Central included Nottingham, Loughborough, Leicester and Rugby, all of which were already well served by other major railway companies and the company soon ran into trouble as the actual cost of building the new line was nearly double the original estimate of £6 million.

Watkins retired as Chairman of the Great Central in 1899 and his place was taken by Alexander Henderson. Sam Fay took over as General Manager in 1902 and, in the same year, John Robinson was appointed Chief Mechanical Engineer. The headquarters of the company moved to Marylebone in 1905. In Robinson the Great Central had found a very able locomotive and rolling stock designer and soon the company was living up to its publicity for 'Rapid Travel in Luxury'. Despite this, passenger traffic never lived up to expectations but the railway did achieve much success as a freight carrier. In the '1923 Grouping' the Great Central became part of the newly formed London & North Eastern Railway and, on Nationalisation in 1948, was allocated to the Eastern Region of British Railways.

The Great Central's fortunes took a severe downturn in 1960 when it was transferred to the London Midland Region of BR. Marylebone to Manchester expresses were withdrawn and other services were placed in the hands of worn-out steam locomotives. At a time when railway rationalisation and full-scale closures were becoming a reality, the duplication of north–south routes into London soon brought about the Great Central's demise. Through freight services were withdrawn on 14 June 1965 and the railway closed as a through route completely on 3 September 1966. Apart from the suburban services from Marylebone to Aylesbury and a short-lived section that was retained for passenger traffic between Rugby Central and Nottingham Victoria, the Great Central ceased to exist. Today, the section from Loughborough to Leicester North is run as an 8¼-mile steam-operated mainline heritage railway while the section from Ruddington, on the southern outskirts of Nottingham, to Loughborough is a 10-mile heritage railway. Only a missing girder bridge separates the two at Loughborough.

LEFT: *Carriages and horse-drawn buses outside Marylebone station c.1910. It also had a hotel, reached by a covered way, which later became the headquarters of British Railways from 1948 to 1991.*

BELOW: *Postcard published in 1907 depicting a Great Central Railway 'Atlantic' 4-4-2 at speed with the 'Manchester Express'.*

A kind of hush

LMS experiments with the Michelin Train

Prior to his death in 1931 Andre Michelin, the French industrialist and manufacturer of pneumatic rubber tyres, spent a sleepless night on board a sleeper train – the noise of the steel wheels on the track kept him awake and inspired him to come up with a quieter solution.

Thus was the rubber-tyred train born – not only was it quieter but it was also more comfortable. Early in 1932, following successful tests made with pneumatic-tyred petrol-engined railcars in France, a single railcar was tested by the LMS on the Bletchley to Oxford line. This strange looking vehicle seated 24 passengers, had 10 pneumatic-tyred wheels, three pairs in front and two at the back, and was driven by a 27 hp Panhard et Levassor sleeve-valve petrol engine. The pneumatic tyres, fitted with a metal flange to keep the wheels on the rail, were inflated to 85lb/in^2 and contained a wooden hoop which kept the wheels on the track if the tyre deflated.

Following their trials with this vehicle on the Bletchley to Oxford line and in the Midlands the LMS then investigated a much larger vehicle. Known as the Coventry Pneumatic Rail-Car it was powered by a 240 hp 12-cylinder engine and seated 56 passengers. The driver sat in a raised turret at one end allowing unobstructed views for running in either direction. Weighing 6.5 tons, the 54ft-long railcar also had rapid acceleration with a top speed in excess of 60 mph. Trials were carried out in 1935 on the mainline between Euston and Leighton Buzzard – following a stop at Watford the next 22¾ miles were covered in 25 minutes with a top speed of 67 mph. The return non-stop journey of 40¼ miles was covered in 42½ minutes – a creditable performance that clearly demonstrated the vehicle's comfort and quietness and impressive acceleration and braking capabilities.

While the UK experiment ended here, pneumatic-tyred railcars continued to operate successfully in France and in some French colonies – one of the last in service still operates short tourist trips on the Fianarantsoa Cote Est (FCE) in Madagascar. Rubber-tyred trains also operate on parts of the Paris Metro.

The Michelin pneumatic-tyred train as used in an experiment by the London Midland & Scottish Railway on its Bletchley to Oxford route in 1932.

Bog off!

Oliver Bulleid's turf-burner experiment

Following his 11-year term as Chief Mechanical Engineer for the Southern Railway the innovative locomotive designer Oliver Bulleid moved to Ireland where he became the CME for the newly-formed Córas Iompair Éireann (CIE/Irish Railways) in 1949. Faced with an acute shortage of coal – the Republic had virtually no coal reserves and imports during and immediately after World War II had slowed to a trickle – Bulleid's first task was to solve the vexed shortage of motive power on CIE. Early dieselisation became a priority and by the early 1950s imported diesels were soon replacing the clapped-out vintage steam locomotives.

Bulleid was not only a radical innovator but also possessed what one can only describe as extremely imaginative lateral thought! He had already experimented with the unique 'Leader' Class of steam locomotive during his latter years as CME of the SR but Nationalisation had killed any further development of this futuristic locomotive. Once in Ireland Bulleid came up with the brilliant idea of using the country's seemingly unlimited supply of indigenous peat reserves to fuel a steam locomotive. He first experimented by converting K3 Class 2-6-0 No 356 to a turf-burning loco – modifications were extensive and included a screw-feed mechanical stoker, twin Crosti pre-heaters and a Franco-Crosti boiler. The pre-heaters on each side of the boiler looking very much like torpedo tubes coupled with the absence of a chimney made this a very strange looking machine indeed. Steaming qualities were initially appalling but in true Irish style a forced-draught fan was later added and powered by an old Leyland bus engine mounted on a wagon behind the tender!

Spurred on by this experiment Bulleid went ahead with the design for a modern turf/oil-burning locomotive. Numbered CC1 it was built at Inchicore Works in Dublin and externally looked similar to his double-ended box-shaped 'Leader' Class of the SR. With a length of 60ft and a driving cab at each end the loco had a 0-6-6-0 wheel arrangement similar to the 19th-century double Fairlies of the Ffestiniog Railway in North Wales. The firebox and boiler were mounted centrally between the cabs and the fuel bunker and water capacity were located at each end. Trials started in the Dublin area in 1957 but with the retirement of its inventor a year later and the mass-dieselisation of CIE already underway the locomotive was shunted into a siding at Inchicore never to steam again. Sadly this unique piece of Irish railway history was scrapped in 1965.

BELOW: *Oliver Bulleid's brand new but ill-fated turf-burning locomotive CC1 is seen here at Inchicore Works in Dublin in 1957. The experiment, which used local turf as a fuel instead of imported coal, was a dismal failure.*

A railway coalition

The Cheshire Lines Committee

What became the second largest (by route miles after the Midland & Great Northern Joint Railway) and certainly the most profitable jointly owned railway in Britain, the Cheshire Lines Committee (CLC) was made up of five independent railways in the Manchester and Liverpool area. Its formation allowed its parent companies access to the lucrative trade from Liverpool Docks and the Manchester area, which were previously the domain of the London & North Western Railway and the Lancashire & Yorkshire Railway.

1. Backed by the Manchester, Sheffield & Lincolnshire Railway (successor to the Great Central Railway) and the Great Northern Railway, the 12¾-mile Cheshire Midland Railway opened throughout between Altrincham and Northwich in 1863.

2. The 2¾-mile Stockport & Woodley Junction Railway was also backed by the MS&LR and the GNR and opened in 1863.

3. The 8-mile Stockport, Timperley & Altrincham Junction Railway (backed by the MS&LR and the GNR) opened between Portwood and Deansgate (Altrincham) in 1865.

4. The 22¾-mile West Cheshire Railway from Northwich to Helsby opened completely in 1870 by which time it had become part of the CLC.

5. The 7-mile Chester & West Cheshire Junction Railway had already become part of the CLC when it opened between Mouldsworth Junction and Chester Northgate in 1875.

The CLC also worked trains on the independent 14-mile Southport & Cheshire Lines Committee Extension Railway which opened between Aintree and Southport in 1884.

The Cheshire Lines Committee was officially formed as an independent concern on 15 August 1867 with equal shares held by the GNR, MS&LR (later to become the Great Central Railway) and the Midland Railway. While the company owned its own rolling stock (including four Sentinel steam railcars from 1929) its locomotives were supplied by the owning companies, predominantly the Great Central until the 'Big Four Grouping' of 1923 when that company became part of the LNER. The CLC remained independent until Nationalisation at the beginning of 1948. Several of its engine sheds, notably Heaton Mersey, Northwich and Trafford Park, remained in use until 1968, the last year of steam on BR.

During its lifetime the CLC was an extremely successful and profitable undertaking, running the most popular passenger service between its termini at Liverpool Central and Manchester Central and between Manchester and Chester. Opened in 1880, Manchester Central became one of the busiest stations in the UK. It closed in 1969 and is now an exhibition and conference centre while Liverpool Central, once the headquarters of the CLC, closed in 1972 and was demolished. The CLC routes between Manchester and Liverpool and between Manchester and Chester are still open to passengers today.

Freight traffic was even more important with the company serving the coalfields and industrial belt around Liverpool and Manchester, as well as Liverpool Docks and the salt mines and chemical works around Northwich.

LEFT: *The CLC's Manchester Central station in 1966. It closed in 1969 and is now an exhibition and conference centre.*

BELOW: *Built in 1880, the CLC's Manchester Central was once one of the busiest stations in the UK. Here ex-LMS 'Jubilee' Class 4-6-0 No 45579 Punjab waits to depart with 'The Palatine' express to London St Pancras on 18 June 1958. To the right is Fairburn Class '4' 2-6-4T No 42111 on a local train.*

Chinese laundries

Bulleid's ill-fated 'Leader' Class

Oliver Bulleid, the Chief Mechanical Engineer of the Southern Railway from 1937 to 1947 and for the Southern Region of BR until 1950, was an innovative railway engineer best known for his air-smoothed 'Light Pacifics' and 'Merchant Navy' Pacifics which did such sterling service on the Southern Region until the end of steam in 1967. Employing the most up-to-date technology, Bulleid was a world-leader in steam locomotive design but his final fling for the Southern Railway before departing for Ireland must surely rate as one of the most ill-conceived and poorly-designed steam locomotive classes in the history of Britain's railways.

The 'Leader' Class started life in 1944 as a replacement for the ageing 'M7' 0-4-4 tank locos and was designed to incorporate many of the features found in Bulleid's utilitarian 'Q1' 0-6-0 locos. Following various drawing board proposals a 0-6-0+0-6-0 design was chosen. It featured two interchangeable six-wheeled steam driving bogies, an offset boiler placed inside a slab-sided

bodywork not dissimilar to a modern diesel, duplicated driving cabs at each end linked by a corridor and a separate centrally-located cab for the firebox and fireman. The driving bogies were each powered by three cylinders with the power transmitted to the driving wheels by an enclosed oil-bathed chain drive. Just to add to this nightmare scenario was the highly unusual sleeve-valve arrangement which was hurriedly tested on an old LBSCR 'Atlantic' loco while 'Leader No 1' was being built.

An order for five 'Leader' Class locos was placed and work started on the prototype at Brighton Works in July 1947. Constant modifications to the design were made while work was hurriedly in progress and a start was also made on the other four members of the class. Nationalisation of Britain's railways in 1948 saw work continue on the prototype loco at Brighton and it emerged for trials, painted in grey with red and white lining, in June 1949. Sequentially following on from the 'Merchant Navy' numbering of 35XXX, the loco was

numbered 36001. By then work had halted on the other four locos: No 36002 was nearly complete; No 36003 just needed its outer bodywork fitting; Nos 36004 and 36005 had barely risen above their frames.

Untried and untested, the slab-sided diesel-lookalike No 36001 sallied forth around the South Eastern Division of the Southern Region, towing a dynamometer car and a train of empty carriages but immediately proved to be unreliable – the list of faults was endless and included heavy fuel and water consumption, badly fitted cylinder rings, poor braking, collapsed firebox linings and uneven balance. The crew worked in confined spaces in appallingly hot conditions leading to the locomotive being nicknamed the 'Chinese Laundry'! While some of these problems were addressed it was all to no avail despite Oliver Bulleid postponing his departure to Ireland in order to oversee the trials. The loco made its last run, reportedly with

some success, on 2 November 1950, but having already spent large amounts of taxpayers' money on the unreliable locomotive British Railways was having none of it and the project was cancelled in 1951.

Not surprisingly neither No 36001 nor the four other unfinished locos survived and they were quietly broken up for scrap. Bulleid went on to become CME of Irish Railways (CIE) where he designed his famous turf-burning locomotive (see page 59).

LEFT: *The locomotive boilers for the Southern Railway's Bulleid 'Leader' Class 0-6-0+0-6-0 Nos 36001–36003 are seen at Brighton Works in 1947.*

BELOW: *'Leader' Class No 36001 at the head of a test train in 1949 which included a former North Eastern Railway dynamometer car. This strange loco proved to be too unreliable and the project was cancelled by British Railways in 1951.*

GWR famous trains 1

Cheltenham Flyer

During the 1920s and 1930s there was fierce rivalry not only between the British 'Big Four' railway companies but also among railways throughout the world to lay claim that they ran the fastest scheduled passenger service in the world. For many years the GWR had run the 'Cheltenham Spa Express' between Cheltenham and Paddington but the introduction of Collett's 'Castle' Class 4-6-0s in 1923 led to a rapid speed up of this service and a change of name to 'Cheltenham Flyer'. Timings were increasingly accelerated until 1929 when the 77¼ miles between Swindon and Paddington was scheduled to take only 70 minutes at an average speed of 66.2 mph. In 1931 the timing for Swindon to Paddington was further accelerated to an average speed of 69.2 mph but by now the tantalising 70 mph average speed was within the GWR's reach.

On 6 June 1932 Driver Ruddock and Fireman Thorp of Old Oak Common shed handed the GWR publicity department a glittering prize when they shattered all previous timings and broke all railway speed records. Headed by No 5006 *Tregenna Castle* the 'Cheltenham Flyer' left the town of its name promptly at 2.30 p.m. and after a leisurely journey through the Cotswolds reached Swindon for its final stop before Paddington. At 3.48 p.m. *Tregenna Castle* and its six coaches left Swindon and then the fireworks started – the train accelerating continuously until Didcot (24.2 miles from Swindon) was passed in 18 min 55 sec at a speed of over 90 mph. This high speed was maintained for mile after mile and despite a slight slowing past Twyford the train was still travelling at 84.4 mph just 2 miles short of Paddington which was reached in 56 min 47 sec from Swindon at an average speed of 81.6 mph. What a journey! Three months later the 'Cheltenham Flyer' was accelerated again and was rescheduled to take only 65 minutes between Swindon and Paddington at an average speed of 71.3 mph – it was now officially the fastest scheduled train in the world.

RIGHT: *Built by the ill-fated North British Locomotive Company, 'Warship' Class 41 diesel hydraulic D601* Ark Royal *heads the 'Cornish Riviera Express' out of Dainton Tunnel on 19 June 1958.*

BELOW: *Built at Swindon Works in 1923 and the first of its class, GWR 'Castle' Class 4-6-0 No 4073* Caerphilly Castle *can be seen today in Swindon Steam Railway Museum. The loco proudly carries the headboard of the 'Cheltenham Flyer', once the world's fastest train.*

Until 1906 trains from Paddington to Devon and Cornwall had to travel the 'Great Way Round' via Bristol but with the opening of new lines between Patney & Chirton to Westbury in 1900 and from Castle Cary to Cogload Junction (near Taunton) in 1906 the journey was shortened by just over 20 miles. New track bypassing Westbury and Frome which opened in 1933, further reduced travelling times.

With the new, shorter route in mind the GWR held a competition in 1904 to find a name for the daily premier express between Paddington and Penzance – thus was the 'Cornish Riviera Limited' born. Initially the train ran via Bristol but in 1906 it took the shorter route via Castle Cary. Slip coaches were included to serve other popular holiday destinations such as Weymouth, Ilfracombe and Newquay. The train became so popular with holidaymakers that it ran in two portions on summer Saturdays until World War I when it was suspended. The train resumed service in 1919 and in 1923 the introduction of new carriages and the 'Castle' Class locomotives saw a further improvement in service. The introduction of the more powerful 'King' Class locos in 1927 allowed heavier trains to reach Plymouth in 4 hours and two years later through coaches were added for Falmouth and St Ives. In 1935 new 'Centenary' carriages were introduced and the

regular 10.30 a.m. departure from Paddington carried reserved seat passengers only and ran (officially) non-stop to Truro – in fact the train halted at Devonport to change engines, the 'King' being too heavy to cross the Royal Albert Bridge. On summer Saturdays such was the demand for the train that it ran 'non-stop' to St Erth with passengers for Falmouth and Helston being conveyed in a relief express.

By 1939 the 'Limited' normally consisted of eight portions: the main portion with restaurant car for Penzance, one through coach each for St Ives, Falmouth, Newquay, Kingsbridge, the Taunton slip with coaches for Ilfracombe and Minehead and the two Weymouth coaches slipped at Westbury. The train continued to run during World War II but via Bristol and it wasn't until 1955 that pre-war schedules had been regained. Steam haulage was ousted in the late 1950s with the introduction of 'Warship' Class diesel hydraulics followed in the 1960s by the more powerful 'Western' Class locos. By the end of the decade the journey time to Penzance had come down to 5hr 35min and more was in the pipeline – following haulage for some years by Class 47 and Class 50 diesel electrics the 'Cornish Riviera' (as it was then known) became an HST working in 1979 and by 1983 Plymouth was being reached in 3hr 13min and Penzance in 4hr 55min.

The joy of trainspotting

How one boy fell in love with trains

As a young child I couldn't fail to get excited about railways. Born in Gloucester, for many years I lived just across the road from the old Midland mainline from Eastgate Station to Bristol. Behind our house and just across the park was the High Orchard Docks branch worked by the diminutive MR Deeley 0-4-0s complete with driver's bicycle slung over the front buffers. Along this line also trundled brand new London Underground trains, narrow-gauge carriages for far-flung railways of the British empire and, later, sparkling new single-car DMUs for British Railways – all of these emerging from the Gloucester Carriage & Wagon Works like newly-built full-size Airfix kits. To gain access to the mainline, these trains had to cross the main road at California Crossing, where road traffic was stopped by a man with a red flag. It was quite a sight to see an aging '3F' 0-6-0 hauling a long train of wagons slowly across the road with wagons filled with timber that had just been offloaded from a coaster in Gloucester Docks.

As a youngster I attended Tredworth Road Junior School and to get there entailed crossing the Midland mainline either at Painswick Road or Farm Street crossings. Inevitably, my perambulations were often interrupted by the passage of a train, sometimes a long slow goods train hauled by a '4F' or '8F' belching steam and smoke as it tackled the gradient out of Gloucester. At other times there was the sheer excitement of seeing a named train, usually hauled by a 'Jubilee' or a 'Black Five', such as the 'Pines Express' or 'The Devonian'.

My father didn't own a car (nor a TV or phone) and because of this my holidays were pure bliss. Each year we usually had one week of holiday in either Swanage, Lyme Regis, Exmouth or Woolacombe and the journey there and back was the highlight of the whole week. My favourite journey was to Lyme Regis. Invariably, this entailed lugging our suitcases down to Eastgate Station where we would catch a stopping train for Mangotsfield, usually hauled by a '2P' 4-4-0. Here, at this draughty

triangular station, we would alight to await the train for Bath Green Park. What a delightful station Bath GP was – wooden platforms and an overall roof (its still there as a covered venue and for parking at the nearby Sainsburys). The next stage of our epic journey was over the Mendips on the Slow and Dirty to Templecombe. Apart from smokey Devonshire and Combe Down tunnels I would invariably spend the rest of the trip with my head out of the window, much to my mother's concern. Templecombe was very exciting as I watched the 'Merchant Navies' thunder through at great speed on their switchback ride to Exeter or Waterloo. During a lull between the holiday expresses we would embark on the fourth stage of our journey to Axminster where would make our final change

on to the Lyme Regis branch. Invariably the train was hauled by one of the veteran Adams radial tanks which wound its way through leafy cuttings and across Cannington Viaduct before depositing us and our luggage at our destination. If only I had a time machine… (for the full story see pages 54–5).

LEFT: *A wonderful scene from the late 1950s as young trainspotters enjoy their packed lunch at Liverpool Street station while BR Standard Class '7' 4-6-2 No 70003* John Bunyan *looks on.*

BELOW: *Clutching the regulation notebook two young trainspotters are deep in conversation alongside BR Standard Class '7' 4-6-2 No 70054* Dornoch Firth *at Preston in 1963.*

Back at home my father had built me (or was it really for himself?) a splendid '0' gauge layout on trestles around one of our attics. With Hornby and Bassett-Lowke locos racing around the tracks and the sound of a 'Jubilee' passing outside on the Bristol to Newcastle mail train how could a small boy not be totally absorbed in railways?

I distinctly remember the first time I went trainspotting. Having just passed my 11+ exam I went on to attend the Crypt Grammar School where several of my classmates had already been bitten by the craze. I was determined that one Saturday I would catch the bus to Gloucester Central station to investigate this phenomenon. I have still got my Sterling No. 3 Notebook from that fateful day in 1957 when I hung around Central Station, taking in the smell of smoke, steam and oil – it was like being let loose in a sweetshop! I can still 'remember' that smell today. Here are the first ever locomotives that I spotted:

2242, 2826, 7208
7810 *Draycott Manor*
7920 *Coney Hall*
5042 *Winchester Castle*
4085 *Berkeley Castle*
6838 *Goodmoor Grange*
4088 *Dartmouth Castle*
5917 *Westminster Hall*
5914 *Ripon Hall*
2266, 4139, 2227
5418, 6394, 6354
5017 *The Gloucestershire Regiment 28th 61st*
3848, 2815, 73011, 1631, 6354
5041 *Tiverton Castle*
6865 *Hopton Grange*

There used to be a very long footbridge that spanned a multitude of carriage and wagon sidings that connected Gloucester Central and Eastgate Stations. I wandered over this on to the platform at Eastgate and here are the locomotives that I spotted there:

73073, 73054, 48523, 41078, 44045, 44818, 58165, 44757, 43932, 1605, 44962

Needless to say, after that first trip I got the bug really badly. Within a short space of time I was travelling far and wide, to Swindon Works, Derby Works and Bristol. Gloucester itself was a fascinating place with the comings and goings of both WR and LMR expresses, coal trains from and iron ore trains to South Wales, local workings to Hereford and Bristol, the Chalford push-pull plus all of the local traffic from the docks, carriage and wagon works and gas works. It was not unusual to see a gleaming ex-works WR loco running in on a Swindon stopping train and one of the highlights of each day was 'The Cornishman' express, its brown and cream coaches always hauled by an immaculate Wolverhampton Stafford Road (84A) 'Castle' class loco such as No 5045 *Earl of Dudley*.

As the years passed, my trainspotting trips became more and more adventurous taking in most of Scotland, Wales and England and usually spent in the company of a fellow enthusiast. One of my craziest and last trips took place on the early morning of 8 May 1966 when, after staying with friends in London, I caught the 00.15 a.m. train out of Euston behind one of the newly introduced AC electrics, E3122. The purpose of this journey was to travel back to London via the Great Central mainline which was due for imminent closure. After alighting at Rugby Midland in the wee hours of the morning I walked across to a completely deserted Rugby Central where I caught the York to Swindon train hauled by Hymek diesel-hydraulic D7093. In the company of a couple of railway workers I travelled down to Woodford Halse where I alighted before the train set off again for its journey to Swindon via Banbury and Didcot. Woodford Halse station in the middle of the night was a pretty scary place to be on your own! The Great Central was in its death throes, the once-busy station was completely deserted, there were no lights and I was the only passenger waiting for the early morning train to Marylebone. It duly arrived and I am sure that the driver of D5016 looked astonished as he spotted me waiting on the gloomy platform. The last leg of the journey to Marylebone was duly completed and I returned to my friend's flat in St John's Wood – nobody was any the wiser of my night time antics as they were all still asleep! The Great Central was finally put to sleep only four months later.

RIGHT: Teenage trainspotters enjoy a chat to the driver of ex-LMS 'Jubilee' Class 4-6-0 No 45573 Newfoundland at soggy Carlisle station on 10 July 1965.

Locomotive builders to the world 1

The North British Locomotive Company

Formed in 1903 by the merger of three Glasgow locomotive manufacturers – Dübs, Neilson, and Sharp, Stewart – the North British Locomotive Company became the largest locomotive manufacturer in Europe with the capacity to build 600 per year. With its headquarters in Springburn the NBL went on until the mid-1950s to build thousands of steam locos not only for British companies such as the SR and LMS, but also for the War Department in World War II and railways in Australia, New Zealand, Malaysia, Pakistan, India and South Africa – some of these locos have since been preserved and are still in steam.

Notable examples of British steam locos built by NBL were as follows:

- Southern Railway:
  30 'King Arthur' Class 4-6-0 (763–792) in 1925.
- London Midland & Scottish Railway:
  25 Compound '4P' 4-4-0, 50 'Royal Scot' 4-6-0s (6100–6149) in 1927, 50 'Jubilee' Class 4-6-0 (5557–5606) in 1934–5.
- War Department:
  208 Stanier '8F' 2-8-0, 150 '8F' 2-10-0 and 545 '8F' 2-8-0 in 1943.

Sadly the NBL failed to continue its long and illustrious record when it moved from steam to diesel production in the late 1950s. After signing a deal with the German company MAN to build diesel engines under licence it went on to build some of the most unreliable locomotives ever ordered by BR. With the taxpayer footing the bill, the list of dismal failures are as follows:

- 58 Type 2 Bo-Bo diesel electric (Class 21) D6100–D6157 1958–60. Apart from 20 which were rebuilt as Class 29, all had been withdrawn by 1968. The Class 29 fared little better and were all withdrawn by 1971.
- 58 Type 2 B-B diesel hydraulic (Class 22) D6300–D6357 1959–62. The class had become extinct by 1972.
- 5 Type 4 A1A-A1A diesel hydraulic (Class 41) D600–D604 1958–9. All withdrawn at the end of 1967.
- 33 Type 4 B-B diesel hydraulic (Class 43) D833–D865 1960–62. All withdrawn by 1971.

NBL also built 10 Class AL4 Bo-Bo electric locos (E3036–E3045) in 1960–61 for the WCML. Even these were unreliable and, despite rebuilding in the early '70s, had all been withdrawn by 1980.

The poor workmanship and unreliability of NBL diesel locos brought the company to its knees. Warranty claims and guarantees finally pushed the company over the brink and it went bankrupt in April 1962. All that remains today are the company's former offices in Flemington Street, Springburn, which are now part of North Glasgow College.

LEFT: *Built for the LMS by the NBL in 1927, 'Royal Scot' Class 4-6-0 No 6137* The Prince of Wales's Volunteers (South Lancashire) *is seen here in all its glory. Willesden engine shed, 16 August 1945.*

BELOW: *NBL-built diesel hydraulic 'Warship' Class 43 D834* Pathfinder *emerges from Box Tunnel with the 'Bristol Pullman' replacement train, c.1962.*

Push me – pull you 1

The GWR's autotrains

During the 19th century the workers at the numerous mills, foundries, breweries and other manufacturing companies dotted up and down the length of the Golden Valley in Gloucestershire had to content themselves with a slow journey to work on a horse-drawn bus or on foot. Although railways had already come to the area as early as 1845 when the Cheltenham & Great Western Union Railway (later part of the GWR) opened for business, the only stations being served by the end of the century were at Chalford, Brimscombe, Stroud and Stonehouse. The proposal for an electric tramway to serve the valley spurred the GWR into action and in 1903 the company introduced a new steam railmotor on a frequent regular interval service between Chalford and Stonehouse. With new small halts eventually built along the 7-mile stretch at St Mary's Crossing, Brimscombe Bridge, Ham Mill, Bowbridge Crossing, Downfield Crossing, Cashes Green and Ebley Crossing the service was an immediate hit with local people.

Designed by G. J. Churchward the new railmotors had internally located vertical boilers and, unusually for the GWR, were fitted with outside Walshaerts valve gear. They could be driven from either end, seated 52 and had a top speed of 45 mph but were difficult to service. Soon after opening, the Chalford to Stonehouse service was in such great demand that extra non-motorised trailer coaches were added but this extra weight reduced performance.

To counter this the GWR started to equip certain small classes of tank engine ('455' Class 2-4-0T, '517' Class 0-4-2T, '1076' Class 0-6-0ST/PT and '2021' Class 0-6-0ST/PT) with auto-control gear that could be operated by the driver, when the locomotive was at the rear, from a driving compartment at the front of a trailer coach. The trains, the forerunners of modern diesel multiple units,

could therefore operate in a push-pull mode and the extra power greatly speeded up the service. The Golden Valley autotrain service was extended to Gloucester Central in the 1920s and other autotrains were also introduced on some South Wales valley lines, the Cheltenham to Honeybourne route, on other West Country branches and on suburban services out of Paddington. Some '4575' Class 2-6-2s and all '5400' and '6400' Class 0-6-0PTs were also auto-fitted at later dates and in the early 1960s could be seen operating services on some ex-LSWR East Devon branch lines and on the Yeovil Town to Yeovil Junction shuttle.

However, the most successful design of auto-fitted locos by far were the '1400' Class 0-4-2Ts which were introduced in 1932 and, with their larger driving wheels, on mainline service, such as that between Standish Junction and Tuffley Junction which paralleled the Midland's Bristol to Gloucester mainline, could achieve speeds of 80 mph.

Sadly, despite profitability and much local support, the popular autotrain service between Chalford and Gloucester was listed for closure in the 1963 'Beeching Report'. Headed by '1400' Class 0-4-2T No 1472 hauling two packed autotrailers, the last train ran on 31 October 1964 and its return journey from Chalford was delayed by throngs of local people paying their last respects at every station and halt along the line. The author, who was on this train, can vividly remember some enthusiasts helping themselves to rather lengthy halt nameboards as souvenirs! Fortunately four members of the '1400' Class along with many autotrailers have since been preserved.

LEFT: *Ex-GWR push-pull fitted '6400' Class 0-6-0PT No 6412 with the 'Chalford Titch' autotrain halts at Brimscombe station on 17 October 1964. Two weeks later this popular and profitable service from Gloucester was withdrawn.*

OVERLEAF: *Viewed from the driving compartment of an autocoach at Bishops Lydeard station on 25 March 2012, preserved ex-GWR 'King' Class 4-6-0 No 6024 King Edward I has just arrived from Minehead with a train of happy passengers on the West Somerset Railway.*

BELOW: *Ex-GWR push-pull fitted '1400' Class No 1426 propels a train full of school children into Severn Bridge station before crossing the Severn Railway Bridge to Sharpness and Berkeley Road in July 1959.*

Small is beautiful 1

Two long-lost narrow-gauge railways

Snailbeach District Railways

Set in the shadow of the craggy Stiperstones Hills in Shropshire, the 2ft-4in. (some sources say 2ft-3¾in.) -gauge Snailbeach District Railways was opened from Pontesbury (on the joint GWR/LNWR branch line from Shrewsbury to Minsterley) to lead mines at Snailbeach in 1877. With a total length of only 3¾ miles this curiously-gauged line was initially profitable but the closure of the largest mine in 1884 led to a decline in the railway's fortunes – during this moribund time the Snailbeach's two locomotives were loaned to the expanding Glyn Valley Tramway in the Ceiriog Valley to the north.

The Snailbeach came back to life again in 1905 when a rail-linked granite quarry near Habberley was opened – to work this traffic the railway borrowed one of the Glyn Valley Tramway's 2ft-4½in.-gauge locos but soon returned it because of the slight difference in gauge, instead buying a Bagnall 0-6-0T *Dennis*. Granite stone traffic remained buoyant for a few years but by 1915 this had dwindled considerably and the line closed.

Following the end of World War I granite for road building came back in demand and Shropshire County Council leased the granite quarry. Seeing another money-making venture beckoning, Colonel Holman Fred Stephens, owner of a ramshackle railway empire (see pages 32–4), bought the line and re-equipped it with two Baldwin 2-6-0 tanks that had previously worked in northern France during the war. The opening of a stone-crushing plant soon brought plenty of work for the railway and through the 1930s it prospered carrying crushed granite to the exchange sidings at Pontesbury.

By 1947 the Snailbeach's three steam locomotives were on their last legs and they were soon scrapped. Shropshire County Council leased what was left of the railway, sending loaded stone wagons by gravity downhill to Pontesbury and hauling them back to the quarry by a tractor straddling the line. This antiquated operation ceased in 1959 when the line from the quarry was converted into a road.

Today, the granite quarry no longer operates although the engine shed at Snailbeach, along with some track to the long-closed lead mines, still survives.

Once dubbed the 'Whisky Capital of the World' the harbour town of Campbeltown at the far south of the isolated Mull of Kintyre was also once home to an eccentric narrow-gauge railway. Opened in 1877 to replace a disused canal, the 2ft-3in.-gauge 4½-mile Campbeltown & Machrihanish Light Railway served coal mines near Machrihanish.

The line initially flourished, carrying coal to the harbour at Campbeltown and was rebuilt and extended as a passenger-carrying light railway in 1906. Carried on fast turbine steamers from Glasgow, daytrippers were conveyed the 6½ miles from Argyll Street station in Campbeltown to the beaches and golf links at Machrihanish. After a break during World War I the railway continued to flourish through the 1920s but competition from road buses and the closure of the Argyll Colliery in 1929 soon brought about its demise. The line closed in November 1931, briefly reopening early in 1932 but closing for good in May of that year. Within a year the track had been lifted, the two 0-6-2 tank locomotives *Atlantic* and *Argyll* scrapped and the company wound up.

Nothing much remains of this unique Scottish narrow-gauge line today although the scene in Argyll Street, Campbeltown, is much the same. The route of the railway alongside Campbeltown Loch and through a long cutting up to Limecraigs can easily be followed – the latter is now a footpath and cycleway. Elsewhere the trackbed has long since disappeared under ploughed fields but at Machrihanish the route of the railway can still be traced close to the site of the terminus behind the former Ugadale Arms Hotel.

LEFT: *Built by Lennox Lange of Glasgow in 1881, Snailbeach District Railways 0-6-0ST Fernhill and some very young railway workers have their photograph taken at Snailbeach, c.1883.*

BELOW: *Argyll Street in Campbeltown in the 1920s with C&MR 0-6-2T Argyll loco and its four-coach train having just disembarked a trainload of daytrippers who make their way to board the steamer back to the Clyde. Apart from the absence of trains the view on Argyll Street is much the same today.*

Up in the clouds

The Snowdon Mountain Railway

Although other mountain railways were proposed on mainland Britain at the end of the 19th century, the only one to be built, the Snowdon Mountain Railway, was opened on 6 April 1896. Operating on the Swiss Abt rack system, the 2ft-7½in.-gauge line climbs from the terminus at Llanberis for 4½ miles on gradients as steep as 1-in-5.5 to the summit terminus at an altitude of 3,493ft above sea level. Motive power is provided by Swiss-built 0-4-2T steam and British-built diesel locomotives which push their coach up the mountain using a series of cogs and a double rack laid between the track. This rack and pinion system also provides braking on the downward journey. The steam locomotives, two of which date from 1895, have a forward-tilted firebox and boiler so that water levels remain fairly horizontal on the steep gradient. To supplement the ageing steam locomotives, four 320 hp diesel locomotives and three diesel-electric railcars were delivered to the line between 1986 and 1995.

A mountain railway to the summit of Snowdon was first proposed as early as 1869 but construction did not start until December 1894. Completed in February 1896 at a cost of £76,000, the line was opened to the public on Easter Monday, 6 April. However, this happy event turned into a disaster when locomotive No 1 *Ladas* became derailed on its downward journey from the summit with the first official train. In accordance with the railway's operating rules, the engine was at the front of the train and the two carriages, which were not coupled to it, were able to stop with their own brakes. Just before the engine hurtled down the mountainside the driver and fireman were able to jump out of the cab but a passenger in one of the carriages who did likewise was not so lucky and was killed. If all of this wasn't bad enough, the following train pulled by locomotive No 2 *Enid* also became derailed at the same spot and ran into the carriages of the first train – fortunately nobody else was killed.

Soon after the opening day accident the Board of Trade halted all services on the line and set up a Board of Enquiry. It found that the accident had been caused by settlement of the ground under the track and recommended improvements to the rack rail and a reduction of the maximum load for locomotives. The line was finally re-opened on 9 April 1897 and has been operating without any major incident ever since. The current summit station buildings were designed in the 1930s by the architect responsible for the famous village of Portmeirion, Clough Williams-Ellis. Weather permitting, trains currently operate from mid-March to the first week of November.

LEFT: *Two descending Snowdon Mountain Railway trains approach Clogwyn station on 16 September 1971.*

A railway-owned electric tramway

The Grimsby & Immingham Tramway

Originally conceived by the Manchester, Sheffield & Lincolnshire Railway, the forerunner of the Great Central Railway, the massive new docks at Immingham at the mouth of the River Humber in north Lincolnshire were officially opened by King George V in 1912. With his eye on the European market, the GCR's forward-looking director Sam Fay was knighted by the king at the same time.

Equipped with state-of-the-art coal-handling facilities, the docks covered an area of 45 acres and had their own internal railway system. The workforce for the construction of the docks and later to run them was mainly drawn from the neighbouring port of Grimsby and a key factor to the smooth running of the operation was the building of an electric tramway linking the two locations. This replaced a steam railcar service on the earlier Grimsby District Light Railway which had been built by the dock's contractor.

Opened in 1912 by the Great Central Railway, the electric tramway ran for 5 miles, mainly on a straight route across marshland but partly through the streets of Immingham and Grimsby, from Immingham Town to Corporation Bridge at Grimsby. A short branch also led to Immingham Dock Eastern Jetty. The depot for the line was at Pyewipe north of Grimsby and passing places were provided on the single track mainline across the marshes.

Operating on a 500V DC current, the trams collected current from an overhead line held up by wooden poles.

Initially services were provided by a fleet of twelve 54ft-long single-decker bogie trams along with four shorter versions for working in the streets of Grimsby.

The tramway became part of the LNER in 1923 and then the nationalised British Railways in 1948 when the trams were repainted in a green livery complete with BR logo. To cope with increased demand after World War II when new industries were being built along the Humber, a large fleet of redundant second-hand trams was purchased from the Gateshead & District Tramways Company in 1951. With business booming in the 1950s the tramway continued to operate until 1961 when the building of new roads and the introduction of buses finally brought about its closure. Even the Ian Allan ABC locospotters' guide of Summer 1961 lists 26 Grimsby & Immingham electric trams on the stockbooks at this late stage. Fortunately one of the original Great Central tramcars has been preserved as part of the National Collection and two of the former Gateshead tramcars, Nos 20 and 26, have been preserved and can be seen at Crich Tramway Museum and Beamish Open Air Museum respectively.

BELOW: *Grimsby & Immingham tramcars await customers at the Immingham Dock terminus, late 1950s – note the 'Lion & Wheel' emblem of British Railways on the leading tramcar, No 14.*

D 09824
BRITISH TRANSPORT COMMISSION (E)
Grimsby & Immingham
Electric Railway
Retain ticket for inspection
1/-
1 SINGLE 1
For Conditions See Over
Bell Punch Co., Ltd., London.

Famous locomotive engineers 1

George Jackson Churchward (1857–1933)

Probably one of the most influential railway engineers of all time, George Jackson Churchward was born into a farming family in Stoke Gabriel, Devon, on 31 January 1857. Surrounded by the beautiful countryside of the Dart Estuary, it is not surprising that he never lost his love for this part of the world and of country pursuits. However, at school he excelled in mathematics and in 1873 he joined the Newton Abbot railway works of the broad-gauge South Devon Railway where he was apprenticed to John Wright, the railway's Locomotive Superintendent. In 1876 the South Devon Railway became part of the Great Western Railway and the young George was transferred to the drawing office at that company's Swindon Works. Here he worked for a brief period under the young Joseph Armstrong, the son of the then GWR's locomotive superintendent. A year later William Dean took over this important post and both Churchward and the young Armstrong were given the task

of developing a vacuum automatic braking system. In 1881, impressed with Churchward's work, William Dean promoted him to Assistant Manager in the Carriage and Wagon Works. Churchward's career certainly progressed from here as he became manager of the C&W Works in 1885, locomotive works manager in 1895 and principal assistant to William Dean in 1897.

Apart from his love of countryside pursuits, such as fishing and shooting, and railways, Churchward, who never married, also had a passion for cars and, at an early age, had built himself a steam-driven vehicle. Around 1900 he took delivery of a very early petrol-driven car which he used to attend countryside events not accessible by train. In the same year, Churchward was unanimously elected as the first Mayor of the new Borough of Swindon and, in 1902, reached the pinnacle of his career when he took over as Locomotive, Carriage and Wagon

Superintendent from the ailing William Dean. In 1916 this title was changed to Chief Mechanical Engineer – a position he held until his retirement in 1922.

To reduce both construction and maintenance costs and borrowing well-tried ideas from French and American locomotive designers, Churchward set about standardising the GWR's locomotives. Between 1903 and 1911 his four standard tapered boiler types, ingenious valve gear and the application of superheating were put to good use in the construction of nine standard locomotive designs. The first of these, the powerful inside-cylinder 'City' class 4-4-0s, was widely based on a successful American design. He went on to design an even more powerful 4-6-0 known as the 'Star' class from which his successor, Charles Collett, developed the famous 'Castle' class locomotives. His only failure was the unique 4-6-2 'Pacific' No 111 *The Great Bear* which, although extremely powerful, was much too heavy for most of the GWRs routes and was prone to derailment. Apart from his advanced locomotive designs, Churchward also designed revolutionary new coaching stock for the GWR and was responsible for the building of the 'A' erecting shop at Swindon Works.

LEFT: *One of Churchward's finest designs – 'Saint' Class 4-6-0 No 2909* Lady of Provence *is seen here at the head of an empty milk train at Paddington station on 31 May 1913.*

RIGHT: *The man himself, George Jackson Churchward, Chief Mechanical Engineer of God's Wonderful Railway.*

BELOW: *Designed by Churchward and built at Swindon in 1914, versatile '4300' Class 2-6-0 No 4358 is seen at rest outside Swindon shed in 1957.*

Churchward retired in 1922 and continued to live in the house provided for him by a grateful GWR, Newburn House in Dean Street, Swindon, where he was provided with a chauffeur, housekeeper and two maids. In his later years he suffered from deafness and this may well have contributed to his death on the misty morning of 19 December 1933 when he was killed by the Paddington to Fishguard express, hauled by No 4085 *Berkeley Castle*, as he went to inspect a loose rail connection close to his home. He is buried in Christ Church graveyard in Swindon Old Town.

Happy Christmas!

A railway Christmas in 1903

Christmas was once the busiest period of the year for the railways and the extra passenger and parcels traffic generated placed an enormous burden on the system. At the beginning of the 20th century paid holidays didn't exist and most people worked up to Christmas Eve, taking only two days off before returning to their city toils. To cope with this mass exodus special trains were run at midnight on Christmas Eve from London termini to principal stations, carrying to their country homes thousands of worn out workers – if the part that our railways played at Christmas had been properly understood then there would have been a collection for the Railway Benevolent Institution at every Christmas dinner table.

Figures released by the London & South Western Railway at the end of 1903 show just how busy this period was for them. On the four days preceding Christmas nearly 100,000 tickets were issued at Waterloo station – these excluded previously bought season tickets or tickets that had been bought at the company's city offices. In the course of an ordinary day there were about 1,000 trains working in and out of Waterloo but on 23 and 24 December the magnitude of bookings necessitated the running of most mainline trains in duplicate, adding about 50 more trains to the daily total.

The majority of the post and parcels sent around the country in the days preceding Christmas were also carried by the railways. This was a massive undertaking with

railway porters employed to load and unload vast quantities of mail and parcels on and off trains – during the seven days prior to Christmas 1903 the London & North Western Railway handled 35,000 food hampers at Euston alone and to facilitate this work a special large shed, 2340ft long and 40ft wide was erected in Maiden Lane. The company ran six special trains to and from Euston on these days just to carry parcels and hampers while at the Midland Railway's terminus of St Pancras around 100,000 parcels were handled. Special milk, fruit, meat and fish trains were also run from the provinces into London – the LSWR had to run four extra trains just for the conveyance of milk churns on each of the four days before Christmas, while the meat specials carrying 'prime Scotch' from north of the border were considered even more important than the progress of 'The Flying Scotsman'! With the Smithfield Show also taking place the LNWR's Broad Street and Camden goods stations handled 2,214 tons of meat in the week ending 23 December.

The special working notice book issued by the GWR to its staff for Christmas 1903 makes interesting reading. Special trains laid on included the 'Marlborough College Special', the 'Cheltenham Lady Collegians', and trains to carry boys home from Clifton College, Malvern College and Cheltenham College. 'Special Parcels Trains' were also run that had precedence over goods trains. Special vans were attached to the New Milford to Paddington parcels train to carry Irish poultry traffic. Altogether there were no less than 90 pages in the GWR's special Christmas notice, all referring to extra trains laid on between 18 and 25 December.

Needless to say, despite railway staff's hard work, there were some parcels that failed to reach their destination, usually because of incomplete or incorrect addresses. As some of these parcels contained perishable goods they were sold for what they could fetch. Items from the 'salvaged' parcels list included a barrel of oysters, a brace of pheasants, a hare, a turkey in feathers, a goose, four rabbits, goose dressed, box containing cake, puddings and photo and a box containing pork pies, sausages and pork. One parcel containing four pieces of beef was condemned by an inspector as unfit for human consumption. A few people obviously had their Christmas festivities spoilt by the non-arrival of these goodies. Non-perishable items that also failed to get delivered for the same reason ranged from a tin tray, a parrot's cage and a parcel of trouser linings to two motor car tyres.

Severe frost and fog at this time of the year also brought its problems – out of 313 down passenger trains arriving at Crewe during the four days before Christmas, 1903, 80 were 30 minutes late, 83 were from 1–2 hours late, and 15 were over 2 hours behind time. Up passenger trains fared just as badly and goods trains were shunted out of the way into sidings to wait until the pressure was over.

GREAT WESTERN RAILWAY.

XMAS

EXCURSIONS

TO CORNWALL
THE RIVIERA OF ENGLAND

TO NORTH & SOUTH WALES

TO THE DORSET COAST

AND OTHER PARTS OF THE LINE

FULL PARTICULARS AT THE STATIONS AND OFFICES OF THE COMPANY.

PADDINGTON STATION. DECEMBER   JAMES C. INGLIS General Manager.

FAR LEFT: *With seasonally decorated ex-GWR 'Manor' Class 4-6-0 No 7802 Bradley Manor at its head, the 'Cambrian Coast Express' waits to depart for Paddington from Aberystwyth station on Christmas Eve 1958.*

LEFT: *This colourful Great Western Railway poster, c.1902, advertises Christmas excursion trains to Wales, the West of England, and Dorset.*

The "Royal Scot" and the "Broadway Limited" at Harrisburg, Pennsylvania, 1933.

"THE ROYAL SCOT" IN AMERICA

LMS

The Royal Scot train of the London Midland and Scottish Railway toured the Dominion of Canada and the United States of America from May 1st to November 11th, 1933, covering under her own steam 11,194 miles over railroads of the North American Continent.

During this tour the train was exhibited at 80 cities and towns and was inspected by 3,021,601 people, of whom 2,074,348 passed through the train during its five-months' stay at "A Century of Progress" Exposition, Chicago, U.S.A.

E.R.G. 55501

PRINTED IN GREAT BRITAIN BY S·CALLER & COMPANY LTD 4, LISLE ST LONDON W.C.2

Foreign travels

Flying the flag for Britain

GWR 4-6-0 No 6000 *King George V*

Built at Swindon in 1927, the 'King' Class locos were the GWR's response to the Southern Railway's powerful 'Lord Nelson' Class 4-6-0s which had been introduced a year earlier. With a tractive effort of 40,300lb/f the 'Kings' became the most powerful 4-6-0s in Britain. The first of the Class, No 6000 *King George V*, entered service at the end of June 1927 and was allocated to Old Oak Common shed and was soon at work on the GWR's premier train, the 'Cornish Rivera Express'. At the beginning of August the loco, along with broad-gauge 2-2-2 *North Star*, was shipped from Cardiff to Baltimore, USA, to represent the GWR at the Baltimore & Ohio Railway's Centenary Exhibition, which took place between 24 September and 15 October. After appearing at the exhibition, where the 'King' was fitted with a commemorative brass bell and cabside plaque, the loco and her GWR crew, Driver Young and Fireman Pearce, made runs between Baltimore, Washington and Philadelphia. Returning to the UK in November 1927 the 'King' went on to haul the principal expresses out of Paddington until withdrawal from service at the end of 1962. Fortunately this historic loco was saved for preservation and, in 1971, became the first preserved steam locomotive to be approved for mainline running since the end of steam on BR. It is now a static exhibit at the Steam Museum in Swindon.

LMS 4-6-0 No 6100 *Royal Scot*

Built as No 6152 *The Royal Dragoon Guardsman* at Derby in 1930 this loco permanently swapped identities with the first engine of this class in 1933 when it was sent with a train of carriages to the Century of Progress Exposition in Chicago. Fitted with a large headlamp, the engine and train then covered over 11,000 miles of the railroads of Canada and the USA and was visited by over 3 million people. On return to the UK the loco remained on mainline duties on the West Coast Main Line between Euston and Glasgow until being withdrawn by BR as No 46100 in October 1962. Fortunately the loco was saved for preservation, firstly by Billy Butlin and then by the Bressingham Steam Museum in Norfolk, and has recently returned to steam on mainline and preserved railways around the UK.

LMS 4-6-2 No 6220 *Coronation*

The loco that was sent to represent Britain at the 1939–40 New York World's Fair was built by the London Midland & Scottish Railway as No 6229 *Duchess of Hamilton* at Crewe in 1938. Her number and nameplate was swapped with the first engine of the class for the duration of what turned out to be a much longer-than-planned visit. Fitted with a streamlined casing and accompanied by eight matching crimson-lake and gold striped carriages, the loco was also fitted with a headlight, brass bell and special couplings for the duration of her stay in North America. After completing a tour of over 3,000 miles around the continent, the loco and her train were exhibited at the World's Fair but became stranded in the US following the outbreak of World War II. The loco was finally shipped back to the UK in 1942 where she reverted back to No 6229 *Duchess of Hamilton*. Used as officers' messes, the carriages only returned back to the UK in 1946. The loco was de-streamlined in 1947 and withdrawn in 1964. Since then she has been preserved and was returned to mainline working order. The loco has been fitted with her original streamlined casing and is exhibited at the National Railway Museum in York.

LNER 4-6-2 No 4472 *Flying Scotsman*

Although this famous LNER 'A3' Class 4-6-2 did not travel abroad until after preservation, *Flying Scotsman* has certainly attracted much public and media attention in recent years. Following withdrawal by BR as No 60103 in 1963 the loco was purchased for £3,000 by Alan Pegler who

LEFT TOP: *LMS poster of 1933 celebrating the tour of the* Royal Scot *around USA and Canada.*

LEFT BOTTOM: *Seen here in 1940 LMS No 6220* Coronation *(aka No 6229* Duchess of Hamilton*) was stranded in the USA due to the outbreak of the Second World War. The loco was shipped back to the UK in 1942.*

restored her back to her original condition. With the addition of a second tender the loco worked rail tours around Britain in 1968 including a non-stop run between London and Edinburgh. In 1969 the loco embarked on a promotional a tour of the USA for which it was fitted with a headlamp, bell and cowcatcher. Initially a success, the visit came to grief in 1972 when Pegler became bankrupt and the loco was only returned to the UK in 1973 when Sir William McAlpine stepped in to save it.

In 1988 the *Flying Scotsman* was shipped to Australia to take part in bicentenary celebrations and while there covered more than 28,000 miles including a run across the Nullarbor Desert from Sydney to Perth. On return to the UK the loco faced an uncertain future when mounting restoration costs led to its sale to Dr Tony Marchington in 1996. By now there was much public outcry about this famous locomotive's future and it was finally bought by the National Collection in 2004. It has now been completely rebuilt and returned to the mainline again.

BELOW: *Complete with bell, headlight, cowcatcher and double tender, ex-LNER 'A3' Class 4-6-2 No 4472 Flying Scotsman visited the USA in 1969 for a promotional tour.*

I'm all right, Jack!

Railway unions — the NUR (aka No Use Rushing) and ASLEF

The National Union of Railwaymen

Before the formation of unions in the 1870s, life for a railway worker in Britain was very dangerous – hundreds were killed in accidents every year, many of these deaths caused by the long hours that they were asked to work. The modern idea of 'Health & Safety' did not exist and passengers' lives were also being put at risk. Although railway employees had at times tried to form workers' associations these were always suppressed in their infancy by the all-powerful railway companies. The first railway union to be recognised was the Amalgamated Society of Railway Servants of England, Ireland, Scotland & Wales (ASRS), which came into being in 1871. Initially membership was small and did not include drivers and firemen who later formed their own union, the Associated Society of Locomotive Engineers and Firemen (ASLEF). By the turn of the century the ASRS was powerful enough to help found the fledgling Labour Party but got into trouble when using union funds to support parliamentary representation.

In 1913 the ASRS merged with two other railway unions – the General Railway Workers' Union and the Pointsmen & Signalmen's Society – to form the National Union of Railwaymen (NUR). Then with a total membership of 267,000, it certainly became a force to be reckoned with especially during the strike-torn years of the 1920s. Just prior to Nationalisation in 1948 membership had risen to a high of 462,000 – from then on the numbers declined due to railway closures, which peaked in the 1960s. The NUR's last General Secretary, Jimmy Knapp, was a gruff ex-railway signalman from Ayrshire who played a central role in the merger of his union with the National Union of Seamen in 1990 – this new union is the National Union of Rail, Maritime and Transport Workers (RMT for short) which currently has a membership of 80,000 from almost every sector of the transport industry.

Associated Society of Locomotive Engineers and Firemen

Although comparatively small in numbers, members of ASLEF have always been among the elite of railway employees. Comprising engine drivers and firemen, the union was born out of a dispute in October 1879 when the GWR cut the wages and extended the working hours of their longest-serving engine drivers and firemen. Receiving no support from the then recently-formed Amalgamated Society of Railway Servants (ASRS) a total of 56 drivers and firemen got together and formed the Associated Society of Locomotive Engineers and Firemen (ASLEF) in February 1880. By 1884 membership had reached 1,000; 20 years later it had grown to 12,000 members and the union had achieved a cut in working hours for these elite men. Although often expressing solidarity with other unions ASLEF has always remained proudly independent and self-sufficient and today has a membership of over 18,500.

BELOW: *News of the imminent and very damaging national rail strike of 1955 is chalked on the side tank of ex-LBSCR 'E4' Class 0-6-2T No 32502 at Guildford, 29 May.*

Island railways

Famous and lesser-known island railways and tramways
around the coastline of Britain

Alderney, Channel Islands

Opened in 1847 to carry stone from Mannez Quarry for the construction of forts and the Braye breakwater, the standard-gauge Alderney Railway was operated for many years by the British Admiralty. In 1980 the 2-mile line was leased from the Home Office by the Alderney Railway Society. The railway is now open to the public between Easter and the end of September, with trains departing from Braye Road station for the journey to Mannez Quarry. Passengers are conveyed in former London Underground cars pushed and pulled by a small diesel locomotive. Beyond Braye Road station it is still possible to follow the disused and rusting rails down to the harbour and along the top of the breakwater. During the winter of 1911/12, a loaded train ran off the end of the breakwater and, after that incident, all locomotives travelling along it had to carry lifebelts!

Anglesey/Holy Island

Both Anglesey, the largest island off the Welsh coast, and Holy Island have been connected to the national railway system since the opening of the Chester & Holyhead Railway in 1850. To carry trains across the Menai Strait, a new wrought-iron tubular bridge, Britannia Bridge, was built by the railway's engineer, Robert Stephenson. The bridge was extensively damaged by fire in 1970 but has since been rebuilt on two levels, the upper one carrying a road and the lower one the railway. Mainline trains still connect Holyhead with North Wales, Chester, Crewe and London. Branch lines ran from Gaerwen to Amlwch (opened 1864, closed to passengers 1964) and Holland Arms to Red Wharf Bay (opened 1909, closed to passengers 1930, to goods 1950). Freight traffic continued to Amlwch until 1993 when the line was mothballed. A 99-year lease was agreed in April 2021 between the Anglesey Central Railway and Network Rail for the Amlwch branch to be brought back into use, for both local passenger and heritage services.

Brownsea Island

Located in Poole Harbour and now owned by the National Trust, Brownsea Island is probably best known as the site of Robert Baden-Powell's first Scout camp that was held there in 1907. However, in 1852, a certain Colonel William Waugh bought Brownsea and embarked upon a massive development of the island. Included in his ambitious scheme was a pottery that was built on the south west coast and linked by a horse-drawn tramway to a pier at the west end of the island. Within five years, Waugh's ambitious business empire on Brownsea had collapsed and the pottery and tramway closed. The route of the tramway southwards along the coast from Pottery Pier to the edge of the Scout Camp can still be followed today.

Flat Holm

Due to its strategic position on the approaches to Bristol and Cardiff in the Bristol Channel, Flat Holm was taken over by the military during World War II. From 1941, over 300 soldiers were based on the island, manning a range of heavy and light anti-aircraft guns and a radar station in the defence of the Bristol Channel ports. A light railway was constructed to convey provisions and ammunition from the pier at the north of the island to the various gun batteries, magazines and searchlight sites scattered around the island. Materials for the railway came from German 60cm-gauge lines that had been captured during World War I and stored between the wars at Longmoor Military Railway depot in Hampshire. The lines were lifted at the end of World War II by German prisoners of war and, apart from traces of the track alignment, nothing remains of the railway today.

Hayling Island

A branch line from Havant to Hayling was opened for goods trains as far as Langstone in 1865. The route to South Hayling was completed in 1867 and passenger services started in July of that year. There were intermediate stations at Langstone and North Hayling. From 1872 the line was operated by the London Brighton & South Coast Railway, becoming part of the Southern Railway in 1923. Due to the cost of replacing the old timber railway bridge across Langstone Harbour, the line closed on 2 November 1963. The trackbed now forms the route of the Hayling Billy Trail and the old station buildings at Hayling are now a theatre. There is still one railway operating on Hayling – opened in 2003, the 2ft-gauge East Hayling Light Railway runs for about a mile through the sand dunes between the funfair at Beachlands and Eastoke Corner.

Isle of Bute

A 4ft-gauge horse-drawn passenger-carrying tramway was opened on the Isle of Bute in 1882. The only tramway on a Scottish island, it was re-gauged to 3ft-6in. and electrified in 1902. The route originally ran along the promenade at Rothesay and ended at Port Bannatyne. The double-track line was extended across the island to Ettrick Bay in 1905, giving the tramway a total length of nearly 5 miles, and remained in use until complete closure in 1936.

Isle of Grain

O pened throughout in 1880 the Hundred of Hoo Railway on the Isle of Grain in Kent lost its passenger service to Allhallows and Port Victoria in 1961. However the line from Hoo Junction to Grain is still open for traffic from an oil refinery and an aggregates terminal.

Isle of Man

T he 3ft-gauge Isle of Man Railway was opened in stages between 1873 and 1879 and did much to help the development of the island. Radiating out from Douglas, the lines to Peel, Ramsey and Port Erin were all closed in 1965. A privately-funded and partially successful attempt was made to reopen the railway in 1967, but by the following year the lines to Peel and Ramsey had finally closed. Under private ownership and with support from railway enthusiasts, the line to Port Erin soldiered on. Nationalised since 1976, the 15½-mile steam-operated line from Douglas to Port Erin still remains in operation and its future seems assured.

During the height of the Victorian tourist boom on the Isle of Man a unique and, at that time, technologically advanced electric railway was built northwards from Douglas following the beautiful and rugged coastline to the port of Ramsey. The 18-mile line was opened in stages between 1893 and 1899, with a 5-mile branch to the summit of the island's only mountain Snaefell (2,036ft above sea level), the line became an instant success with visitors. Surprisingly

BELOW: *Class 'A1X' 0-6-0T No 32678 crosses the timber viaduct across Langstone Harbour with a train for Hayling Island on 3 February 1963. This charming island railway closed nine months later.*

the mainline operates on a 3ft-gauge while the Snaefell branch is 3ft-6in.-gauge. This scenic railway with its unique American-style trams was saved from closure in 1957 when it was nationalised by the Manx government. With much of the rolling stock still in its original form a trip on this historic line is a journey back in time.

Isle of Mull

Opened in 1984, Mull Rail was the only passenger-carrying railway to operate on a Scottish island. This 10¼in.-gauge miniature railway carried visitors for 1¼ miles from a station near Craignure Pier, served by Caledonian MacBrayne ferries from Oban, to Torosay Castle. Building this little railway was no mean feat as it involved rock blasting and crossing a bog. Sadly the railway has now closed.

Isle of Sheppey

Located just off the Kent coast, the Isle of Sheppey has been linked by rail to the mainland since 1860 when the London Chatham & Dover Railway opened its line to the port of Sheerness. The railway crosses the stretch of water known as The Swale on the combined road and rail Kingsferry Bridge which has an electrically operated lifting section to allow the passage of ships. Passenger trains currently operate between Sheerness and Sittingbourne where there are connections with mainline services.

During the early 20th century attempts were made to develop the eastern coast of the Isle of Sheppey as a seaside resort. A light railway was opened in 1901 from the main railway line at Queenborough to the new resort of Leysdown-on-Sea. The attempts to popularise Leysdown as a resort for Londoners was never a complete success and the railway closed in 1950.

Ex-SECR 'H' Class 0-4-4T No 31512 is seen at Grain terminus on 13 June 1961. The Hundred of Hoo Railway closed to passengers less than six months later although it remains open today for freight.

Isle of Wight

Once upon a time the Isle of Wight boasted 56 miles of standard-gauge public railway. Today, apart from the 5-mile Isle of Wight Steam Railway, which operates a steam-hauled service between Smallbrook Junction and Wootton, and the electrified 8½-mile section from Ryde Pier Head to Shanklin, until recently served by veteran former London Underground stock, all this has disappeared.

Between 1862 and 1900, a total of six routes were built and, until the Grouping of 1923, these were operated by three separate companies. The Isle of Wight Central Railway operated the lines between Smallbrook Junction to Cowes via Newport, Newport to Sandown via Merstone, and Merstone to Ventnor West. The Freshwater, Yarmouth & Newport Railway operated the line between Freshwater and Newport and the Isle of Wight Railway ran services between Ryde (St Johns Road) and Ventnor and the branch from Brading to Bembridge. A joint line was opened between Ryde (St John's Road) and Ryde Pier Head by the LSWR and LBSCR in 1880. Closures began under British Railways in the 1950s and culminated in 1966 with the ending of steam haulage and closure of all remaining routes apart from the Ryde to Shanklin section.

Sections of trackbed from Freshwater to Yarmouth, Newport to Sandown, and from Shanklin to Wroxall are now footpaths and cycleways.

Ex-SR Class '02' 0-4-4T No 20 Shanklin *in the headshunt of Ventnor station, Isle of Wight, after arriving with a train from Ryde Pier Head on 15 August 1965.*

Jersey, Channel Islands

Two separate railways were built on the Channel Island of Jersey during the 19th century. The Jersey Railway opened between St Helier and St Aubin in 1870. The railway was built to the British standard-gauge but later converted to 3ft-6in.-gauge when it was extended to Corbière. Plans to electrify the 7-mile-long line in 1906 did not materialise, and the railway closed for good in 1936 following a serious fire at St Aubin station when most of the rolling stock was destroyed. Today, the former terminus building at St Aubin is now a police station and the trackbed of the railway line between St Aubin and Corbière has been converted to a cycleway and footpath.

The second railway on Jersey, the Jersey Eastern Railway, ran from St Helier to Gorey and was opened in 1872. However, increasing competition from buses led to its closure in 1929.

The trackbeds of both these railways were incorporated into the military network of railway lines that were built to link stone quarries and construction sites on Jersey during the German Occupation of World War II.

Lindisfarne (Holy Island)

Located just off the coast of Northumberland, the island of Lindisfarne is an unlikely place to find the remains of a tramway. However, in 1860, a Scottish company greatly expanded the limestone quarrying industry on the island and constructed lime kilns, a horse-drawn tramway and a jetty adjacent to the historic Lindisfarne Castle. Although this ambitious venture had closed by 1900, visitors to the island and its castle can still walk along the well-preserved remains of the old tramway trackbed with its embankments and stone bridges.

Lundy Island

Located 7 miles north of Hartland Point in Devon, windswept Lundy Island was purchased by William Hudson Heaven in 1834. In an attempt to bring employment to Lundy, Heaven opened granite quarries on the east side of the island in 1863 and built a horse-drawn tramway to convey stone from the quarries to a landing stage where it was loaded on to ships. The quarries did not prove to be commercially viable and were closed in 1868. Today, visitors to the island, which is owned by the National Trust

and managed by the Landmark Trust, can still follow the clearly defined route of the old tramway.

Orkney Islands

A group of about 50 islands lying off the north coast of Scotland, the Orkneys have a fascinating railway history. Many standard-gauge and narrow-gauge lines were built between the end of the 19th century through to World War II to serve quarries, military installations and a lighthouse service depot. By far the largest network of lines were those built by Balfour Beatty during the construction of the Churchill Barriers during World War II. These enormous concrete barriers, designed to protect the strategic naval anchorage at Scapa Flow, connected the Orkney mainland with South Ronaldsay across the islands of Burray, Glimsholm and Lambholm. Both 3ft-gauge and standard-gauge lines were used to convey the vast amount of building material required to construct the barriers. Shorter, 2ft-gauge lines were also used in and around quarries and other military installations on several other islands including Hoy, Fara and Flotta. Today, discerning visitors to these islands can still find many traces of this once strategically important network of the most northerly of our railway lines.

Steep Holm

As with the neighbouring island of Flat Holm, the little island of Steep Holm was taken over by the military during World War II to protect the approaches to Bristol and Cardiff. Starting in 1941, army engineers installed four 6-inch naval guns, dating from World War I, together with their emplacements, lookouts and ammunition stores, at strategic points around the edge of the island's plateau. Faced with the difficult task of transporting huge amounts of building materials for the gun emplacements the army built a new jetty that was linked to the plateau by a narrow-gauge switchback railway. The railway was built from captured German World War I prefabricated 60cm-gauge lines that had been stored at Longmoor between the wars. This switchback route was cable-operated with diesel-powered winches hauling wagons up the three inclines from the jetty. Unlike Flat Holm, nearly all of the track is still in situ and visitors to this delightful island follow the railway's zig-zag route to the top of the island after disembarking from their boat.

Made in Scotland

Five Scottish locomotive works

St Rollox

Located in Springburn, Glasgow, St Rollox Works opened in 1856 as the locomotive and carriage and wagon works for the Caledonian Railway. At the height of production in the early 20th century St Rollox works covered an area of 190 acres and employed around 5,000 men building classic steam locomotives designed by such luminaries as Dugald Drummond, John McIntosh (famous for his 'Oban Bogies', 'Dunalastair' and 'Cardean' Classes) and William Pickergill. During the Second World War the works produced Horsa gliders and parts for the Rolls-Royce Merlin engine. In 1948 St Rollox became the chief locomotive works for British Railways in Scotland, overhauling steam locomotives until 1966, but, despite modernisation in the 1960s at a cost of £1.5 million, the Works had been slimmed-down by the early 1980s. Since then a much-reduced St Rollox Works has been run by a succession of owners with Locomotive Services Ltd being the next possible candidate.

Cowlairs

Also located in Springburn, Glasgow, Cowlairs Works was built in 1841 for the Edinburgh & Glasgow Railway, before going on to become the main locomotive and carriage and wagon works for the North British Railway. The first two locomotives built at the works were powerful 0-6-0 banking engines for use on the nearby Cowlairs Incline out of Queen Street station. Under the watchful eye of Chief Mechanical Engineers such as Dugald Drummond, Matthew Holmes and William Reid, Cowlairs Works turned out some classic steam locomotives culminating in Reid's famous 'Glen' Class (LNER Class 'D34') 4-4-0s which remained in service on the West Highland Line through to the BR era. Like nearby St Rollox, the Works produced Horsa gliders and parts for Rolls-Royce

BELOW: *Inside Cowlairs Works on 20 May 1961 with BR Standard Class '6' 4-6-2 No 72006* Clan Mackenzie *receiving a heavy overhaul.*

Merlin engines during the Second World War. Locomotive construction ended following the 'Big Four Grouping' of 1923 although locomotive, carriage and wagon repair work continued through the LNER era until 1948. The works closed in 1968 and the site is now an industrial estate.

Inverurie

Located 16¾ miles north of Aberdeen, Inverurie Locomotive Works was opened in 1903 by the Great North of Scotland Railway, replacing the cramped works they had been using previously at Kittybrewster. Despite only building 10 new locomotives in its lifetime the Works continued to repair locomotives and rolling stock, through the LNER and BR eras until 1969 when it closed. Designed by William Pickersgill, eight of the Class 'V' and two of their Class 'F' 4-4-0s (both later classified by the LNER as Class 'D34') were built at

Inverurie while the rest of these graceful locomotives were built by the North British Locomotive Company in Glasgow. One NBL loco, No 49 *Gordon Highlander*, has since been preserved.

Lochgorm

Located in the triangle of lines outside Inverness station, Lochgorm Railway Works was built by the Inverness & Nairn Railway in 1855 and became the main locomotive works for its eventual successor, the Highland Railway. Under William Stroudley the works first turned out three diminutive 0-6-0 tanks which were the predecessors of his famous 'Terrier' tank locomotives designed for the London, Brighton & South Coast Railway. Under his successor, David Jones, Lochgorm went on to build 4-4-0 and 2-4-0s tender locos, 2-4-0 tank locos and the famous 4-4-0 'Skye Bogies'. Despite

this, many of the Highland Railway's locomotives, such as the famous 'Jones Goods', were built by outside contractors, for example Sharp, Stewart, Dübs, Neilson and Hawthorn, Leslie.

Jones was succeeded by Peter Drummond as the Highland Railway's locomotive superintendent. Nine of his 'Small Ben' 4-4-0s were built at Lochgorm along with three 0-6-0 tank locos and four 0-4-0 tanks locos.

Lochgorm became part of the LMS in 1923 and continued to repair locomotives and rolling stock until the BR era. The works were used as a diesel maintenance and running shed following closure of Inverness steam shed in 1961.

Kilmarnock

Originally located in Glasgow, the Glasgow & South Western Railway's locomotive works was moved to Kilmarnock in 1854. Under successive locomotive superintendents such as Patrick Stirling and James Stirling, Hugh Smellie, James Manson, Peter Drummond and Robert Whitelegg, Kilmarnock produced around 400 steam locomotives for the company. Despite this, many of the company's locos were built by outside contractors such as the North British Locomotive Company. From 1923 the G&SWR became part of the LMS with most of the heavy repair work being transferred to St Rollox. Loco repair work ended in 1952 with rolling stock repair ceasing in 1959. The LMS was quick to rid itself of ex-G&SWR locos with most them having been withdrawn by the mid-1930s.

BELOW: *Diminutive 0-6-0ST Strathpeffer was designed by William Stroudley and built at the Highland Railway's Lochgorm Works in Inverness in 1869. It is seen here as LMS No 16118 at Strathpeffer terminus with its train from Dingwall in August 1926.*

Made by the Great Western Railway

The GWR's Swindon Works

Located to the west of Swindon station in the fork between the Swindon to Gloucester and Swindon to Bristol mainlines, Swindon Works was the principal locomotive, carriage and wagon works for the Great Western Railway and, from 1948, the Western Region of British Railways.

The Works were opened in 1843. The decision to build at Swindon was made in 1840 by 24-year-old Daniel Gooch, the first Superintendent for Locomotive Engines of the GWR. The Works transformed what was then just a rural village into a large railway town. Under the GWR's

famous locomotive superintendents – Daniel Gooch, Joseph Armstrong, William Dean, G. J. Churchward, C. B. Collett and F. W. Hawksworth – the Works turned out firstly such broad-gauge giants as the single-wheeler 2-2-2 and 4-2-2 express locos followed by the famous standard-gauge 'City' and 'County' Class 4-4-0s, 'Star', 'Castle' and 'King' Class 4-6-0s and, at its peak in the 1930s, employed around 14,000 people. Following Nationalisation in 1948 Swindon turned its hand to building many of the BR Standard Class locos including 45 Class 3 2-6-2 tanks (Nos 82000–82044), 80 Class 4 4-6-0s,

20 Class 3 2-6-0 (Nos 77000–77019) and 53 Class '9F' 2-10-0 including the last steam loco to be built for BR, No 92220 *Evening Star*. The ill-thought-out 'Modernisation Plan' of 1955 brought more work for Swindon including the building of 38 of the 'Warship' Class diesel-hydraulics (Class 42 D800–D832 and D866–D870) between 1958 and 1961, 35 'Western' Class diesel-hydraulics (Class 52 D1000–D1034) between 1961 and 1964, and 56 of the short-lived Type 1 diesel-hydraulics (Class 14 D9500–D9555) between 1964 and 1965, along with some of the more successful Class 03 0-6-0 diesel shunters and diesel multiple units – including some of the Inter-City, Cross-Country and Trans-Pennine units. Although building of locomotives ended in 1965, diesel locomotives continued to be repaired along with carriage and wagon work until March 1986 when the Works closed.

Today the Swindon Steam Railway Museum is housed in one of the Grade II listed buildings of the Works and English Heritage have their headquarters in another. A large retail outfit is located in other buildings.

LEFT: *King George V and Queen Mary visited Swindon Works on 28 April 1924. Here the King tries his hand at driving brand new 'Castle' Class 4-6-0 No 4082 Windsor Castle back to Swindon station. Beside him are the Queen, the Chairman of the GWR, Viscount Churchill, and the Chief Mechanical Engineer, Charles Collett.*

BELOW: *With No 4252 in the foreground, two GWR '4200' 2-8-0Ts are nearing the completion of their heavy overhaul in 'A' Shop of Swindon Works on 4 May 1958.*

My local station

Gloucester Eastgate

I suppose there is always one railway location that has a special place in our hearts. In my case it has to be Gloucester Eastgate station – only a 5-minute walk from my childhood home and my regular stamping ground during my trainspotting days in the early 1960s. It was also the station from where we embarked on our annual summer holiday – my father didn't own a car and we always headed south on a convoluted train journey to our destination. Whether it was Exmouth, Lyme Regis, Woolacombe or Perranporth the journey there and back was always the highlight of the holiday for me.

I first discovered the delights of Gloucester Eastgate when I was around 11 years old by which age I had caught the trainspotting bug badly and, armed with notebook and pencil, would spend most Saturdays at the north end of the curving island platform of this former Midland Railway station watching the comings and goings of trains on the Bristol to Birmingham mainline. It was also a good vantage point to watch activity at Horton Road shed and trains on the ex-GWR line out of Central station. There was never a dull moment!

Summer Saturdays were pure bliss at Eastgate, despite missing some holiday expresses which ran via the Gloucester avoiding line there was a never-ending procession of trains: ex-LMS 'Black 5' and 'Jubilee' Class 4-6-0s on trains between the north and south such as 'The Devonian' and 'Pines Express' with Bristol Barrow Road 'Patriot' Class '5' 4-6-0s (No 45506 *The Royal Pioneer Corps* and No 45519 *Lady Godiva* were regular performers) and Gloucester Barnwood's ancient '2P' 4-4-0s or BR Standard Class 5 4-6-0s on local stopping trains to Bristol or Birmingham. In 1960 Barrow Road had a total of nine 'Jubilees' and regulars such as No 45651 *Shovell*, No 45662 *Kempenfelt,* No 45682 *Trafalgar* and No 45699 *Galatea* were seen on an almost daily basis heading Bristol to Newcastle expresses and the evening Travelling Post Office. Despite all of this mainly ex-LMS scene the one daily intruder (but most welcome) was 'The Cornishman' from Wolverhampton Low Level to Penzance which was always headed by an immaculate Stafford Road 'Castle' such as No 5045 *Earl of Dudley* or No 5088 *Llanthony Abbey* hauling a rake of smart Mk 1 brown and cream coaches – on a summer Saturday

On 27 May 1961 I travelled behind restored Midland Railway Compound No 1000 from Gloucester Eastgate to Derby Works on a trip organised by the Gloucestershire Railway Society. Here is No 1000 before departure on this circuitous trip which included travelling over the Stratford-upon-Avon & Midland Junction Railway.

this train ran in two portions with the second part heading for Paignton.

By 1962 this scene had started to change with newly-introduced 'Peak' Type 4 diesels allocated to Bristol Bath Road having taken over many of the north-south expresses and even the rerouted 'The Cornishman' succumbed to their doubtful charms after the end of that summer's timetable. However, even at this late stage, some steam newcomers also appeared with downgraded and dishevelled ex-LMS 'Royal Scot' 4-6-0s and BR Standard 'Britannia' Class 7MT 4-6-2s appearing for a couple of years on summer-Saturday trains from the north. The former working out of Saltley, Nottingham and Millhouses depots and the latter from Aston added a perpetual sense of heightened expectation for me during these last years of steam. To add to this glorious scene the comings and goings from Horton Road shed and in and out of Central station could also be witnessed from the north end of Eastgate's island platform – trains to and from Paddington arriving or departing behind one of 85B's well-groomed Castle' 4-6-0s such as No 5017 *The Gloucestershire Regiment 28th, 61st*, No 5071 *Spitfire* or No 7000 *Viscount Portal* while Class '5101' 2-6-2Ts or even

occasionally '9400' 0-6-0PTs struggled manfully with the eight-coach trains to and from Cheltenham St James. The one interloper was the daily Cardiff to Newcastle express which changed engines at Central. A Cardiff 'Hall' would come off here in favour of a Midland-allocated 'Jubilee' which had backed down from Barnwood shed before heading north with its train towards Birmingham. In amongst all this activity were the diminutive but fast Class '1400' 0-4-2Ts on the Chalford auto-trains and a continuous procession of heavy freight, coal and iron ore trains to and from South Wales usually headed by ex-GWR '2800' Class 2-8-0s, '4200' Class 2-6-2Ts, '7200' Class 2-8-2Ts, ex-WD 2-8-0s and BR Standard Class '9F' 2-10-0s. Pure heaven for a teenage trainspotter!

Sadly this idyllic scene ended on 31 December 1965 when steam was ousted from the Western Region. From then on the rail scene in Gloucester went from bad to worse – Eastgate station and the ex-Midland line south to Tuffley Junction were closed on 1 December 1975 and north-south trains then had to use Central station where they reversed. Consequently many of these trains do not even stop at Gloucester today, taking the avoiding line instead, thus putting a city of 130,000 souls at a serious disadvantage.

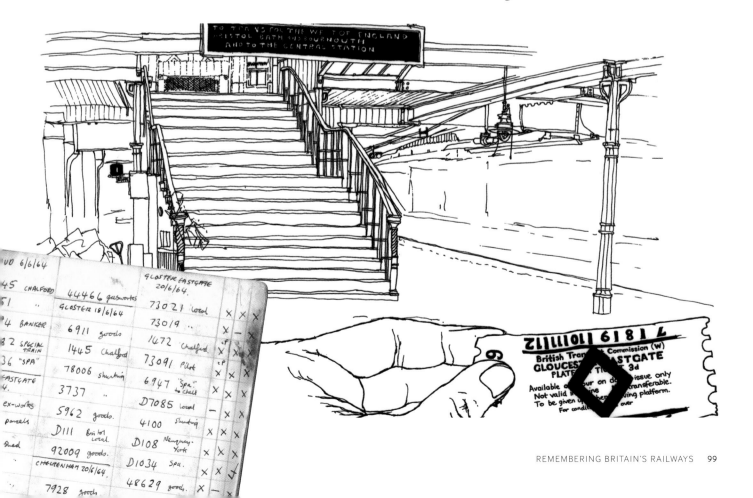

What a Boer!

How the London & South Western Railway saved the British Empire

Until the London & South Western Railway came to the rescue in 1892 Southampton Docks was in deep trouble. Within a few years the railway company had modernised the moribund concern including the installation of 25 miles of railway, new hydraulic cranes, new warehouses, new graving docks (amongst the largest in the world), thousands of feet of sheltered deep-water quayage and the finest cold storage installations in Europe. By the early 20th century goods traffic was up by 90%, coal traffic over 100% and passenger traffic by 70%. However its proximity to the great military centres of Southern England also gave it supreme importance for the embarkation and disembarkation of troops and their supplies during the Second Boer War. It is no exaggeration to say that during this period the L&SWR materially helped to save the British Empire from the terrible calamity of the over-running of Natal by the Boers between 1899 and 1902 – an opinion voiced by Lord Kitchener on his return from South Africa.

Joint naval and military manoeuvres were also mounted by the government in 1904 to test the capabilities of Southampton Docks in an even more striking way. On 5 September, in connection with this expedition, 10 transports totalling 90,000 tons gross were simultaneously berthed in Empress Docks and along the ocean quays. Transported to the docks by the L&SWR, the force consisted of 12,000 officers and men, 2,900 horses, 61 guns, 315 transport, engineer and ambulance wagons and 55 landing boats. The work commenced at 7 a.m. and by 3 p.m. 9 out of the 10 transports had finished loading and got away – the tenth transport was delayed for 2 hours by a steering fault.

The disembarkation test on 16 September was even more successful. All 10 transports returned simultaneously, commencing at 9 a.m., and in 1 hour they had all been berthed, 9,000 of the troops and many of their horses were entrained at the docks immediately on disembarkation and the remainder marched away with the cavalry, guns and wagons. The whole expedition was clear of the docks by 3 p.m. – only 6 hours after the arrival of the first ship. The Duke of Connaught, who was present with this expedition, personally expressed thanks to Mr Williams, the L&SWR's superintendent at the docks, for his appreciation of the arrangements and facilities by which this remarkable feat had been achieved. During later conflicts, in particular the two World Wars, Southampton Docks once again showed its vital military importance – thanks to the far-sighted planning of the L&SWR during the late 19th century.

BELOW: *The Empress Dock in Southampton was owned by the London & South Western Railway. This photograph was taken at the time of the Joint Naval and Military Expedition to South Africa in September 1904 and shows some of the transports berthed.*

One-offs

Seven unique British steam locomotives

Caledonian Railway 4-2-2 No 123

Known as the 'Caley Single' this elegant and unique single-wheeler was built for the Caledonian Railway by Neilson & Company in Springburn, Glasgow, in 1886. In the same year the loco was exhibited at the Edinburgh International Exhibition where it won a gold medal. In service the loco was employed hauling express trains on the West Coast route to Carlisle before taking on the important task of hauling the Directors' saloon in the 1920s. The loco became LMS No 14010 in 1923 and was withdrawn for preservation in 1935. Returned to working order in the late 1950s No 123 spent a few years hauling enthusiasts' specials before becoming a static exhibit at the Glasgow Museum of Transport. It was then transferred to the new Riverside Museum in the city.

GWR 4-6-2 No 111 *The Great Bear*

Designed by G. J. Churchward and built at Swindon in 1908, *The Great Bear* became the first Pacific type locomotive in Britain and the only one to be built for the GWR. More of a publicity stunt, the locomotive and its eight-wheeled tender was not a great success as the heavy axle loading restricted its operations to the Paddington to Bristol route. Retaining its number of 111 the loco was rebuilt as a 4-6-0 'Castle Class' in 1924 and renamed *Viscount Churchill*. It remained in service until withdrawal in 1953.

BELOW: *Unique and handsome Caledonian Railway 4-2-2 No 123, here seen at Carlisle Kingmoor on 13 June 1964, spent the late 1950s and early '60s hauling enthusiasts' specials around Scotland.*

MR 0-10-0 'Big Bertha'

Only two 0-10-0 (known as 'decapod') steam locos were built for service in Britain. One was a tank engine built for the Great Eastern Railway in 1902, the other was a tender locomotive, nicknamed 'Big Bertha', designed for the Midland Railway by James Clayton specifically for use as a banker on the 1-in-37 Lickey Incline south of Birmingham. Built at Derby in 1919, No 2290 weighed 107 tons and its 10 driving wheels were driven by four cylinders. Complete with electric headlight, 'Big Bertha' was renumbered 58100 by British Railways in 1948 and remained in service as a Lickey banker until 1956 when it was replaced by a new BR Standard '9F' 2-10-0.

LMS 4-6-0 No 6399 *Fury*

Based on the frames of one of Fowler's 'Royal Scot' Class 4-6-0, this unique high-pressure locomotive was built in 1929 by the North British Locomotive Company. Despite a fatal accident in 1930 when a high-pressure tube burst, the loco underwent four years of trials but never entered service. It was rebuilt in 1935 with a normal Stanier taper boiler and became No 6170 *British Legion*. As No 46170 the loco was withdrawn by British Railways in 1962.

LNER 4-6-4 No 10000 'Hush-Hush'

Designed by Nigel Gresley for the LNER, the Class 'W1' was the only 4-6-4 tender locomotive to operate in Britain. Its unusual features included a high-pressure marine-type water boiler built by Yarrow & Co. Under a cloak of utmost secrecy, No 10000 was part-assembled at Doncaster before being completed at Darlington at the end of 1929. There then followed six months of tests and modifications before the loco entered service in June 1930 – between that date and August 1935 the loco was in and out of Darlington Works many times for repairs and further modifications, the last visit including the fitting

BELOW: *Built by the Midland Railway in 1919, 0-10-0 No 58100 'Big Bertha' spent its whole working life banking trains from the rear up the 1-in-37 Lickey Incline in Worcestershire. It is seen here between duties at Bromsgrove station on 21 May 1950.*

of a Kylchap exhaust in May 1935. No 10000 finally emerged from Doncaster at the end of 1937 with a conventional boiler and a streamlined casing similar to the 'A4' Class. Entering BR service the loco was renumbered 60700 in 1948 and withdrawn in June 1959.

LMS 4-6-2 No 6202 'Turbomotive'

Designed by William Stanier, the 'Turbomotive' was a modified 'Princess Royal' Class 4-6-2 built in 1935. Using turbines instead of cylinders the loco was considered a great success but fell foul of British Railways' management in 1949 when it required a new turbine. As No 46202 the loco was eventually rebuilt as a conventional loco in 1952 and named *Princess Anne* after the Queen's daughter who had been born two years earlier. After only two months of service the loco was involved in the Harrow & Wealdstone crash on 8 October 1952 (see pages 104–5) and subsequently scrapped. It was replaced in 1954 by BR Class 8 4-6-2 No 71000 *Duke of Gloucester*.

BR 4-6-2 No 71000 *Duke of Gloucester*

Designed by R. A. Riddles (see pages 173–5) this unique three-cylinder Standard Class '8' loco was built at Crewe in 1954. With its design based on the 'Britannia' Class 7 Pacifics, No 71000 differed in having modern Caprotti valve gear but suffered in service due to high fuel consumption and poor steaming resulting from draughting problems. It was withdrawn in 1962 after only eight years of service and languished at Dai Woodhams scrapyard at Barry until 1975 when it was bought for preservation. Since then it has been completely rebuilt with modifications that have resulted in a highly efficient and powerful steam locomotive.

LMS 4-6-2 No 6202 'Turbomotive' is the subject of intense scrutiny at Euston station in 1935.

Peacetime horrors

Britain's worst peacetime rail crashes

Harrow & Wealdstone: 8 October 1952

Involving two collisions between three trains, the worst peacetime rail crash in Britain occurred at Harrow & Wealdstone station on the mainline out of Euston during the morning of 8 October 1952. At 8.19 a.m. a stationary stopping train from Tring to Euston was hit in the rear by 'Coronation' Class 4-6-2 No 46242 *City of Glasgow* travelling at 50–60 mph with the Perth to Euston sleeping car train – the loco was not fitted with an Automatic Warning System and its driver had failed to observe both 'caution' and 'danger' signals to the north of the station. Wreckage was strewn across the down mainline and this was hit seconds later by a Euston to Liverpool and Manchester express travelling at 50 mph and double-headed by 'Jubilee' Class 4-6-0 No 45637 *Windward Isles* and 'Princess Royal' Class 4-6-2 No 46202 *Princess Anne*. The latter engine had only emerged from Crewe two months earlier after being rebuilt as a conventional locomotive from the steam turbine 'Turbomotive' (see page 103). The resulting scene of death and destruction was horrific – 112 people lost their lives (including the driver and fireman of the train that caused the accident) and 340 were injured. *City of Glasgow* was repaired and returned to service but both *Windward Isles* and *Princess Anne* were scrapped.

Ex LMS 'Coronation' Class No 46242 City of Glasgow *after the crash at Harrow & Wealdstone. Although badly damaged the loco was rebuilt and remained in service until 1963.*

The second-worst peacetime rail crash in Britain occurred near St Johns station in Lewisham on the evening of 4 December 1957. In thick fog a Charing Cross to Hayes electric train was halted by a red signal shortly after passing St Johns station – its last carriage left standing underneath a railway flyover. In the meantime, on the same line, the much-delayed express from Cannon Street to Ramsgate was powering towards Lewisham behind 'Battle of Britain' 4-6-2 No 34066 *Spitfire*. In the dense fog neither driver or fireman saw the yellow caution signals and only when the red danger signal was spotted at the end of St Johns station did the driver attempt an emergency stop – all in vain as the heavy express piled into the rear of the electric train at 35 mph. Not only were the rear coaches of the latter train completely demolished but the lead coach of the express was derailed bringing the railway viaduct crashing down on the next two coaches. To add to this scene from Hell a train about to cross the viaduct narrowly avoided being brought down into the wreckage. Ninety people were killed and 173 injured. As at Harrow & Wealdstone, although driver error was mainly to blame the lack of an Automatic Warning System on the locomotive was a major contributory factor in the crash. No 34066 was repaired and returned to service. It became one of the last unrebuilt Bulleid Pacifics to remain in service until withdrawal in September 1966.

No more buckets and spades

Britain's lost seaside branch lines

It is a sad fact that many seaside branch lines were closed in the 1930s and after World War 2. Many of the places that they once served owe their existence today to the Victorian railway builders and their backers – for example, on the Yorkshire coast the resorts of Hornsea and Withernsea were insignificant villages until the coming of the railways in the mid-19th century but both lines fell victim to Dr Beeching's Axe in 1964. Fortunately a few seaside branch lines that once faced closure were reprieved and are today being used by growing numbers of visitors – for example the Looe Valley Line in Cornwall, promoted by the Devon and Cornwall Rail Partnership, has seen passenger numbers nearly double since the beginning of the 21st century.

The South of England in particular suffered greatly from the post-'Beeching Report' cuts. With passenger closure dates given in brackets, the resorts in Cornwall that lost their rail links were: Perranporth (1963), Fowey (1965), Padstow (1967) and Bude (1966). In Devon Kingsbridge (1963), Brixham (1963), Budleigh Salterton (1967), Sidmouth (1967), Instow (1965) and Ilfracombe (1970) all went the same way, although Lynton lost its narrow-gauge railway as early as 1935. In Somerset the long branch line to Watchet and Minehead closed in 1971 but was fortunately revived as the West Somerset Railway while Burnham-on-Sea closed in 1951. Back on the south coast the delightful branch line to Lyme Regis closed in 1965, West Bay (1930) and Swanage (1972) but the latter has in more recent years been reopened as a heritage railway. Closures on the Isle of Wight started in the 1950s: Yarmouth and Freshwater (1953), Bembridge (1953), Ventnor and Cowes (1966), although the latter has since reopened between Smallbrook Junction and Wootton as a heritage railway. Back on the mainland the Hayling Island branch closed in 1963, Selsey (1935), Dungeness (1937), New Romney (1967), Sandgate (1931) and Leysdown on the Isle of Sheppey (1950).

There were also many closures in Eastern England: Aldeburgh (1966), Southwold (1929), Gorleston-on-Sea (1970), Caister-on-Sea (1959), Mundesley-on-Sea (1964), Wells-next-the Sea (1964) and Hunstanton (1969). Up in Lincolnshire Sutton-on-Sea and Mablethorpe lost their railway in 1970 while further north in Yorkshire both Withernsea and Hornsea lost theirs in 1964. On the Yorkshire coast Robin Hood's Bay station closed in 1965 and Sandsend, Kettleness and Staithes in 1958. In Northumberland the Newbiggin-on-Sea branch closed in 1964, Amble (1930) and Seahouses (1951).

Over on the west coast the Silloth branch closed in 1964 and the Wirral coast route through Heswall in 1956.

Wales also lost several seaside branch lines: Redwharf Bay (1930), Amlwch (1964), Aberayron (1951), Cardigan (1962), Porthcawl (1965) and Lavernock (1968).

Finally to Scotland where on the east coast the Eyemouth branch closed in 1962, Gullane (1932) and the Fife coast route via Elie and Anstruther closed in 1965. St Andrews lost its rail link in 1969, Inverbervie (1951), Cruden Bay (1932), Peterhead (1965), St Combs (1965), Fraserburgh (1965), Macduff (1951), Banff (1964) and the Morayshire coast route via Portsoy and Cullen (1968).

Along the coastline of the Moray Firth Lossiemouth lost its branch in 1964, Burghead and Hopeman (1931) and Fortrose (1951). Further north the Dornoch branch closed in 1960 while the remote Lybster branch closed as early as 1944. Back down the west coast the Campbeltown & Machrihanish Light Railway closed in 1932 and the Ayrshire coastal route via Turnberry went in 1942 although the stub to Heads of Ayr stayed open until 1968. Finally this long roll of closures ends in Galloway with the Portpatrick branch closing in 1950 and Kirkudbright in 1965.

In memory of happier days.

LEFT: *Former Great Eastern Railway Class 'J15' 0-6-0 No 65447 gets ready to depart from Aldeburgh station with a train for Saxmundham, c.1959. The line closed to passengers on 12 September 1966 although it is still open for nuclear flask trains from Sizewell.*

BELOW: *Ex-LSWR Class 'T9' 4-4-0 No 30715 departs from Padstow with a train for Wadebridge on 1 August 1958. The line closed on 30 January 1967 and today the trackbed forms part of the Camel Trail cycleway and footpath.*

Raised from the dead

Dai Woodham's Barry scrapyard

The 1960s were a boom period for scrapyards up and down the country – the BR 'Modernisation Plan' of 1955 spelt the end for 16,000 steam locomotives, 16,000 carriages and 625,000 goods wagons. These all had to be disposed of and by the end of the 1950s the various railway works around the country were already full to bursting with withdrawn locos, carriages and wagons. Enter scrap metal merchant Dai Woodham, who became the first recipient of withdrawn Western Region locos and wagons from Swindon at his Barry scrapyard.

The first engines sent to Barry, four Moguls and a Prairie tank, arrived in March 1959 and within a few years this slow trickle became a torrent, not only of steam locomotives but also of thousands of wooden goods wagons and brake vans. Soon the scrapping of the steam locomotives was put on the back burner so that Woodham's could concentrate on disposing of the backlog of goods wagons – by 1968 297 locos had been sold to the company but they had only scrapped 80. The picture was very different at other scrapyards around the country where withdrawn locos were disposed of fairly quickly.

By 1968 the railway preservation movement was gaining momentum and Woodham's was the only source of steam engines – albeit many of them by now rusting hulks. Many of them lay at Barry for over 20 years with the longest resident being ex-GWR 2-6-2 tank No 5552 which arrived in May 1961 and was liberated in June 1986 – over 25 years on 'death row'. Western Region locos saved include 11 'Hall', five 'Castle', two 'King', six 'Modified Hall' and eight 'Manor' 4-6-0s. Representatives of the Southern Region, particularly Bulleid Pacifics, fared even better as most of them were withdrawn towards the end of steam on BR and include 10 'West Country', eight 'Battle of Britain' and 10 'Merchant Navy' Pacifics. Forty-five ex-LMS locos were also saved including two 'Jubilees', six 'Black Fives' and six '8Fs'. Even two Somerset & Dorset Joint Railway '7F' 2-8-0s and the unique BR '8P' Pacific

No 71000 *Duke of Gloucester* were saved for posterity. Oddly, only one ex-LNER loco, 'B1' 4-6-0 No 61264, was bought by Dai Woodham and, after spending nearly eight years there, was also saved for preservation.

Steam locos saved from Barry:

38 BR Standard locos

98 ex-GWR locos

41 ex-SR locos

35 ex-LMS locos

1 ex-LNER loco

The site of Barry scrapyard has now been completely cleared and now all traces of this important resting place for Britain's steam locomotives have been erased.

LEFT: *The scene at Dai Woodham's scrapyard in Barry on 12 October 1969. The majority of the locos seen here were eventually bought for preservation.*

RIGHT: *Withdrawn locos seen by the author at Dai Woodham's scrapyard in Barry on 7 April 1963.*

BELOW: *Seen here at Barry on 16 June 1979, rebuilt ex-SR 'Battle of Britain' Class 4-6-2 No 34059 Sir Archibald Sinclair was saved for preservation by the Bulleid Society and can be seen at work on the Bluebell Railway.*

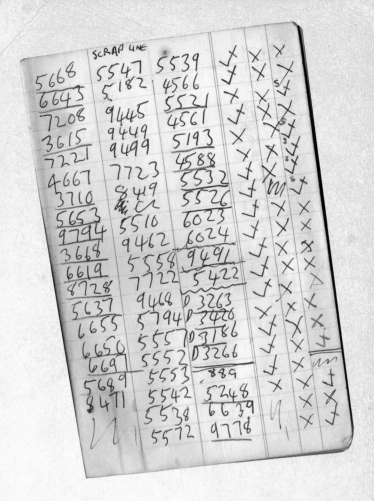

Birth and death of a railway

The Lyme Regis branch

The Dorset seaside town of Lyme Regis, with its ancient Cobb Harbour, had been an important trading centre since medieval times. By the mid-18th century it had also become a popular destination for artists, poets, writers and royalty. The discovery of important dinosaur fossils in the crumbling clay cliffs either side of the town by Mary Anning in 1799 brought more fame to the town and by the early 19th century it had become a popular resort for the wealthy. Despite this growth and although the London & South Western Railway's line from Yeovil to Exeter had opened in July 1860, Lyme Regis had to wait another 43 years before it was connected to the mainline at Axminster.

Although there were several schemes to build a railway to Lyme Regis nothing was done until the passing of the Light Railways Act in 1896. This Act enabled the building of low-cost and lightly constructed railways in sparsely-populated rural areas and soon many optimistic schemes were being put forward to build such lines throughout the country. One of these was the Axminster & Lyme Regis Light Railway Company which obtained a Light Railway Order in 1899. The company appointed Arthur Pain as its engineer and work started on the construction of the line in 1900. Although the steeply graded 6¾-mile line was built to light railway standards there was still one major engineering feat, the 10-arch viaduct across the valley at Cannington, that needed to be accomplished. One of the earliest viaducts in the country to be built of concrete, material for the structure arrived by sea at the Cobb Harbour in Lyme Regis. However, during construction, one of the arches suffered an unforeseen settlement and had to be reinforced by an unsightly jack arch. Once these problems had been overcome the railway was opened on 24 August 1903 with the first train being double-headed by 'Terrier' Class 0-6-0s Nos 734 and 735. Apart from the terminus at Lyme Regis, located high above the town, and the junction with the mainline at Axminster, there was only one intermediate station at Combpyne.

From the outset train services were operated by the L&SWR who, in 1907, took over the line completely. The company then proceeded to upgrade the branch by installing signalling and relaying the track with conventional rail. Passenger traffic on the branch was heavy during the summer months but by the time of the 'Big Four Grouping' in 1923, when the L&SWR became part of the larger Southern Railway, competition from

Ivatt Class '2' 2-6-2T No 41292 halts at bleak Combpyne station with an Axminster to Lyme Regis train on 18 May 1963. On the left is an ancient camping coach which was let out during the summer months.

road transport was already being felt. The location of the terminus at Lyme Regis, 250ft above sea level, necessitating a long walk up hill from the town, certainly did not help the situation. Goods traffic, including livestock, fertilisers and large quantities of coal, was frequently attached to the regular passenger train to form a mixed train.

Under the Southern Railway, the Lyme Regis branch saw the weekday summer service increase to 11 trains each way per day and, from 1930, a Sunday service also operated. The winter Sunday service continued until the Autumn of 1951 when it was replaced by a bus service that connected with mainline trains at Axminster station. The growth of summer holiday traffic after World War II also saw the introduction of through coaches between London Waterloo and Lyme Regis. This service ran from 1953 until 1963 with coaches often being conveyed in one of the many portions of the 'Atlantic Coast Express' before being detached or attached at Axminster. In its final summer of operation this train left Waterloo at 10.45 a.m. and, after pausing at Combpyne station, arrived at Lyme Regis at 2.13 p.m. – the equivalent car journey today along our heavily congested roads would probably take longer. So much for progress! These trains were often so heavily loaded that double-heading was often necessary for the final part of their journey along the branch. For some years an old railway carriage, suitably converted, was parked

in the single siding at Combpyne station and let out to holidaymakers as a camping coach.

Locomotive haulage on this steeply-graded and sharply-curved line was initially in the hands of the diminutive ex-London Brighton & South Coast Railway's 'A1' ('Terrier') Class 0-6-0s but these were replaced by the ancient ex-L&SWR Adams radial 4-4-2 tank engines as early as 1913. Three of these endearing locomotives, all built in 1885, continued to provide the mainstay of motive power on the line until 1961 when they were replaced by more modern ex-LMS Class '2MT' 2-6-2 tanks. These steam locomotives were based at Exmouth Junction shed at Exeter where they returned once a week for routine maintenance. Steam haulage ended in November 1963 and goods services were withdrawn soon after. From then until closure a much-reduced passenger service was handled by two-car and, finally, single-car diesel multiple units. Despite much local opposition, the line finally closed completely on 29 November 1965. Attempts to reopen part of the line in 1970 came to nothing and now picturesque Lyme Regis suffers from traffic gridlock in its narrow streets and appalling car parking problems during summer weekends. Bring back the railway!

BELOW: *Ex-LSWR Class '0415' 4-4-2T No 30582 runs round its train at Lyme Regis station after arriving from Axminster, 16 August 1959. Built in 1885 by Robert Stephenson & Company this veteran loco was withdrawn in 1961.*

Chip vans

Sentinel Steam Railcars

Builders of steam railcars in the early 20th century, the Sentinel Waggon Works started life in Glasgow in 1875 as Alley & MacLellan. Here they not only produced steam road vehicles but also boats. The company moved its steam road vehicle production to a new factory in Shrewsbury in 1915 and was taken over by William Beardmore & Co two years later.

In addition to building geared steam locomotives for the LMS, LNER and the Somerset & Dorset Joint Railway, the company supplied a large number of steam railcars, the first to the narrow-gauge Jersey Railway in 1923. The majority were built mainly for the LNER but also one for the Axholme Joint Railway, one for the Southern Railway, one for New Zealand Railways and 10 for Egyptian National Railways. In 1959 the company started to build diesel locomotives, culminating in Rolls-Royce-engined diesel locomotives for use by the Manchester Ship Canal Company and Stewart & Lloyd's mineral division at Corby. However, redundant and cheaper BR Class 14 diesel-hydraulic locos soon took over work at Stewarts & Lloyd's ironstone quarries and production at Sentinel stopped.

By far the largest order of steam railcars were the 80 bought by the LNER between 1925 and 1932. Exhibited at the 1924 British Empire Exhibition, Sentinel's first standard-gauge steam railcar was loaned to the LNER for trials in northeast England. Competing with an Armstrong-Whitworth diesel-electric railcar the Sentinel steam railcar won the day and the success of these trials led to an order for 80 for use on the LNER and for four for the LNER-controlled Cheshire Lines Committee.

With bodywork built by Cammell Laird, Sentinel's steam railcars were self-contained vehicles with the boiler and driving compartment at the front followed by a luggage compartment and seating for 48–64 passengers, depending on model. At the other end was a remotely-operated driver's compartment for use when running backwards. Delivered between 1925 and 1932, eight different versions were built, some with vertical boilers while others had horizontal boilers. The earlier versions were chain-driven but breakage problems with these led to the introduction of gear-driven versions. Two types were built with an articulated trailer car, while one, built in 1930, came as a twin car. The later versions were capable of speeds in excess of 60 mph.

The Sentinel steam railcars, the majority of them receiving the names of famous stage coaches, were seen at work all over the LNER system, mainly on light branch

RIGHT: *LNER Sentinel steam railcar No 225* True Blue *at West Hartlepool engine shed on 4 June 1932. The railcar was built in 1928 and withdrawn at the end of 1942.*

BELOW: *LNER poster of April 1932 advertising a new Sentinel steam railcar Sunday service between Wigan Central and Irlam & Cadishead.*

NEW SUNDAY SERVICE

COMMENCING 8th MAY

			a.m.	p.m.
Wigan (Central)	...	... dep.	6.45	4. 0
Lower Ince	... ...	... ,,	6.48	4. 3
Hindley and Platt Bridge	... ,,		6.52	4. 7
Irlam and Cadishead	...	... arr.	7.12	4.27
			a.m.	p.m.
Irlam and Cadishead	...	... dep.	7.45	5.52
Hindley and Platt Bridge	...	,,	8. 4	6.12
Lower Ince	...	... ,,	8. 8	6.16
Wigan (Central)	...	... arr.	8.11	6.19

STEAM RAIL CAR

(ONE CLASS ONLY)

London, April, 1932.

L·N·E·R

lines but also on short suburban routes. By 1931, 15 had been allocated to Scotland with one being used for a short period out of Aberdeen Kittybrewster shed for service on ex-GNoSR branches. The confined space of the main driving compartment and their temperamental behaviour made them unpopular with their crews – their box-like appearance and their smoking chimneys soon led to their nickname of 'Chip Vans'. Problems with maintenance eventually led to their demise and the last one, LNER No 2136 *Hope*, just survived into the British Railways era before withdrawal in February 1948.

Four steam railcars were also supplied to the Cheshire Lines Committee and one to the Southern Railway for use on the Brighton to Devil's Dyke branch. None of the British railcars survived but one articulated example from the 10 supplied in 1951 to Egyptian National Railways has been preserved at the Buckinghamshire Railway Centre at Quainton Road.

Days out

Early excursion trains and *Holiday Haunts*

As early as the 1840s the idea dawned upon a few enterprising men, of whom Thomas Cook and James Allport became the most famous, that there might be a 'business of travel' in addition to the travel required by business – from this idea grew the excursion train. One of the first excursion trains known in railway history was run on the Midland Counties Railway from Nottingham to an Exhibition at Leicester on 24 August 1840. Apparently the enormous train of nearly 70 carriages carrying 2,400 people passed majestically before the astonished spectators.

During the following years, Cook went on to arrange railway outings from Leicester for temperance societies and Sunday schools and in 1851 arranged excursions to the Great Exhibition at Crystal Palace for over 150,000 people. Taking a percentage of the cost of railway tickets, his success led to his first foreign adventure in 1855 when he arranged a trip from Leicester to the Paris Exhibition. By the 1860s he was arranging tours further afield to Italy, Egypt and the USA – he never looked back. Railway excursions and day-trips, especially to the seaside, became a popular part of British social life.

Monster railway excursions, such as the Bass annual trip from Burton and the yearly excursion of GWR employees, were run in the late 19th and early 20th centuries.

The GWR annual trip consisted of a succession of trains run to different destinations departing at 10-minute intervals from Swindon. The brewing firm of Bass often chartered up to 17 specials and by the time the last of these had left Burton the first had arrived at its destination, Blackpool, 90 miles away!

Both the 'Big Four' railway companies and British Railways continued in this vein with excursion trains to seaside resorts and large cities playing an important part in opening-up Britain for the masses well into the 1960s.

From 1906 until the outbreak of the Second World War, the Great Western Railway published *Holiday Haunts*, an annual guide to holiday resorts served by the railway which included lists of hotels and boarding establishments. The guide, costing 6d (2½p), was almost 700 pages long and over 200,000 copies were printed each year. To help popularise and give people an opportunity to inspect prospective 'digs', special trains were operated in the 1930s at cheap fares on Sundays during the spring. These trains were appropriately named the 'Holiday Haunts Express' and ran from principal towns and cities on the GWR network to such destinations as Penzance, Minehead, Weymouth, Paignton and Newquay. Fares ranged between 5s (25p) and 10s (50p) and sufficient time was allowed at the destination for passengers to book rooms for a holiday stay later in the year. The train was suspended during the Second World War, but the *Holiday Haunts* series of guides continued to be published by the GWR after the war and British Railways from 1948 until the early 1960s.

FAR LEFT: *South Eastern & Chatham Railway poster of 1921 promoting rail travel to the Grand International Poultry and Pigeon Show at Crystal Palace.*

LEFT: *Great Northern Railway poster of 1907 promoting non-stop excursions from King's Cross to Skegness for 3 shillings (15p).*

BELOW: *Ex-LMS Class '5' 4-6-0 No 44667 arrives at St Pancras station with the 'Derby Holiday Express' in the late 1950s.*

Drinking and driving

Railway water troughs

By the late 1850s, the running of long-distance passenger trains was hampered by the need for regular stops to replenish steam locomotives with water. To remedy this situation, in 1860, John Ramsbottom, an inventor and then locomotive superintendent of the Northern Division of the London & North Western Railway, designed the water trough. First fitted on a stretch of the L&NWR North Wales mainline at Mochdre to the west of Colwyn Bay, the device consisted of a length of water-filled metal trough, fed from a trackside tank, located in the middle of the track. Water was then collected by a scoop, fitted underneath a locomotive's tender, which could be lowered at speed thus replenishing supplies without the need for stopping.

Soon water troughs were being fitted at strategic locations on mainlines throughout Britain, usually at distances of between 30 and 60 miles apart. The London & South Western Railway was the only major company not to use them, instead choosing to fit their express locomotives with larger capacity eight-wheeled tenders.

Locomotives refuelling from water troughs often presented the onlooker with an impressive spectacle when an overfilled tender produced a vast fountain of water – trainspotters were often drenched when inadvertently leaning out of a carriage window at the wrong time! By the 20th century there was an extensive network of water troughs on mainlines around Britain – by 1930 the GWR had 14 fitted, the majority with a length of 560yds, at the following strategic locations:

Paddington to Plymouth
Between Aldermaston and Midgham
Between Frome and Westbury
Between Durston and Creech St Michael
Between Exminster and Starcross

Paddington to Bristol and S Wales
Between Pangbourne and Goring & Streatley
Between Keynsham and St Anne's Park
Between Badminton and Chipping Sodbury
Between Severn Tunnel Junction and Magor
Between Ferryside and Carmarthen Junction

Oxford to Worcester
Between Charlbury and Ascott under Wychwood

Paddington to Birmingham Snow Hill
Between Ruislip & Ickenham and Denham
Between Aynho and King's Sutton
Between Hatton and Lapworth

North-West route Shrewsbury to Newport
Between Bromfield and Ludlow

Only two water troughs were fitted in Scotland: at Strawfrank on the WCML south of Carstairs and at New Cumnock on the ex-G&SWR mainline. Both the LMS and LNER also made extensive use of water troughs especially on the rival West Coast and East Coast mainlines between London and Scotland. Early BR diesels such as the Class 40 and 55 were initially fitted with steam-heated boilers and these continued to replenish supplies from water troughs until the introduction of electrically-heated carriages. Now that water troughs are a dim and distant memory the newly-built Peppercorn Class 'A1' Pacific No 60163 Tornado has been fitted with a larger capacity tender – an extra 1,000 gallons taking up the space previously used for a scoop mechanism – thus enabling it to complete longer distances while on mainline operations.

Hauling a West of England express, one of Charles Collett's new 'Castle' Class 4-6-0s picks up water while travelling at speed.

Let the train take the strain

Car-carrying trains

Before the age of the car privately-owned horse-drawn carriages were regularly transported around Britain by train. They were usually conveyed in special carriage trucks attached to scheduled passenger trains. By the beginning of the 20th century early motor cars were also being carried in the same manner with the Midland Railway being one of the first companies to offer this service. In Scotland, with the opening of the Ballachulish branch in 1903, road vehicles were carried across the Connel Bridge from Connel Ferry station to North Connel on a specially adapted goods wagon until 1914 when the bridge was then resurfaced to accommodate both road and rail traffic.

A scheduled car-carrying service was introduced in 1924 by the GWR between Severn Tunnel Junction and Pilning High Level as an alternative to the erratic Aust Ferry across the River Severn. Passengers were conveyed in separate carriages while the cars travelled on open bogie trucks attached to the rear. Cars were usually filthy at the end of their journey after being conveyed through the dripping tunnel by a steam engine! The scheduled service ended in 1966 with the opening of the Severn Bridge.

The Motorail services as we knew them started in 1955 with the introduction by the Eastern Region of BR of an overnight London to Perth service. A daytime service between London Holloway and Edinburgh was introduced in 1960 and within a few years the network had expanded to include destinations from London such as Stirling, Inverness, Fishguard and St Austell. Outside of London

there were services between Manchester and Dover, Sutton Coldfield and Inverness, Newcastle and Exeter, Newcastle and Dover and York and Inverness. The majority of the trains ran overnight and were made up of sleeping cars attached to either flat car transporter wagons or converted end-loading GUV covered wagons. Cars were loaded on and off the train via an end-loading dock at a station – the one at the west end of Reading station could be seen for many years after falling into disuse. The only purpose-built Motorail terminal opened at Kensington Olympia in London in 1961 – this remained in use until 1981.

Motorail services peaked in the late 1970s with around 30 destinations served but the opening of new motorways and the increasing reliability of cars led to a gradual decline in routes. The last Motorail service ran in 1995 but in 1999 First Great Western re-introduced a Motorail service which was attached to its overnight 'Night Riviera' sleeping car train. It last ran with a Motorail van in 2005.

FAR LEFT: *King's Cross shed's ex-LNER Class 'A3' 4-6-2 No 60061 Pretty Polly halts at Newcastle Central to take on water while hauling the up 'Anglo-Scottish Car Carrier' on 21 June 1959 (the author's birthday!).*

LEFT: *The 1961 timetable for 'Anglo-Scottish Car Carrier' daytime service.*

BELOW: *The network of Motorail services around Britain in the summer of 1968.*

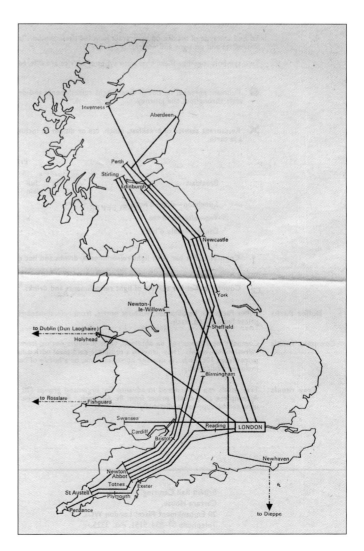

Prepare for take-off

Railway Air Services – Britain's railway-owned airline

Even back in the late 1920s the railways saw domestic airlines as a serious threat and in 1929 the 'Big Four' – GWR, LMS, LNER and SR – obtained Parliamentary approval to run their own air services. Apart from the Southern Railway's unsuccessful attempt to take control of Imperial Airways nothing much happened until 1933 when the GWR started an air service for mail and passengers linking Cardiff and Plymouth – an obvious choice as the meandering rail journey via Bristol was 164¾ miles while the direct air route across the Bristol Channel was around 90 miles. Birmingham, Teignmouth and Torquay were also soon added to the GWR's network.

In March 1934 the 'Big Four' railway companies and Imperial Airways formed Railway Air Services Ltd – the first chairman of RAS was Sir Harold Hartley of the LMS and the first flight was by a de Havilland Dragon on the Plymouth-Haldon-Cardiff-Birmingham route. The RAS network soon expanded to include Croydon, Brighton & Hove, Portsmouth, Isle of Wight, Southampton, Bournemouth, Exeter, Plymouth, Bristol, Cardiff, Cheltenham & Gloucester, Birmingham, Stoke-on-Trent, Manchester, Liverpool, Belfast and Glasgow using de Havilland Dragon, Dragon Rapide and Express 'airliners'.

Apart from the Liverpool-Belfast-Glasgow route, the airline ceased operations during World War II but resumed in 1946 with Avro Ansons and DC3s. Railway Air Services were taken over by the newly-formed state-owned British European Airways in 1947.

RIGHT: *Late 1930s' posters promoting Railway Air Services flights.*

BELOW: *De Havilland DH84 Dragon II No 6075 G-ACPX of the Railway Air Services preparing to take off from Speke Airport on the inaugural flight from Liverpool to Plymouth, 7 May 1934.*

Railways that never were

Scottish light railways that were never built

During the latter part of the 19th century and the early years of the 20th century a surprising number of hairbrained schemes were put forward to build new railway lines in the sparsely populated region of northwest Scotland and on some of the Western Isles. Despite much optimism from their promoters about their future prospects, if built, the lines would never have returned a profit.

The first scheme was the Garve & Ullapool Railway which received authorisation in 1890 to build a 32-mile line from Garve, on the Dingwall & Skye Railway, to the fishing village of Ullapool on the west coast. Nothing came of this due to lack of capital but it was revived a couple of years later by the Great North of Scotland Railway – their nearest railhead was at Elgin and to work the Ullapool line the company would have needed to obtain running powers over the existing Highland Railway line between that town and Garve via Inverness and Dingwall. Naturally the Highland Railway would have none of this and the scheme quietly died. A similar fate befell a scheme to build a 35-mile line from Achnasheen, also on the Dingwall & Skye Railway, to Gairloch and Aultbea.

The passing of the Light Railways Act in 1896 brought about hundreds of schemes to build low-cost railways in rural areas throughout Great Britain and Ireland. Taking advantage of the provisions within the Act, the Highland Railway was quick off the mark and within a year the company had put forward an ambitious programme for the building of nearly 250 miles of new lines in the region. These included reviving the already proposed lines to Ullapool and Aultbea, a 41-mile line from Culrain, on the Inverness to Far North line, to Lochinver and a 42-mile line from Lairg to Loch Laxford – all of these schemes were designed to provide an outlet for the west coast's fishing industry, provide new links with ferries to the Outer Hebrides and take advantage of the up-and-coming tourist industry. Probably fortunately for the Highland Railway, none of them ever saw the light of day!

In the far northeast of Scotland the company also proposed building new lines from Forsinard to Melvich and Portskerra (14 miles), from Thurso to Scrabster and also to Gills Bay (17 miles) and from Wick to Dunbeath (20 miles). Of these only the line to Lybster (7 miles north of Dunbeath) was built. Apart from the branch line from The Mound to Dornoch, another scheme further down the east coast from Fearn to Portmahomack (9 miles) also never materialised. A 19-mile line was also proposed from Dingwall to Cromarty and the first 6 miles was actually built – then along came World War I and the line was abandoned. Its route can still be seen today.

Narrow-gauge railways with a 3ft-6in.-gauge were also proposed by the Highland Railway on the Hebridean islands of Lewis and Harris, and Skye. On Lewis and Harris proposals included lines from Stornoway westwards to Carloway and Dunan Pier and south to Tarbert while on Skye lines were to be built from Kyleakin to Torrin and from Isleornsay in the south to Broadford, Portree and Uig in the north with a branch to Dunvegan. As with the majority of the company's schemes none of these lines were ever built.

Parliamentary Committee findings, 1919

The question of rural transport in Scotland was studied by a Parliamentary Committee which published its findings in 1919. It makes interesting reading following on from earlier stillborn proposals by the Highland Railway to build new railways in the northwest of Scotland and on Lewis and Skye.

In their report the Committee advocated the building of 382 miles of new railway, 85 miles of new road, road improvements and the introduction of new bus and steamer services. As the majority of these proposed schemes would pass through sparsely populated and remote countryside the Committee pressed the point that Government funding would be necessary.

It must be remembered that at this time the UK was just starting to recover from the First World War and was seriously in debt – at home there were shortages of raw materials, food and fuel, unrest among the workforce with strikes already making themselves felt, while abroad revolution and political shockwaves were spreading around the world. However well-meaning, the

Committee's schemes to liberate unpopulated regions of Scotland never had a cat's chance of succeeding.

Theoretically, the majority of their new railway proposals would have been possible under the 1896 Light Railways Act, which did away with a lot of red tape and Health & Safety nonsense, enabling lines to be built and operated at less expense than normal railways. The narrow-gauge lines were to be built to a 60cm-gauge using German military railway equipment 'liberated' at the end of the war. The following list of these new routes is fascinating as some of them had already been proposed years before (with no success) and none, apart from the Cromarty branch which was started but not finished, were actually built.

Standard-gauge lines
Culrain to Lochinver, 40 miles
Garve to Ullapool, 33 miles
Parton to Dalmellington, 28 miles
Turriff to Maud, 21½ miles
Alford to Bellabeg, 19 miles
Conon to Cromarty, 18 miles
Ballater to Braemar, 17 miles
Stranraer to Drummore, 14½ miles
Fraserburgh to Aberdour, 9 miles
Lybster to Dunbeath, 8 miles
Pinwherry to Ballantrae, 8 miles
Balfron to Fintry, 8 miles
Thurso to Scrabster, 2 miles

Narrow-gauge lines
Isle of Skye, 75 miles
Isle of Lewis, 40 miles
Dunoon to Strachur, 21 miles
Isle of Arran, 20 miles

FOOTNOTE: The Committee also proposed a revolutionary new road system, constructing concrete wheel tracks either on or at the side of existing roads, and at the same level. They suggested that bye-laws should make it obligatory on motor drivers to use these tracks. The Committee recommended a test of its practicability on a stretch of road at some suitable locality. It seems they eventually got their way when £116.2 million was earmarked for the controversial Cambridgeshire Guided Busway in 2009! It follows the course of the closed Cambridge to St Ives railway but, quite frankly, it would have been cheaper to have reopened the railway...

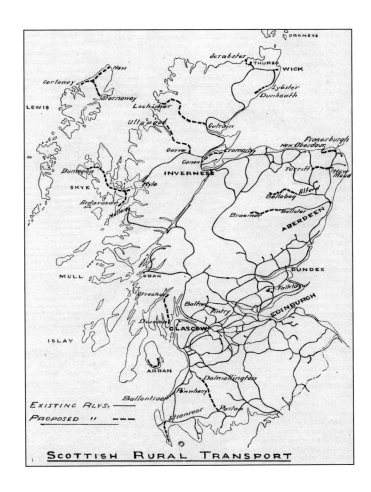

ABOVE: Early-20th-century map showing the proposed new light and narrow-gauge railways around Scotland. Construction of the Cromarty & Dingwall Light Railway was started but never completed and it was abandoned in 1914. None of the others got off the ground at all.

BELOW: The Light Railway Commission's application of 1898 for compulsory purchase of land in connection with the planned construction of the Rhins of Galloway Light Railway. The railway was never built.

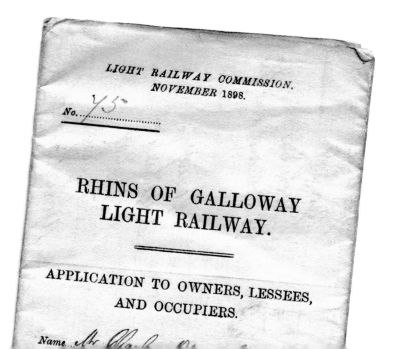

LIGHT RAILWAY COMMISSION,
NOVEMBER 1898.

No. 45

RHINS OF GALLOWAY
LIGHT RAILWAY.

APPLICATION TO OWNERS, LESSEES,
AND OCCUPIERS.

Name. Mr

We've run out of coal

British oil-fired steam locomotives

Until the mass introduction of diesel locomotives in the late 1950s Britain's railways depended on a regular supply of good quality steam coal to keep the trains running. Fortunately Britain has always been well endowed with such fuel and it was only during periods of industrial unrest or Arctic weather conditions that railway companies temporarily converted some of their steam locomotives to oil-burning.

The first oil-fired steam locomotive in Britain, appropriately named Petrolea, was built by James Holden for the Great Eastern Railway in 1893. Its success led to 100 suburban and express oil-fired locomotives being built for the railway until the cost of waste oil rose to a prohibitive level and the experiment was ended.

During the prolonged coalminers' strikes of 1912, 1921 and 1926 coal was in very short supply and many locomotives were temporarily converted to oil-burning. Apart from the obvious increase in costs when importing fuel from abroad, oil-burning locomotives were generally cleaner to operate and were more efficient. The largest number of British steam locomotives converted to oil-burning occurred early in 1947 when the country was hit by one of the coldest winters on record. Heavy snowfalls and freezing weather caused roads and railways to be blocked. Coal supplies, already low following the privations of World War II, couldn't reach power stations – which were then forced to shut down. The UK not only suffered mass power blackouts but also severe food shortages. Faced with this crisis, and to keep the railways running, the Labour Government drew up emergency plans to fund the conversion of 1,200 steam locomotives to oil-burning. Faced with the looming coal shortage the GWR, under its CME F. W. Hawksworth (see opposite page) had already begun experimenting with converting examples of 2-8-0 freight locos, 'Halls' and 'Castles'. In typical British fashion the oil conversion scheme soon collapsed as the country did not have enough foreign exchange to purchase the oil!

Converted to oil burning, ex-London & South Western Railway 'L11' Class 4-4-0 No 157 (built in 1903) is seen at Eastleigh Works on 2 June 1951, one year before withdrawal. Eight of these locos were converted to oil burning in 1947 and 1948.

Swindon's last great man

F. W. Hawksworth – the last Chief Mechanical Engineer of the GWR

Frederick W. Hawksworth was born in Swindon in 1884 and joined the GWR in 1898. After working his way up the corporate ladder to the company's drawing office he was appointed Chief Locomotive Draughtsman at the time of the introduction of the 'King' Class locos in 1927. When his famous boss, Charles Collett, retired in 1941 Hawksworth was appointed as Chief Mechanical Engineer. This was a difficult time for the GWR with World War II in full swing and shortages of good quality coal adding to their problems.

Hawksworth assembled a team of 100% GWR men and by 1944 had introduced the 'Modified Hall' Class 4-6-0s which were a notable development of Collett's 'Hall' Class and considered a resounding success. Although plans for a powerful Pacific-type loco never got beyond the drawing board the period 1945–47 was busy with the introduction of new powerful 'County' Class and improved 'Castles' with double chimneys and four-row superheaters. Despite being two-cylinder engines the 'County' Cass was certainly

a break away from GWR tradition with their high-pressure Stanier '8F' boiler and 6ft-3in. driving wheels.

Other loco types introduced under Hawksworth were the '1600' Class and '9400' Class 0-6-0 pannier tanks (the latter with taper boiler) and the '1500' Class 0-6-0 pannier tank, the latter the only mainline locos designed by the GWR with Walschaerts valve gear.

Following Nationalisation in 1948 Hawksworth remained in control at Swindon but was now responsible to the new Railway Executive. He retired at the end of 1949 and died at the age of 92 in 1976.

BELOW: *Built at Swindon Works in 1945, ex-GWR 'County' Class 4-6-0 No 1002* County of Berks *at rest at Bristol Bath Road shed in April 1949. This loco was later fitted with a double chimney and withdrawn in September 1963.*

Push me – pull you 2

The Lancashire & Yorkshire Railway's railmotors

Unlike the Great Western Railway's railmotors which had an integral vertical boiler and driving cab, the Lancashire & Yorkshire Railway under its Locomotive Superintendent George Hughes opted for a more novel approach when designing its own railmotor.

However, prior to building his own railmotors, Hughes had bought two such vehicles from the Taff Vale Railway (TVR) in 1905. They were built by Kerr Stuart with bodies supplied by the Bristol Carriage & Wagon Works and were used for several years on branch line services around Bury and Bolton. These test bed vehicles provided important lessons for Hughes and in 1906 he introduced the first of 18 railmotors which were built at Horwich Works. At one end of the railmotor was a diminutive but conventional 0-4-0 tank locomotive, fitted with outside cylinders and Walschaerts valve gear, which

was permanently attached to a single coach. The coach was supported at one end by the locomotive and the other end by a bogie. As with the GWR's railmotors and auto trains a driving compartment at the far end of the trailer coach allowed the driver to operate the train when the locomotive was pushing from the rear. A cost-effective and successful design, the train was totally self-contained and did not even need to be turned.

The two TVR railmotors were withdrawn in 1909 and by 1911 Horwich had completed the production run of Hughes's own design. They could be seen at work throughout Lancashire including the Bury to Holcombe Brook branch, the Southport to Altcar branch and along the Colne Valley. All of the L&YR's railmotors survived into LMS ownership with one (No 10617) just scraping into the British Railway's era before it was withdrawn in 1948.

Built by the Lancashire & Yorkshire Railway at Horwich works in 1911, diminutive LMS 0-4-0T No 10617 (minus its carriage) is seen here in ex-works grey paint in 1925. It just survived into British Railways ownership, being withdrawn in March 1948.

Vital statistics

Engine: 2 cylinders, 12in. diameter × 16in. stroke

Wheels: 3ft-75/8in. diameter on tread

Wheelbase (engine): 8ft; total wheelbase 54ft-8in.

Boiler diameter: 4ft-3in.

Heating surface (total): 509 sq ft

Grate area: 9.4 sq ft

Working pressure: 180lbs per sq in.

Capacity of water tank: 550 gallons

Capacity of coal bunker: 1 ton

Trailer car: length over buffers: 69ft-5in.

               width of car body: 8ft-6¾ in.

               length of car body: 47ft-6in.

               seating capacity: 56 passengers (all one class)

               luggage compartment: 340 cu ft

Total weight (loco and trailer): 47½ tons

BELOW: *LMS steam railmotor No 10617 on a local service at Bolton Trinity Street station, 1947.*

On shed, 29 March 1964

An almighty shed bash around Glasgow and Edinburgh

Spurred on by the imminent end to steam haulage on British Railways many railway societies, including the Warwickshire Railway Society and the Home Counties Railway Society, organised trips during the early 1960s to distant engine sheds and railway works for their members. Known as 'shed bashes', many of these trips had to be undertaken by motor coach due to the difficulties in organising an itinerary, usually on a Sunday, that took in obscure destinations that had long lost their passenger service. Fortunately, not all of these trips were made by road and one of them, organised by (I believe) the Warwickshire Railway Society for 28–30 March 1964, was a shed bash to end all shed bashes!

On 28 March hundreds of fellow trainspotters and I gathered in the gloomy depths of Birmingham New Street station to await the arrival of our overnight special to Glasgow and Edinburgh. By that date the diesel invasion was well underway and my trip up from

Gloucester on a Bristol to Newcastle train that evening had been behind BR Sulzer Type 4 D35. However, I was not to be disappointed when our special train drew into New Street behind gleaming maroon-liveried 'Coronation' Class 4-6-2 No 46256 *Sir William A. Stanier, F.R.S.* – with only six months to go before withdrawal this powerful machine was much in demand for specials such as ours. Departure from New Street was prompt at 11 p.m. and with pick-ups at Crewe (12.35 a.m.) and Preston (1.47 a.m.) we arrived at Glasgow Central at 6.20 a.m. on the 29th.

There must have been around 400 or so trainspotters who alighted bleary-eyed from that train and in a monumental exercise that would have done justice to the British Army we were transported in a fleet of motor coaches to 10 engine sheds around the Glasgow and Edinburgh areas. From early morning until early evening this vast army with notebooks and cameras to hand visited engine sheds at Polmadie (66A), Motherwell (66B),

Freshly shopped out from St Rollox Works, Stanier 'Black Five' 4-6-0 No 45312 was seen at Glasgow Corkerhill shed (67A) on this momentous day.

Corkerhill (67A), Dawsholm (65D), Eastfield (65A), St Rollox (65B), Bathgate (64F), Haymarket (64B), Dalry Road (64C), and St Margarets (64A). At the end of that day we were dumped at Waverley station until our train arrived to take us back to Birmingham. Departure from Waverley was at 10.35 p.m. and there were drop-offs at Preston (3.20 a.m.) and Crewe (4.34 a.m.) – however I must have fallen asleep soon after departure as I cannot remember much of the journey back (I suppose we must have travelled back via the Waverley Route). *Sir William* came off at Crewe where 'Black Five' 4-6-0 No 44765 took over for the rest of the journey to New Street where we arrived at 6.08 a.m. on the 30th. Weary and exhausted after spotting a total of 675 locos (353 steam, 313 diesel, 9 electric) I snoozed on the way back to Gloucester behind BR Sulzer Type 4 D126. What a trip!

RIGHT: *The page from my notebook recording locos seen at Glasgow Polmadie shed (66A) on 29 March 1964.*

BELOW: *Bathgate shed (64F) was a treasure trove of wonderful old locos awaiting preservation or scrapping in 1964. Here is ex-NBR Class 'Y9' 0-4-0ST No 68095, built by Neilson in 1887 and withdrawn at the end of 1962. It is now on static display at the Bo'ness & Kinneil Railway.*

Flying bananas

The GWR's streamlined railcars

The Great Western Railway was never slow in keeping up with the latest trends and their publicity department often put other railway companies to shame. The introduction by the GWR of their first streamlined diesel railcar in 1933 was no exception to this and its initial success led to a total of 38 being built by 1942, their streamlined shape and their brown and cream livery giving them the nickname 'Flying Banana'. Powered by AEC diesel engines similar to those used in a London bus, they were built in three batches by Park Royal, Gloucester Railway Carriage & Wagon Company and by the GWR at Swindon. Apart from No 1 which only had one engine, all of the other units were fitted with twin engines. Various versions were built including some with a small buffet section, parcels cars and two twin-sets with buffet and lavatory for longer cross-country journeys – the latter were capable of running back-to-back or with a single ordinary carriage between them.

When used on loss-making branch lines the introduction of the single railcars led to a steady increase in passengers and the twin-set railcars transformed services on the Cardiff to Birmingham Snow Hill (via Gloucester Central) route to such an extent that longer steam-hauled trains had to be introduced to cater for the extra passengers. The latter units were then transferred to the Bristol to Weymouth and Reading to Newbury routes. All but one railcar (No 9 had been destroyed in a fire in 1946) passed into British Railways ownership in 1948. Withdrawal started in 1954 with the last examples surviving until 1962. Three examples, W4W, W20W and W22W have since been preserved.

BELOW: *Ex-GWR diesel railcar W20 arrives at Woofferton station on 30 April 1960 with a train from Bewdley and Tenbury Wells. Woofferton station and the line from Tenbury Wells closed on 31 July 1961.*

How rats ruined a railway

Brunel's atmospheric South Devon Railway

Isambard Kingdom Brunel, not a man to ignore the latest technology, had just completed the building of the Bristol & Exeter Railway. His next project was to extend the railway line from Exeter to Plymouth which would involve some steep gradients west of Newton Abbot. Concerned about the steam locomotive's ability to pull heavy trains on this section, in 1844 he made the decision to build an atmospheric railway. The atmospheric system had been patented by Clegg, Samuda & Samuda in 1838 and, on witnessing early trials in West London, Brunel was highly impressed with the results.

Obviating the need for normal steam locomotives, the system consisted of a 20-inch-diameter iron pipe located between the rails from which stationary steam engines pumped out air to create a vacuum. The iron pipe had a slot in the top, sealed by a leather flap, and a 15ft-long piston, secured on a rod beneath the leading carriage, fitted into the pipe. The pressure of the air that was sucked into the vacuum pipe as the flap was opened moved the piston, and the train, forward. As the piston moved forward, two small wheels in front of and behind it first opened the flap and then resealed it. Stationary pumping houses located at intervals of 3 miles along the line were used to keep a permanent vacuum in the pipe.

However, the equipment for the atmospheric railway had not been delivered when the railway opened as far as Teignmouth on 30 May 1846 and locomotives, hired from the Great Western Railway, had to be used to haul trains. The next section of line to Newton Abbot was opened on 30 December 1846 but there was still no sign of the atmospheric equipment. Finally, in February 1847, enough equipment had been delivered for Brunel to start trials with the system. Although fairly successful with lightly loaded trains problems were encountered at this stage with early deterioration of the leather flap that was supposed to keep the pipe air-tight. Tallow, grease that was produced from melting animal fat, was liberally applied to the slot in the pipe in an effort to ensure an air-tight seal but it was soon found that rats found it tasty and that it melted in hot sunshine!

Finally, passenger-carrying atmospheric trains started operation between Exeter and Teignmouth on 13 September 1847 and were extended to Newton Abbot on 10 January 1848. On 23 February all trains, including freight, were operating on the atmospheric system. By July the system was operating as far as Totnes and work went ahead to complete the remaining steeply-graded section to Plymouth. However, escalating costs due to the high maintenance required to ensure an air-tight seal along with the system's eccentric uniqueness soon brought about its demise. A more or less unanimous vote to abandon the system was taken by South Devon Railway shareholders at the end of August and it ceased to operate on 6 September.

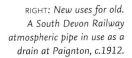

RIGHT: *New uses for old. A South Devon Railway atmospheric pipe in use as a drain at Paignton, c.1912.*

FAR RIGHT: *The South Devon Railway atmospheric pumping station at Exeter in 1923. The tall chimney was for the large stationary steam engine that powered the hydraulic pumps.*

It's a small world

The miniature railways of W. J. Bassett-Lowke and Henry Greenly

The model company founded in Northampton at the end of the 19th century by Wenman Joseph Bassett-Lowke (1877–1953) became a leading sub-contractor and distributor of scale model ships and railways for over 50 years. By the beginning of World War I the company, working closely with model railway engineer Henry Greenly, was offering a range of well-detailed railway models from 15-in.-gauge to Gauge '2', Gauge '1' and the increasingly popular '0' gauge. A whole range of British outline model trains were built for Bassett-Lowke by the German company Bing and the French company Carette – many of these faithful reproductions of their full-size counterparts were powered by steam or clockwork. In 1923 Basset-Lowke also introduced the first '00' gauge tabletop railway – versions were available with clockwork or third-rail electric power. These were first manufactured by Bing and then, after that company's demise in 1932, by Trix.

Bassett-Lowke also built complete miniature railways such as the Gauge 1 layout at the Bekonscot Model Village in Beaconsfield and larger 15-in.-gauge locomotives for miniature railways such as the Ravenglass & Eskdale Railway in Cumbria. The latter line was converted by Bassett-Lowke from 3ft-gauge in 1915 and operated using that company's 4-4-2 steam loco *Sans Pareil*.

Bassett-Lowke's fortunes declined after World War II and the company closed in 1965. The name was bought by Corgi in 1996 and is currently owned by Hornby which has restarted production of detailed '0' gauge locomotives and rolling stock.

Born in Birkenhead, Henry Greenly (1876–1947) trained as a draughtsman at the Neasden Works of the Metropolitan Railway and went on to become a leading designer of miniature passenger-carrying railways. By the early 20th century he had become a much sought-after consultant model engineer and, as such, worked closely with W. J. Bassett-Lowke designing miniature steam locomotives.

Perhaps Greenly's greatest moment was when he teamed up with millionaire Captain 'Jack' Howey as Chief Engineer of the 13½-mile 18in.-gauge Romney, Hythe & Dymchurch Railway which opened in 1927. Built by Davey, Paxman, his one-third scale steam locomotives still operate on the line today and are a living testimony to his skill as a miniature locomotive designer. Greenly also edited a model railways magazine and wrote several groundbreaking books on model railways in the 1920s – he is generally considered to have had an enormous impact on the British model railway scene.

BELOW: Passengers waiting for a train at Eskdale Green station on the Ravenglass & Eskdale Railway, c.1927. The locomotive is 2-8-2 River Esk which was designed by Henry Greenly and built by Davey, Paxman in 1923.

OVERLEAF: Romney Hythe & Dymchurch Railway 4-8-2 'Mountain' Class Samson was designed by Henry Greenly and built by Davey, Paxman in 1927. It is seen at the head of a train to Hythe at Dungeness station in 2019.

Fair exchange

Locomotive exchanges

In the days before and just after Nationalisation, Britain's railways often tested their locomotives against those of their rivals. Hauling similar loads along the same demanding route, the performance of these engines could be measured against each other and the outcome was quite often surprising!

The 1925 Exchanges

Probably one of the most famous of these locomotive exchanges took place in April 1925 when the Great Western Railway's latest design, the 'Castle' Class 4-6-0 was tested against the much larger London & North Eastern Railway's Class 'A1' 4-6-2. During the trials GWR No 4079 *Pendennis Castle* and LNER No 2545 *Diamond Jubilee* were tested to their limits first by hauling heavy trains on the East Coast mainline out of King's Cross. While the 'Castle' performed faultlessly, the 'A3' lost time on several of its journeys even though it was performing on its home ground – much to the chagrin of the LNER

bosses! Similar tests were conducted on the GWR mainline from Paddington to Plymouth and the 'Castle', this time pitted against 'A3' Class *Victor Wild*, again came out on top – not only was the 'Castle' 15 minutes faster than the 'A3' on both the outward and return journeys but it also used considerably less coal. The GWR had proved once and for all that its locomotive design was far superior to that of its rivals.

The 1948 Exchanges

When the 'Big Four' railway companies were nationalised on 1 January 1948 the newly-formed British Railways were faced with the mammoth problem of taking over thousands of non-standard steam locomotives, many of them well past their 'sell-by' date. To overcome this, BR planned to build a completely new range of standard steam locomotives that would incorporate all of the best design features from the locomotive stock of the 'Big Four'. Before they could proceed with the building programme a series of locomotive

exchanges were made between four express passenger classes and four mixed traffic classes to ascertain the relative merits of each one. They all had to haul the same weight along designated routes using the same, Yorkshire, coal.

Express passenger locomotive trials

The routes used for the trials were as follows:
London Euston to Carlisle
London Paddington to Plymouth
London Waterloo to Exeter
London Kings Cross to Leeds

For the express passenger classes the following classes of locomotives were used, each one being required to haul the same weight train along each of the designated routes and burning the same, Yorkshire, coal:
LMS – Stanier 'Coronation' Class 4-6-2
GWR – Collett 'King' Class 4-6-0
LNER – Gresley Class 'A4' 4-6-2
SR – Bulleid 'Merchant Navy' Class 4-6-2

A fifth locomotive class, the LMS Stanier 'Royal Scot' Class 4-6-0, was added to the list at the last moment.

It must be remembered that while these locomotives were designed to haul expresses on their own home ground, some of them were not particularly well-suited for the testing uphill sections that they encountered in the trials. The results were a mixed bag with, surprisingly, the smaller and less powerful 'Royal Scot' probably giving the best overall performance, particularly with its exhilarating run from Taunton to Paddington where it arrived over 16 minutes ahead of schedule. The 'King' probably suffered most because it had to burn Yorkshire coal instead of the South Wales coal that it was designed to use. Apart from one amazing performance between Salisbury and Waterloo, the 'Duchess', too, did not fare too well. The 'Merchant Navy' put in some worthy runs on the formidable section between Penrith and Carlisle but paid for this performance with very high oil and coal consumption. Finally, the 'A4', despite some mechanical problems, probably gave the best performance out of the four larger locos, turning in a scintillating run on the former GWR mainline.

LEFT: *Ex-Southern Railway 'West Country' Class 4-6-2 No 34006* Bude *is seen here at Aylesbury in June 1948 while taking part in the mixed traffic locomotive exchanges on the former Great Central Railway mainline between Marylebone and Manchester.*

BELOW: *Ex-LNER 'A4' Class 4-6-2 No 60033* Seagull *departs from Paddington station on a test run to Plymouth while taking part in the locomotive exchanges of 1948. Immediately behind the loco is a dynamometer car for measuring performance.*

Ex-GWR 'King' Class 4-6-0 No 6018 King Henry VI at Wakefield Westgate in May 1948 while taking part in the locomotive exchanges on the Eastern Region between King's Cross and Leeds.

While not perfect, these trials provided much useful data, some of which was incorporated into the design of the new Standard 'Britannia' Class 4-6-2s introduced by British Railways in 1951.

Mixed traffic locomotive exchanges

The routes used for the trials were as follows:
London St Pancras to Manchester
Exeter to Bristol
London Marylebone to Manchester
Perth to Inverness

For the mixed traffic classes the following classes of locomotives were used and, as before, each one was required to haul the same weight train along each of the designated routes and burn the same, Yorkshire, coal:
LMS – Stanier Class '5' 4-6-0
GWR – Collett 'Hall' Class 4-6-0
LNER – Thompson Class 'B1' 4-6-0
SR – Bulleid 'West Country' Class 4-6-2

Unlike the mixed bag of results with the express locomotives there was one clear winner from these trials. Without a doubt, the 'West Country' excelled on all of the routes giving extremely impressive performances on even the most demanding sections. Both the 'Hall' and 'B1' performed well in a workmanlike way but, surprisingly, the Stanier Class '5' turned in very poor times. One eminent railway historian and recorder of locomotive performances of that time, Cecil J. Allen, was shocked that this highly regarded locomotive that had put in such sterling work for the LMS had failed so miserably! It did appear that the problem probably didn't lie with the locomotive at all but with the driver and fireman who had obviously lost the plot and decided to break the world-record for the most amount of fuel consumed in the trials!

Although the 'West Country' was the undoubted winner, its heavy consumption of fuel let it down and it was the already tried-and-tested Class '5' that was used as the blueprint for the design of the new Standard Class '5' 4-6-0s that were introduced by British Railways in 1951. As with the Class '5', these new locomotives gave sterling service on British Railways up until the end of steam in 1968.

Attention!

The military names of locomotives

The naming of locomotives has been a popular public relations exercise since the early railways. Names ranging from abbeys, Arthurian legends and the British Empire to castles, fox hunts, monarchs and schools that adorned many steam locomotives lent further glamour to the already perceived romanticism of rail travel. The GWR's large brass nameplates were a work of art in themselves. Giving military names to locomotives became a regular practice after World War I when 25 North British Railway's 'C' Class 0-6-0s were named after generals and sites of battles after returning from active duty in northern France. The height of engine naming came in the 1930s and 1940s and the practice continued after Nationalisation with the naming of whole classes of Western Region mainline diesel locomotives after famous warships.

NOTE: BR numbering is used throughout.

Great Western Railway

'Castle' Class — 11 were renamed after World War II military aeroplanes (Nos 5071–5082). Their original names were given to newer 7000 series locos when built. No 5017 was renamed in 1954 after the Gloucestershire Regiment following its famous exploits in the Korean War. Former 'Star' Class locos rebuilt as 'Castles' with military names were No 4016 *The Somerset Light Infantry (Prince Albert's)* and No 4037 *The South Wales Borderers*.

Southern Railway

'Lord Nelson' Class — the entire class of 16 (30850–30865) was named after famous admirals.
'Battle of Britain' Class — Nos 34049–34090 and 34109/34110 were named after World War II RAF fighter squadrons, airfields and military leaders.

London Midland & Scottish Railway

'Black Five' – four of this class (45154 and 45156–45158) were given names of Scottish regiments.

'Patriot' Class – military names (including regiments and VC holders) were given in a very haphazard manner to around one-third of the 52 locos of this class.

'Jubilee' Class – despite many of this class being named after colonies of the British Empire, 48 (Nos 45639–45686) were named after famous admirals and sea battles and 44 (Nos 45687–45730) were named after famous British warships.

'Royal Scot' Class – when originally built this class had a mix of regimental names and names of famous L&NWR locomotives. By the mid-'30s all of the class carried regimental names except the last three – 46168 *The Girl Guide*, 46169 *The Boy Scout* and 46170 *British Legion*.

London & North Eastern Railway

'V2' Class – four locos were named after north-eastern regiments (Nos 60809, 60835, 60872, 60964).

'J36' Class – 25 of these humble 0-6-0 locos were given names of World War I generals and names of battles after returning from active service in Northern France. Unlike other named engines the names were only painted onto the wheel arch and these disappeared over time.

British Railways steam locomotives

'Britannia' Class – five of this class (70040–70044) were given names of former army commanders and No 70048 was later named *The Territorial Army 1908–1958*.

British Railways mainline diesel locos

BR Sulzer Type 4 (Class 45) – 25 were named after regiments.

BR Sulzer Type 4 (Class 46) – only one of these, D163/46026, was named, which was Leicestershire and Derbyshire Yeomanry.

North British Type 4 'Warship' – all five (D600–D604) were named after famous warships.

BR/NBR Type 4 'Warship' (Class 42/43) – apart from D800, all the remaining 70 locos were named after famous warships.

English Electric Type 5 ('Deltic'/Class 55) – 14 were named after Scottish and north-eastern regiments.

English Electric Type 4 (Class 50) – the entire class of 50 were named after warships in 1978.

LEFT: *The nameplate of Class '55' 'Deltic' diesel-electric D9013, seen at Edinburgh Haymarket depot on 29 March 1964. The loco was withdrawn in December 1981.*

BELOW: *The nameplate of ex-LMS 'Black Five' 4-6-0 No 45156. Built in 1935 by Armstrong Whitworth the loco was withdrawn from Rose Grove shed (10F) in August 1968.*

The infernal combustion engine

Early diesel and gas-turbine locomotives

The GWR's experiment with gas-turbine technology

Even before World War II problems with coal supplies caused by industrial unrest had led many American railroads to invest heavily in diesel electric technology as a replacement for steam traction. Apart from a few faltering steps in the 1930s Britain lagged behind until after World War II when two of the 'Big Four' railway companies built experimental diesel-electric mainline locomotives and the Great Western Railway dabbled with gas-turbine technology. Although the gas-turbines led up a cul-de-sac, the diesel-electric prototypes paved the way for the introduction of British Railways' first generation of mainline diesels in the late 1950s.

Seeking an alternative source for mainline motive power in the 1940s the GWR decided to investigate gas-turbine technology. Their reasoning for this decision was that a gas-turbine locomotive could produce enough power to equal their 'King' Class 4-6-0 whereas they would need two diesel-electric locomotives to do the same job. Delayed by World War II, the GWR finally ordered the prototype gas-turbine locomotive No 18000 in 1946. The A1A-A1A loco was built in Switzerland by the Swiss Locomotive Works and Brown, Boveri and was delivered to British Railways in 1950. A slightly more powerful Co-Co loco, No 18100, was built by Metropolitan-Vickers of Manchester and delivered a year later. Operating mainline services out of Paddington both locos proved to be unreliable and heavy on fuel – No 18100 was withdrawn in 1958 and later converted to run as a test bed 25kv AC electric loco. In this new guise it ran as E1000 (later E2001) until it was withdrawn from service in 1968. No 18000 (nicknamed 'Kerosene Castle') was withdrawn in 1960 and returned to Europe where it was used, firstly as a test bed (minus its gas-turbine equipment) by the International Union of Railways and, secondly, as a static exhibit in Vienna. It was later returned to the UK for preservation and is on display at Didcot Railway Centre.

LMS's prototype
diesel-electric locomotives

Quick off the mark after World War II, the London Midland & Scottish Railway were the first to introduce mainline diesel-electric locos. Designed by H. G. Ivatt, CME of the LMS, two Co-Co locos, Nos 10000 and 10001, were built at Derby Works with the first one being delivered towards the end of 1947, only two months before Nationalisation. No 10001 followed later in 1948. Powered by English Electric units both locos had a power output of 1,600 hp and, because of their low power output compared to the 'Coronation' Pacifics, had to work in multiple when hauling heavy passenger trains. To enable this a connecting corridor was fitted in the front nose of each loco. After operating on the Midland and West Coast Main Lines the pair were transferred to the Southern Region in 1953 where their performance was able to be compared with the more powerful Bulleid diesel-electric locos Nos 10201–10203. The five locos were permanently transferred to the LMR in 1955 where they were allocated to Willesden depot. For some years they made regular appearances working in multiple on the WCML hauling expresses such as the 'Royal Scot'. No 10001 was withdrawn in 1962 and 10000 was withdrawn in 1966. Neither of these ground-breaking machines was preserved despite their considerable contribution to the design of BR's first generation diesel-electric locos.

LEFT: *The GWR's gas-turbine locomotive No 18000 seen here at Swindon in British Railways' livery shortly before withdrawal in 1960.*

BELOW: *The LMS's brand new diesel-electric loco No 10000 shortly after completion at Derby Works in 1947. This ground-breaking loco was withdrawn in 1966.*

The Southern Railway's prototype diesel-electric locomotives

Designed by Oliver Bulleid for the Southern Railway these slab-fronted mainline diesels were actually built by BR after Nationalisation. With English Electric power units the first two locos (Nos 10201 and 10202), with a power output of 1,750 hp, emerged from Ashford Works in 1950 and were soon put to work hauling expresses out of Waterloo. These two locos were joined in 1953 by the two LMS diesels, Nos 10000 and 10001, for joint performance trials. A third Bulleid-designed loco, No 10203, with a power output of 2,000 hp, was built at Brighton in 1954. All five locos were permanently transferred to the LMR in 1955 where they were allocated to Willesden and operated trains on the WCML. All three of the SR locos were withdrawn in 1963. None has been preserved.

BELOW: *Designed by Oliver Bulleid, diesel-electric loco No 10203 was built at Brighton Works in 1954. It worked on the London Midland Region for most of its life before withdrawal in 1963.*

Shed bashing on the straight and narrow

Engine shed, locomotive works and lineside permits

During the 1950s and early '60s it was considered rather a 'cissy' thing to apply for a permit to visit an engine shed! 'Shed bashing', as it was known, was a term used by trainspotters to describe their frenetic trips to as many engine sheds (usually without permits) as was possible in one day. Without an official permit some sheds were easier to visit than others depending on the friendliness of the shed foreman or the deviousness of the trainspotter. All manner of tricks were employed to gain access to the hallowed ground and once inside it was often a game of cat and mouse before we were eventually thrown out.

However, many visits were official and highly organised by the myriad of railway societies up and down the country whose members were whisked from shed to shed by the coachload. It was a sad fact that many of these trips had to be made by road but a) the trips were usually held on Sundays when the sheds were full and, because it was the Sabbath, there was only a limited or non-existent train service to the nearest station, and b) there was no practical way to visit such a large number of sheds in one day as many of them were located on out-of-the-way goods-only lines. Naturally, the proper paperwork had been done by the society and the necessary permits obtained.

The Stoke Division of the LMR issued detailed conditions for visits to their engine sheds including the stipulation that visitors must travel by rail! No wonder so many trainspotters 'bunked' sheds without permission. Prior notification also had to be given if any women wished to travel with the party! There was also a stipulation that any photographs taken were for private collection only – this latter stipulation was obviously not enforced.

Visits to railway works were also often made on Sundays when the workforce was at home digging the garden or reading the *Sunday Express*. Annual open days at Crewe, Derby and Swindon, for instance, also drew large crowds of spotters. To accommodate the young trainspotter Swindon Works also allowed visits without a permit on a Wednesday afternoon during the school holidays.

Lineside passes for photographers were much harder to come by and only the 'chosen few' responsible adults (or BR employees on a 'busman's holiday') were handed one of these!

BELOW: *A familiar occupation by the author – a large group of well-behaved trainspotters armed with notebooks visit Swindon Works on 23 April 1963.*

Gone forever

Long-lost railways

Even before Dr Beeching came on the scene thousands of miles of loss-making railway had been closed following the nationalisation of Britain's railways in 1948. The 'Beeching Report' of 1963 just compounded the destruction of what was once a rail network that served nearly the entire population of Britain. Slowly over the years since then many of these lost railways have experienced a renaissance with the opening of heritage railways, footpaths and cycleways along their routes (see pages 224–6). Despite this many lost railways are certainly gone forever, taken over by nature or built over by man and can only live on in our fading memories and photographs.

Here are a few examples that have gone for good, photographed in their death throes.

BELOW: *The sad remains of Dingestow station on the former Coleford, Monmouth, Usk & Pontypool Railway. Located 3 miles from Monmouth Troy station, Dingestow was closed in May 1955 following a major strike by railwaymen.*

Slowly being overtaken by nature, this sad picture of Cockermouth station was taken after the line from Penrith to Workington closed in 1966. The station was completely demolished to make way for a new fire station.

The lonely remains of Dungeness station on 2 August 1959. The station had been closed on 4 July 1937 with a new one opening at Lydd-on-Sea on the New Romney branch, half-a-mile away. The branch from Appledore closed to passengers in 1967 but remains open as far as Romney Junction for nuclear waste trains.

We never closed!

The Talyllyn Railway — the world's first preserved railway

Opened in 1865 to carry slate from the Bryn Eglwys quarries to the harbour at Towyn in West Wales, this 7-mile-long 2ft-3in. narrow-gauge line became the first railway in the world to be saved from closure and preserved. In 1911 both the quarries and railway were purchased by the local MP for Merioneth, Sir Haydn Jones, who also developed the line as a tourist attraction. Between the wars slate traffic dwindled and passenger traffic was lost to competing buses so, by 1946, when the quarries closed, the line was in a sad state of repair. Somehow, passenger trains still ran in the summer months along the grass-covered tracks but when Sir Haydn Jones died in 1950 it seemed certain that the line would finally close.

A group of railway enthusiasts, led by L. T. C. Rolt amongst others, had already met Sir Haydn before he died with a view to saving the line from closure. On his death the non-profit making Talyllyn Railway Preservation Society was formed to take over the running of the line. Faced with the run-down state of the line, locomotives and rolling stock, the volunteers had to look further afield before they could open the line for the 1951 summer season. A few miles away, the narrow-gauge Corris Railway had ceased to operate in 1947 and two locomotives, rolling stock and a quantity of rail was purchased from the railway's owners, British Railways (Western Region), at a knock down price. Volunteers worked feverishly to get the railway ready for its opening,

new track was laid, the sole steam engine still operating, the temperamental 85-year-old *Dolgoch*, was given a boiler examination, overhanging trees along the lineside were cut back and new signs erected.

Whit Monday (28 May) 1951 dawned, the sun shone from a blue sky and the Talyllyn Railway was back in business operating a limited passenger service between Towyn and Rhydyronen. Watched by Sir Haydn Jones's widow, ancient *Dolgoch* and her train of four-wheeled carriages wheezed out of Wharf station and up the incline to the first stop at Pendre. The railway had been saved! Much work was still to be done but those early enthusiasts

certainly deserve our thanks in saving this beautiful little line for generations to come. The Talyllyn Railway now operates a regular steam-hauled passenger service between Towyn Wharf and Nant Gwernol from the end of March to the beginning of November.

LEFT: *Built in 1864 and still going strong, Talyllyn Railway 0-4-2ST No 1 Talyllyn with admirers at Abergynolwyn station on 15 September 1959.*

BELOW: *Hauled by 0-4-0WT No 6 Douglas, the annual Talyllyn Railway Preservation Society train pauses for water at Dolgoch sation in September 1957. The loco was built in 1918 and worked on the depot railway at RAF Calshot until being given to the Talyllyn Railway in 1953.*

Locomotive builders to the world 2

Beyer, Peacock

The locomotive building company Beyer, Peacock was founded in 1853 by English engineer Richard Peacock, German-born Charles Beyer and Scottish engineer Henry Robertson. With its extensive works at Gorton Foundry in Manchester the company went on to build 4,753 tender locos and 1,735 tank locos for countries ranging from India, Sweden, Spain, Egypt, Turkey, Belgium, Holland, Germany and Italy to Peru, Brazil, Uruguay, the Dutch East Indies and the Australian states as well as for many British railway companies. They also built 1,115 Beyer-Garratt articulated locos between 1909 and 1958 for Australia, India, Brazil, Burma, Chile, Ecuador, Brazil, Russia, New Zealand, Sierra Leone, South Africa, Kenya, Uganda, Rhodesia, Nigeria, Iran, Sudan, Angola and last, but not least, the LMS and the LNER in Britain. Of note was the largest steam engine built in Europe – with a tractive effort of 90,000lb the 4-8-2+2-8-4 Garratt was supplied to Russian Railways in 1932 – and the world's most powerful narrow-gauge locos – the 3ft-6in.-gauge Garratts supplied to South African Railways in 1929. During World War II the company produced tanks and shells alongside continuing loco production – a Garratt for Burma Railways was designed and built in a record time of 118 days!

By 1958 steam engine production was at an end and Beyer, Peacock went on to build electric and diesel mainline locos for BR:

Works photo of a South African Railways 2-6-2+2-6-2 NGG16 Beyer-Garratt locomotive. Several of these locos have found a new lease of life on the Welsh Highland Railway.

BEYER, PEACOCK & CO LTD
7868
BEYER-GARRATT LOCOMOTIVE
MANCHESTER 1958

- 101 Hymek B-B diesel hydraulics D7000–D7100 (Class 35) 1961–64. These strikingly designed diesels were built for the Western Region but their non-standard transmission had led to their demise by 1975.
- 62 Sulzer Type 2 Bo-Bo diesel electric D7598–D7660 (Class 25/3) in 1966. These fairly successful maids-of-all-work had all been withdrawn by 1987.
- 29 Clayton Type 1 Bo-Bo diesel electric D8588–D8616 (Class 17) 1964–65. Not a successful type and the whole class had been withdrawn by 1971.
- 10 Class 82 Bo-Bo electric locos E3046–E3055 for WCML 1960–62. Two of the class were destroyed in fires while the remainder were rebuilt in the 1970s. The last two examples were withdrawn in 1987.

However this changeover to modern traction proved uneconomic for Beyer, Peacock and the company was forced to close in 1966. Happily, many preserved examples of its work can still be seen in operation around the world.

BELOW: *The original artist's drawings of what was to became the Hymek diesel-hydraulic locomotives built for the Western Region of British Railways.*

BOTTOM: *The first of its class, D7000 is seen here at Swindon Works shortly after delivery from Gorton Foundry in May 1961.*

Mr Bradshaw, friend of the railway traveller

The railway timetable

George Bradshaw was born in Pendleton, Lancashire, on 29 July 1801. He became an engraver and printer of canal maps in Manchester and, in 1838, published the world's first railway timetable. Soon, new railways were being opened at an ever increasing rate and to keep pace with these changes Bradshaw started issuing a revised edition once a month. Published in partnership with his London agent, William Jones Adams, and known as *Bradshaw's Monthly Railway Guide* it was sold with a yellow cover and continued to be published until 1961 with the final 1,521st edition. From 1847 Bradshaw also published a *Continental Railway Guide* and, soon, all railway timetables, irrespective of who published them, became known as Bradshaws. The rapid growth of railways in

Britain had a similar effect on the size of his timetable – in 1845 it consisted of only 32 pages but by 1898 it was nearly 1,000 pages!

In addition to introducing the world's first railway timetables, George Bradshaw also published the *Railway Manual* and the *Railway Shareholders' Guide*, both of which continued in print until 1922. In his private life Bradshaw became a Quaker and peace activist and spent much of his time and money in helping the poor in his home city of Manchester. He died at the relatively young age of 52 after contracting cholera in Norway in August 1853 and is buried in the grounds of Oslo Cathedral. A portrait of Bradshaw, painted in 1841 by Richard Evans, hangs in the National Portrait Gallery in London.

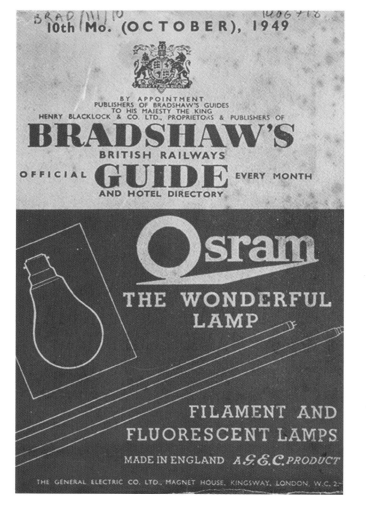

Despite the success of Bradshaw's timetable, most railway companies started issuing their own timetables in the 1930s. On nationalisation of the railways in 1948, individual regional timetables were introduced by British Railways and it was only in 1974 that these were combined into an all-line timetable similar to Bradshaw's original concept. As a topical footnote, it was announced in July 2006 that the all-line UK railway timetable, published by Network Rail, would soon cease to exist. Costing £12 a copy this bulky 2,500-page tome was in its final years, only selling about 12,000 copies per year. Apparently travellers now prefer to use the online timetables available at the touch of a button on their computer or phone.

Lynton to Red Wharf Bay
via the scenic route

Prior to the antics of Messrs Marples and Beeching (see pages 166–7), it was possible to travel from more-or-less-anywhere in Britain to more-or-less-anywhere by train. Just for fun let's look at a real journey that could be accomplished using Bradshaw's July 1922 *Railway Guide*. After staying for a week's restful holiday at the Valley of Rocks Hotel in Lynton, North Devon, the intrepid traveller, for some reason forgotten in the mists of time, needs to travel to Red Wharf Bay in Anglesey during the week. It may be quicker by road in the 21st century but nowhere near as fun. This is how he fared!

Day 1
Lynton & Lynmouth depart 8.15 a.m.
Barnstaple Town arrive 9.37 a.m.
CHANGE
Barnstaple Town depart 10.12 a.m.
Bristol TM arrive 1.34 p.m.
CHANGE
Bristol TM depart 2.00 p.m.
Gloucester Eastgate arrive 2.57 p.m.
CHANGE
Gloucester Central depart 3.47 p.m.
Hereford arrive 5.02 p.m.
CHANGE
Hereford depart 8.45 p.m.
Three Cocks Junction arrive 9.49 p.m.
Stay night in local hostelry

Day 2
Three Cocks Junction depart 7.47 a.m.
Moat Lane Junction arrive 9.40 a.m.
CHANGE
Moat Lane Junction depart 9.55 a.m.
Machynlleth arrive 10.43 a.m.
CHANGE
Machynlleth depart 10.45 a.m.
Afonwen arrive 1.35 p.m.
CHANGE
Afonwen depart 1.55 p.m.
Bangor arrive 3.10 p.m.
CHANGE
Bangor depart 3.35 p.m.
Gaerwen arrive 3.55 p.m.
CHANGE
Gaerwen depart 3.56 p.m.
Holland Arms arrive 4.00 p.m.
CHANGE
Holland Arms depart 4.33 p.m.
Red Wharf Bay arrive 4.54 p.m.
Journey's end!

FAR LEFT: *Oil painting of George Bradshaw (1801–53), the father of railway timetables.*

LEFT: *Cover of the October 1949 edition of 'Bradshaw's British Railways Guide and Hotel Directory'. Printed on the cheapest paper their publisher could find, they were only intended to have a lifespan of one month.*

BELOW: *Pages 44–5 of the Bradshaw railway timetable for June 1850. Timetables for Leeds, Dewsbury, Huddersfield, Manchester and Liverpool. Also for Chester to Holyhead and Chester to Mold.*

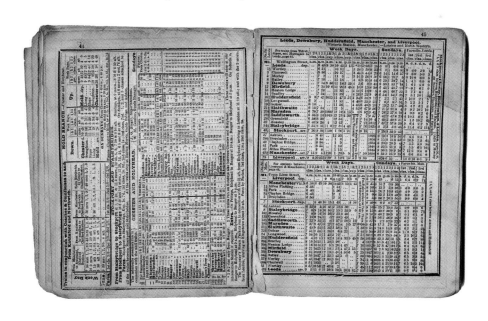

Along the route of the Great Central

Famous named trains

Until HS1 was completed between Folkestone and London St Pancras in 2007 the last mainline to be built to London was the Great Central Railway's London Extension between Sheffield and Marylebone.

Unlike other railways in the country the Great Central London Extension was built to the Continental loading gauge as the route was seen as the first step in a railway linking the North of England with Europe via a Channel Tunnel. The latter project had to wait nearly 100 years before it saw the light of day.

Serving Sheffield, Nottingham, Loughborough, Leicester, Rugby and London Marylebone, the new railway opened in 1899, offering an alternative for freight and passengers to the existing Midland Railway and Great Northern Railway routes between London and the North.

The Great Central Railway (GCR) became a constituent company of the newly formed London & North Eastern Railway (LNER) in 1923. Following nationalisation of the railways in 1948, the Great Central route became part of the Eastern Region of British Railways until 1960 when it was transferred to the London Midland Region. Services on the now downgraded route went into decline, with through expresses being withdrawn leaving just a slow stopping train service between the capital and Nottingham. Through freight services ended in 1965 and the end came in 1966 when much of the GC was closed.

The only named trains that ran on the Great Central route, 'The Master Cutler' and 'The South Yorkshireman', were both introduced after World War 2.

The Master Cutler

Between the two world wars there had been a popular restaurant car express that ran on weekdays between Marylebone and Sheffield. As yet unnamed, it was discontinued during World War 2 and reintroduced by the LNER in the autumn of 1947 with the name 'The Master Cutler'. The train was usually hauled by 'B1' Class 4-6-0s but these were replaced in the mid-1950s by former LNER 'A3' 4-6-2s. The morning up train to Marylebone travelled via the direct line through Aylsebury and Amersham but the evening return service went via the GW/GC Joint Line through High Wycombe and Princes Risborough to avoid commuter traffic. In 1958 the train was rerouted to travel between London King's Cross and Sheffield via the one stop at Retford. Powered by new English Electric Type 4 diesels the, by now, all-Pullman train provided a much faster service for businessmen. The train was discontinued in 1968.

The South Yorkshireman

The second named train to operate along the Great Central route was the weekday-only 'The South Yorkshireman' which was introduced by the Eastern Region of BR in 1948. It wasn't exactly an express as the up service between Bradford (Exchange) and Marylebone via Huddersfield, Sheffield, Nottingham, Loughborough, Leicester, Rugby and Aylesbury took 5hrs 15min. The return down service had the same stops apart from Rugby, which was omitted, and a stop at Penistone was added, the entire journey taking 5hrs 30min. The train was normally hauled by 'B1' 4-6-0s although the final one on 2 January 1960 was headed by BR Standard Class '5' 4-6-0, No 73066.

LEFT: *Ex-LNER Class 'V2' 2-6-2 No 60842 at the head of 'The Master Cutler' express at Leicester Central station in August 1958.*

BELOW: *The early British Railways leaflet for 'The Master Cutler' for the summer timetable of 1948.*

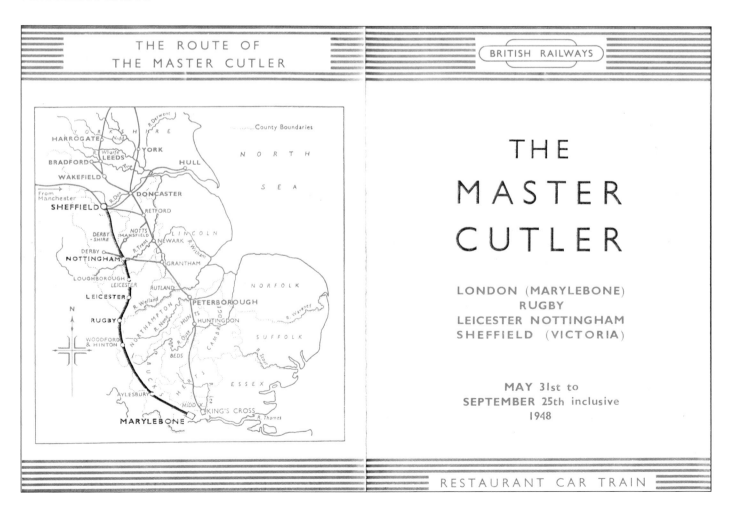

THE ROUTE OF THE MASTER CUTLER

BRITISH RAILWAYS

THE MASTER CUTLER

LONDON (MARYLEBONE)
RUGBY
LEICESTER NOTTINGHAM
SHEFFIELD (VICTORIA)

MAY 31st to
SEPTEMBER 25th inclusive
1948

RESTAURANT CAR TRAIN

Low Moor shed's 'B1' Class 4-6-0 No 61383 climbs out of Bradford Exchange past Mill Lane on 'The South Yorkshireman' bound for London Marylebone, 15 August 1959.

British artics

The Beyer-Garratts of the LMS, LNER and the Welsh Highland Railway

LNER CLASS 'U1' 2-8-0+0-8-2

Articulated Beyer-Garratt steam locomotives had been built for railways of the British Empire by the Manchester company of Beyer, Peacock since 1909 (see pages 150–51). The first to be built for a British railway company was the unique LNER Class 'U1' 2-8-0+0-8-2 No 2395, which was introduced in 1925. This massive loco was specifically designed to bank heavy coal trains over the ex-GCR Woodhead route in South Yorkshire and spent most of its life allocated to Mexborough shed. With a length of over 87ft and a tractive effort of 73,000lbs the Class 'U1' was both the longest and most powerful steam locomotive of its time in Britain.

Following a brief sojourn as a banker on the Lickey Incline south of Birmingham in 1949, the loco, now renumbered 69999, returned to the Woodhead route until electrification of that line in the early 1950s made it redundant. Returning to Bromsgrove for the second time, this time fitted with a large electric headlight, the loco spent its last three months as a banker up the Lickey Incline before withdrawal at the end of 1955.

LMS 2-6-0+0-6-2

As successor to the Midland Railway the LMS was faced with continuing the former company's small engine policy. In short this meant double-heading of all heavy trains including coal trains southwards from the Nottinghamshire coalfields to London. To overcome this expensive operation the LMS took delivery of three 2-6-0+0-6-2 Beyer-Garratt locomotives from Beyer, Peacock in 1927. With another 30 locos built in 1930 the LMS had a large fleet of powerful goods locos for the first time – although slightly longer than the LNER 'U1', they were significantly less powerful with a tractive effort of just over 45,000lb. The majority of the class, now fitted with revolving coal bunkers, were allocated to Toton shed in Nottinghamshire where they were employed on heavy coal trains down the Midland mainline to North London. Renumbered 47967–47999 in 1948, the class was gradually withdrawn between 1955 and 1958.

BELOW: *Built in 1925, the LNER's sole Class 'U1' 2-8-0+0-8-2 Beyer-Garratt was designed to bank heavy coal trains over the Woodhead route in South Yorkshire. It was also used for brief periods on the Lickey Incline, where it is seen in August 1949.*

Seen just before withdrawal from service, ex-LMS 2-6-0+0-6-2 Beyer-Garratt No 47969 hauls a heavy coal train near Wellingborough on 26 June 1957.

Welsh Highland Railway

Recently completely rebuilt and reopened from Caernarfon to Porthmadog the 1ft-11½in.-gauge Welsh Highland Railway possesses no fewer than five Beyer-Garratt articulated steam locomotives, which are among the most powerful narrow-gauge engines in the world. The oldest, the first of its type to be built, is a 0-4-0+0-4-0 that was delivered to Tasmanian Government Railways in 1909. Four larger 2-6-2+2-6-2 locomotives, built between 1937 and 1958, were rescued from South Africa where they once operated on the Alfred County Railway. These 62-ton, 48ft-long monsters are capable of hauling a 12-coach train up 1-in-40 gradients at a speed of 25 mph.

BELOW: *Saved from scrapping in South Africa, Welsh Highland Railway 2-6-2+2-6-2 Garratts Class 'NGG16' No 87 (built 1937) and No 138 (built 1958) double-head a demonstration goods train near Rhyd-Dhu on 3 November 2013.*

Crash

Britain's worst railway disaster

It was just gone 6 o'clock on the morning of 22 May 1915 and George Meakin was nearing the end of his night shift as signalman at Quintinshill, a small block post on the mainline 10 miles north of Carlisle. The two overnight expresses from Euston to Glasgow, running late, were due and a slow-running northbound goods train was already waiting patiently in the down loop line for them to pass before resuming its journey. However, a local passenger train had already left Carlisle ahead of the two expresses and, as the down loop was already occupied, Meakin switched the local onto the up mainline where it came to a halt close to his signalbox. Finally, to complete this busy scene, a Carlisle-bound goods train was directed into the up loop line just as Meakin's colleague, James Tinsley, arrived to start his shift.

Tinsley, who arrived for work on the local train, always started his shift half-an-hour late and this was covered up by Meakin who, instead of recording train movements for this period in the official train register, wrote these details for his mate on a separate piece of paper so that it could be copied in later. However, on this morning, they made one fatal error and, forgetting the local train was standing on the up mainline, sent a signal to the next signalbox at Kirkpatrick which indicated that the up line was clear. He also pulled the signals to clear the passage of the northbound Euston to Glasgow express. There next followed the most appalling series of events which culminated in Britain's worst rail disaster.

BELOW: *Ex-LNER Class 'V2' 2-6-2 No 60954 seems to be in a spot of bother at Mirfield on 7 January 1962.*

With the signals cleared, a crowded troop train consisting of 15 old wooden coaches, all lit by acetylene gas, was now approaching Quintinshill on the up line at speed. It ran head-on into the stationary local with such an enormous force that the wooden coaches of the troop train were completely smashed to pieces and the locomotives ended up on their sides straddling the down mainline. This in itself was a major disaster, but worse was to follow. One minute later, the first of the late-running down expresses, hauled by two locomotives and weighing over 600 tons, was approaching Quintinshill at high speed and ploughed into the debris of the first accident. Colliding with the tender of the troop train engine, the leading engine of the down express left the rails and came into collision with the stationary goods train waiting in the down loop line. This total devastation was then turned into a scene from hell when the escaping gas from the smashed troop-train carriages was ignited by the red-hot coals thrown out from the derailed locomotives. In all, 227 people, of which 215 were soldiers from the Royal Scots Regiment, lost their lives and 245 were injured, however, because of wartime reporting restrictions, the accident was not widely publicised. At a later trial, both Meakin and Tinsley were found guilty of grossly neglecting their duties and also of culpable homicide and were jailed for 18 months and three years respectively.

The aftermath of the rail crash at Quintinshill on 22 May 1915 when 227 people were killed and 245 were injured. It was by far Britain's worst rail disaster.

Britain's worst railway accidents

Date	Location	Deaths/Injuries	Cause
24 December 1841	Sonning	8/17	Landslip
20 August 1868	Abergele	33	Collision and fire
3 August 1873	Wigan	10	Derailment
10 September 1874	Norwich Thorpe	25/100	Collision
21 January 1876	Abbots Ripton	14	Collision in snow
28 December 1879	Tay Bridge	75	Bridge collapse
16 July 1884	Penistone	24	Derailment
12 June 1889	Armagh	80	Collision
10 November 1890	Norton Fitzwarren	10	Collision
1 September 1905	Witham	11	Derailment
1 July 1906	Salisbury	28	Derailment
2 September 1913	Ais Gill	14/38	Collision and fire
22 May 1915	Quintinshill	227/245	Collision and fire
27 June 1928	Darlington	25	Collision
13 October 1928	Charfield	15	Collision and fire
28 September 1934	Winwick Junction	12	Collision
10 December 1937	Castlecary	35/179	Collision in snow
4 November 1940	Norton Fitzwarren	27	Derailment
30 September 1945	Bourne End	43/64	Derailment
24 October 1947	South Croydon	32/183	Collision
8 October 1952	Harrow & Wealdstone	112/340	Collision in fog
23 January 1955	Sutton Coldfield	17/43	Derailment
2 December 1955	Barnes	13/41	Collision and fire
4 December 1957	Lewisham	90/173	Collision
30 January 1958	Dagenham East	10/89	Collision
5 November 1967	Hither Green	49/78	Derailment
11 June 1972	Eltham Well Hall	6/126	Derailment
20 December 1973	Ealing	10/94	Derailment
28 February 1975	Moorgate	43	Collision with buffer stops
12 December 1988	Clapham Common	35/100	Collision
4 March 1989	Purley	6/94	Collision
8 January 1991	Cannon Street	2/200	Collision with buffer stops
19 September 1997	Southall	6/150	Collision
5 October 1999	Ladbroke Grove	31/523	Collision
17 October 2000	Hatfield	4/35	Derailment
28 February 2001	Selby	10/80	Collision with car
10 May 2002	Potters Bar	7/70	Derailment
6 November 2004	Ufton Nervet	7/150	Collision with car

Evenin' all!

The railway policeman

Known since 1948 as the British Transport Police, the first railway policemen in Britain were employed by the Liverpool & Manchester Railway to keep order when it opened in 1830. Even before this men were employed in the capacity of unofficial special constables to control the often unruly navvies who were building the railways – these so-called policemen were actually chosen from among the navvies themselves, in reality a form of self-policing. Soon thousands of these construction workers were swarming over England's green and pleasant land, often creating mayhem in previously peaceful areas. The 1838 Special Constables Act set out to address this problem by forcing the railway companies and their contractors to fund policing around construction sites – the Act's full title was appropriately worded 'An Act for the Payment of Constables for Keeping the Peace near Public Works'.

Once the railways were open police were also needed to protect property and passengers – one of the earliest of these railway policemen was Constable John Metcalfe who was appointed by the Stockton & Darlington Railway in 1846. His portrait now hangs in the National Railway Museum, York.

The GWR was one of the first railway companies granted powers to appoint police – the Great Western Railway Act of 1835 contained provisions for constables to be appointed, but only on its premises. It wasn't until 1877 that they were given powers to operate further afield. In the meantime the railway policeman not only had to deal with a whole range of crimes, from drunkenness and smoking (the latter prohibited on all railway premises and in trains until 1868 when smoking carriages were introduced) to robbery and murder but also the control of trains and to clear the line of obstructions. In the early years of the London & Birmingham Railway constables were placed about a mile apart along the whole length of the line as signalmen, armed with coloured flags for daytime use and lamps for the night-time. On the GWR a policeman was located on average every 1½ miles along the track, housed in wooden shelters at the lineside and required to salute each train as it passed.

Railway employees could also be sworn in as special constables in times of trouble, for instance during the threatened Chartists riots in 1848 when 20,000 special constables were put on alert by the London & North Western Railway.

Beating the criminals

The fast expanding railway network in Britain was a golden opportunity for criminals, enabling them to move quickly around the country, committing crime and avoiding detection. The introduction of the lineside electric telegraph in 1843 (by the GWR between Paddington and Slough) soon brought dramatic results – on 1 January 1845 a murderer who boarded a train at Slough was apprehended in London after his details had been telegraphed along the line. The murderer, John Tawell, was later sentenced to death, becoming the first criminal in the world to be caught by electric telegraph.

By 1921 around 20 British railway companies had their own police force – the North Eastern Railway's police force was the first to introduce dogs , in 1908, when they were used for patrolling Hull Docks. Until the First World War railway constables were also employed to control horse-drawn cabs at London termini by collecting a fee of one penny from those permitted to trade there.

Even from their early days the railways had become a honey pot for criminals bent on robbing wagons and depots of their goods and passengers of their valuables while the carrying of mail on trains also brought further ill-gotten gains. Parcels and mailbags left hanging around on station platforms were easy pickings and child delinquency in the form of stone throwing and placing obstacles on the line was rife. The railway policeman had his hands full!

The Grouping of 1923 saw the police forces of the four newly-formed major railway companies receive extra powers including stop-and-search and arrest of employees suspected of company theft. Following the nationalisation of the railways the British Transport Commission Act of 1949 led to the formation of the British Transport Police (BTP) who were given wide-ranging powers not only on the railways but also on the canals and docks infrastructure around Britain. The BTP continues to this day, now funded mainly by the train operating companies, Network Rail and London Underground, and employs nearly 2,900 police officers along with several hundred special constables, police community support officers and a backroom staff of around 1,300. Their frontline 'police stations' can be found at 88 railway stations around the country.

The original Great Train Robbery

Everyone has heard of the 'Great Train Robbery' of 1963 when £2.6 million was stolen from a travelling post office train in Buckinghamshire but give a thought to the first major train robbery, which happened in 1855 on the South Eastern Railway.

By the late 1840s gold bullion was regularly being carried by boat train from London to Folkestone on the first part of its journey to Paris. A certain Edward Agar hit on the bright idea of robbing one of these trains by availing himself of duplicate keys for the travelling safes and set about making friends with a SER boat train guard and the stationmaster of London Bridge station. After carrying out a successful dummy run in 1854, Agar, with prior knowledge of the weight of the gold consignment and the use of his duplicate keys, was able to swap £14,000 of bullion for the same weight in lead shot before the train arrived at Folkestone. While the 'lead bullion' was taken out of the train Agar and his co-conspirator Edward

Pierce stayed behind and left the train at Dover, returning to London with their ill-gotten gains.

There was uproar in Paris the next morning when the theft was discovered. In the end the French accused the British and vice versa but there were no clues on either side of the Channel as to how it had happened. The gold (at today's price worth around £1.1 million) was melted down by Agar and he nearly got away with it but for a twist of fate. Framed for forging a cheque by his new lover's ex-boyfriend, Agar was sentenced to transportation to Australia for life. Meanwhile, Agar's previous lover, Fanny, was now getting pretty angry with Pierce who had been looking after some of the gold to care for her and her (also Agar's) child. Furious that the double-crossing Pierce wouldn't help her, she reported the whole sorry affair to the authorities – acting promptly they seized Agar from his prison ship in Portland Harbour just before it sailed to the Antipodes. In the subsequent trial Agar turned on his accomplices, two of whom were sentenced to transportation to Australia for 14 years while Pierce received only two years. What was left of the money was divided between the South Eastern Railway and the Police Chief with instructions that it be used to care for Fanny and her child.

BELOW: *A squad of London Midland & Scottish Railway policemen on parade at Euston station on 19 May 1937.*

Dr Beeching, I presume!

The destruction of Britain's railways

Introduced by a Conservative Government, the 1962 Transport Act did away with the bureaucratic British Transport Commission (BTC) and gave British Railways complete autonomy as an independent public corporation for the first time since its formation in 1948. Taking effect on 1 January 1963, the new British Railways Board, chaired by former BTC Chairman Richard Beeching, were immediately faced with the huge problem of ever-increasing railway deficits. A constant drain on the public purse since Nationalisation in 1948, Britain's railways were struggling to survive in a competitive world where more and more people and goods were taking to the roads. Even before the Beeching era, about 3,000 miles of

uneconomic lines had already been closed since Nationalisation. Despite these closures and the implementation of the 1955 Modernisation Plan, in which regional autonomy had destroyed any chance there was of standardisation and subsequent reduction in running costs, vast amounts of public money were still being used to shore up what was basically an antiquated and overmanned railway system.

Prior to his appointment as Chairman of the newly-formed British Railways Board, Richard Beeching, who had been technical director of ICI and had no previous experience in the management or running of railways, had been a member of the Stedeford Committee,

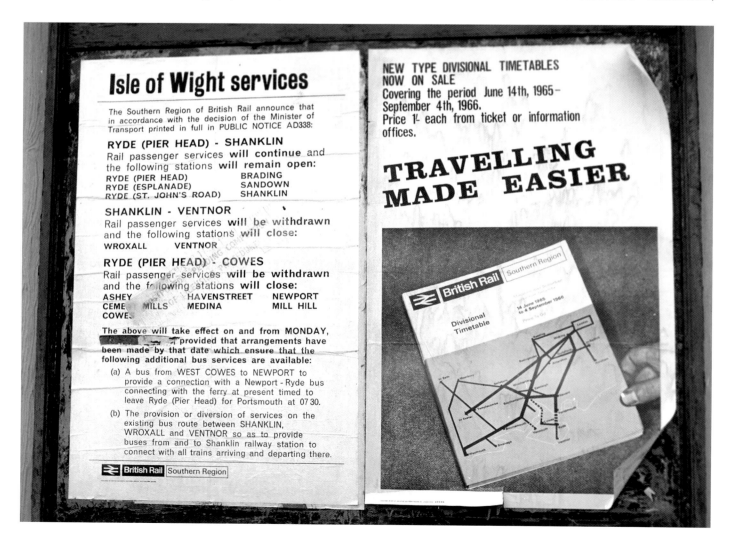

an advisory group set up in 1960 by the then Conservative Transport Minister, Ernest Marples, to report on the state of Britain's transport system and make recommendations for its improvement. Although Beeching proposed wholesale railway closures the report was never published. Therefore, it was no coincidence when Marples appointed Beeching as chairman of the British Railways Board in 1963 – the former already owned a two-thirds share in a major road-building company and the latter wanted to close a third of the railways!

After becoming Chairman of the British Railways Board on 1 January 1963, Richard Beeching did not waste much time in producing his report in which, to be fair, he not only proposed massive railway closures but also the modernisation of the remaining system. Entitled 'The Reshaping of British Railways', the first part of his report, which was seized on by Conservative politicians, proposed closing 6,000 miles of uneconomic rural and cross-country routes, reducing staff by 200,000, closing 2,300 stations, reducing locomotive numbers by 9,000 and scrapping 16,000 carriages and 450,000 freight wagons. The second part of his report, which didn't go down so well with politicians, proposed spending large amounts of taxpayers' money on modernising and streamlining the rest of the railways.

The Conservative government, firstly under the premiership of Harold Macmillan and then of Alec Douglas-Home, also wasted no time in approving the first part of Beeching's report and branch line closures and the wholesale scrapping of steam engines had soon reached a peak by 1964 and continued for some years even under a newly-elected Labour Government who had pledged to halt the cuts. By August 1968, all steam traction (apart from three narrow-gauge locomotives on the state-owned Vale of Rheidol Railway) had been eliminated from British Railways and 3,432 route miles had been closed. Closures, albeit at a much slower rate, continued until 1974 when the system stabilised to more or less that which exists today. The more positive side of Beeching's report, modernisation of the remaining system, was never fully implemented and this legacy of underinvestment by successive governments can still be witnessed on Britain's railways today.

Richard Beeching resigned from the British Railways Board in 1965 after he fell foul of the then Labour Government over his proposal for more swingeing cuts of the rail system (see pages 176–7). As a reward for his services he was made a life peer in the same year and died on 23 March 1985.

LEFT: *Ironic juxtaposition of the closure notice for railways on the Isle of Wight as seen at Havenstreet station in 1965.*

BELOW: *A scene of dereliction at Penygroes station after closure of the Caernarfon to Afonwen line on 7 December 1964. This sad scene was repeated all across Britain in the 1960s.*

Famous locomotive engineers 2

Oliver Bulleid (1882–1970)

Oliver Vaughan Snell Bulleid was born in Invercargill in the South Island of New Zealand on 19 September 1882. His parents had previously emigrated from Britain but on the death of his father, William Bulleid, the seven-year-old Oliver returned to Britain with his mother. On completing his education he began an apprenticeship in 1900 with the Great Northern Railway at that company's Doncaster Works. Under the watchful eye of the railway's Chief Mechanical engineer, H. A. Ivatt, Bulleid became assistant to the GNR Locomotive Running Superintendent in 1904 and a year later was promoted to the position of manager of the Works. At the age of 26 he moved to Paris where he worked as a test engineer for the Westinghouse Electric Corporation in their brake and signal division, later becoming chief draughtsman and assistant works manager. At this time Bulleid also married Marjorie Ivatt, the daughter of his former boss at Doncaster.

Bulleid returned to Britain in 1910 where he worked for the Board of Trade for two years before rejoining the Great Northern Railway as assistant to that company's new Chief Mechanical Engineer, Nigel Gresley. Following service in World War I, Bulleid was promoted to manage the GNR's Carriage and Wagon Works before returning to Doncaster in 1923 as Gresley's assistant in the newly-formed London & North Eastern Railway. Under Gresley, Bulleid worked on the development of many ground-breaking designs including the Class 'U1' 2-8-0+0-8-2 Garratt and the Classes 'P1' and 'P2' 2-8-2 locomotive types.

In 1937 Bulleid was appointed Chief Mechanical Engineer of the Southern Railway following the retirement of Richard Maunsell. This was during a period when that railway was forging ahead with an expensive electrification programme and spending on new steam

locomotive development had been severely restricted. However, there existed a pressing need for more powerful and modern motive power for its non-electrified lines and Bulleid, despite restrictions imposed during the early years of World War II, had by 1941 produced a new class of innovative steam locomotives. Employing the most up-to-date technology, such as high boiler pressure, welded fireboxes, chain activated and oil-bathed valve gears and disc wheel centres, Bulleid's first major locomotive type, the air-smoothed 'Merchant Navy' Class 4-6-2s were way ahead of the competition. It was soon followed by the more lightweight 'West Country/Battle of Britain' Class 4-6-2s and the utilitarian Class 'Q1' 0-6-0 freight engine. In addition to his ground-breaking steam locomotive designs, Bulleid also went on to introduce improved electric rolling stock, the prototype 'Leader' locomotive powered by steam-operated power bogies (see page 59) and was a pioneer in the design of mainline diesel-electric locomotives.

Sadly, Bulleid, who was a devout Catholic, had previously lost his son, Hugh, in a cycling accident in 1938 and this terrible tragedy weighed heavily on him for the rest of his life. In 1949 Bulleid was appointed Chief Mechanical Engineer for Coras Iompair Eireann (CIE, Irish Railways) where he was responsible for the modernisation of that country's antiquated rail system, the early introduction of diesel locomotives and the development of an unusual, but unsuccessful, turf-burning locomotive (see page 59). He retired from CIE in 1958 and lived in Devon for some years until a deterioration in his health led him to move to the warmer climate of Malta where he died on 25 April 1970.

LEFT: *Bulleid's Southern Railway 'Merchant Navy' Class 4-6-2 No 21C20 (35020) Bibby Line in all its glory at Nine Elms shed in 1947.*

BELOW: *Bulleid's utilitarian 'Q1' Class 0-6-0 No 33018 trundles though Virginia Water station hauling a Feltham to Wimbledon freight train via Chertsey, early 1960s.*

LMS famous trains

Royal Scot

One of the most famous long-distance expresses in the world, the 'Royal Scot' was first introduced by the London & North Western Railway and the Caledonian Railway in 1862. Departing at 10 a.m. from London Euston the train travelled the length of the West Coast Main Line to Glasgow, a distance of 401¼ miles. Hauled by one of the L&NWR's crack express locomotives such as the 4-4-0 'Precursor' or the later 4-6-0 'Claughton', the train required banking assistance on the climb to Shap before arriving at Carlisle where a Caledonian Railway loco took over.

Following the 'Big Four Grouping' of 1923 the 'Royal Scot' became the premier express train of the LMS and the introduction of the Fowler-designed '7P' 'Royal Scot' Class 4-6-0s in 1927 led to a greatly improved service with heavier loadings. However, even these powerful locos still needed assistance over Shap – a situation which was only remedied in 1933 with the introduction of Stanier's '8P' 'Princess Royal' Class Pacifics. By then the train had officially become non-stop but in reality it still stopped at Carlisle for a crew change. Streamlined 'Coronation' Class Pacifics took over in 1937, a duty they were to retain until the end of steam haulage in the early 1960s. By 1962 the departure from Euston had been retimed to 9.30 a.m. and with a stop at Carlisle the train reached Glasgow at 4.50 p.m. (Monday–Friday). The Saturday working took 40 minutes longer and on Sundays the train was virtually reduced to stopping-train status with stops at Rugby, Crewe, Carlisle, Beattock and Motherwell, arriving at Glasgow at 7.20 p.m.

Following electrification of the WCML to Glasgow in 1974 the 'Royal Scot' continued to run until 2003 when the name was dropped. Existing Pendolino Class 390 trains from Euston to Glasgow now take only 4hr 31min to complete the journey.

The Thames-Clyde Express

The alternative and more scenic route from London to Glasgow was via the ex-Midland Railway line from St Pancras to Carlisle via Leeds and the Settle & Carlisle line and then to Glasgow St Enoch via Dumfries over ex-G&SWR metals. In 1927 the LMS gave the name 'The Thames-Clyde Express' to its 10 a.m. departure from St Pancras to Glasgow St Enoch and the 9.30 a.m. departure in the opposite direction. Although serving major population centres in the East Midlands and Yorkshire the route was much longer and steeper than the alternative WCML, consequently the journey was much longer. Suspended during World War II the 'Thames-Clyde Express' was restored in 1949. During this post-war period the train was usually headed by either 'Jubilee' or 'Royal Scot' 4-6-0s until these were replaced by BR Sulzer Type 4 diesels. Journey times remained poor – the summer 1962 timetable showed the train departing St Pancras at 10.10 a.m. and after calling at Leicester, Chesterfield, Sheffield, Leeds, Carlisle, Annan, Dumfries and Kilmarnock arrived at St Enoch at 7.50 p.m. – a journey time of 9hr 40min and 2hr 20min slower than the rival 'Royal Scot'. This couldn't go on much longer and with the completion of WCML electrification in 1974 the train lost its title.

LEFT: *Camden shed's ex-LMS 'Coronation' Class 4-6-2 No 46237 City of Bristol at rest at Euston station after arriving with the 'Royal Scot' from Glasgow Central, c.1960.*

BELOW: *Holbeck's shed ex-LMS 'Jubilee' Class 4-6-0 No 45659 Drake at Leeds with 'The Thames-Clyde Express' in October 1959.*

Goods in transit, 1963

British Railways freight facilities

For over 100 years Britain's railways had kept the wheels of industry moving but by the 1960s the writing was on the wall for the conveyance of individual loads by train. By this time the closure of thousands of miles of unprofitable branch lines and secondary routes during the notorious Beeching era left many isolated communities without their once-vital rail link to the outside world. By 1963 the end was in sight for personalised freight services but those that were still being advertised are now difficult to comprehend on today's 'modern' railways with their containerised trainload policy. Is this progress? I don't think so!

So cast your mind back nearly 60 years when British Railways offered an amazing choice of freight train facilities. Here are a few examples:

Express freight services

In addition to providing next-day delivery on overnight services between London and principal provincial stations, and also between the main provincial centres, BR ran seasonal express trains for fruit, vegetables and other kinds of market produce such as fish.

Carriage of perishable goods

Insulated vans and containers specially constructed for the conveyance, under refrigerated conditions, of frozen foodstuffs, quick-frozen commodities and ice-cream were available.

Farm removals

BR undertook to transfer complete farms, including implements, livestock, etc., from one part of the country to another. Special arrangements could be made to enable cows to travel between milking times or, where very long journeys were involved, for them to be milked en route, and all animals to be fed and watered.

Works removals

BR undertook complete works removals, including dismantling plant, etc., and its re-erection in the new works. No job was too large and all-in quotations could be given.

Packaging

In association with BR, Collico Ltd hired out collapsible cases for rail transport. The carriage charged was on net weight of contents only, the empty case being returned free.

For fuller information on any of the above ask your local goods agent or stationmaster for a copy of 'Freight Train Facilities and Services'. Fat chance of that happening now!

BELOW: *Cattle being loaded onto a freight train at Saffron Waldon station, 26 April 1961. The cattle were being taken to Bodmin in Cornwall, along with the rest of the farmer's equipment and stock. This traffic was soon lost to road transport.*

Setting standards

R. A. Riddles – the last great British Chief Mechanical Engineer

Robert Arthur Riddles was born on 23 May 1892 and was a premium apprentice with the London & North Western Railway at Crewe Works between 1909 and 1913. He then became a fitter at the Works before serving with the Royal Engineers during World War I. After the war, during which he was seriously injured, he returned to Crewe where he became responsible for overseeing engine sheds and other locomotive department buildings and the construction of the new erecting shop at the Works. Following this he was promoted to head the production department and was mainly responsible for the reorganisation of Crewe Works in 1925–27.

During the 1926 General Strike Riddles became a volunteer driver – a task which included a run from Crewe to Carlisle with a Scotch express. This practical experience was certainly put to good use when he was appointed as CME of the embryonic British Railways in 1947.

On completion of his task at Crewe Riddles was then moved to Derby to head a similar reorganisation of the former Midland Railway Works. In 1933 he became Locomotive Assistant to William Stanier and two years later was promoted to Principal Assistant during which period he was closely involved in the design and construction of the 'Coronation' Class Pacifics until being transferred to Glasgow as Mechanical & Electrical Engineer in 1937. In the same year he was closely involved with the record-breaking test run of No 6220 *Coronation* when the loco achieved 114 mph south of Crewe before accompanying this famous streamlined locomotive on its tour of North America in 1939. Riddles drove *Coronation* on much of its North American tour due to the illness of its regular driver.

BELOW: *British Railways Standard Class '4' 2-6-4T No 80010 seen here at Eastleigh in September 1957. A total of 155 of this class were built – 130 at Brighton, 15 at Derby and 10 at Doncaster – between 1951 and 1956. They had a short working life with withdrawals taking place between 1962 and 1967.*

World War II saw Riddles step up to the plate – first becoming Director of Transportation Equipment for the Ministry of Supply and then, in 1941, as Deputy Director General, Royal Engineer Equipment. In this role he was not only involved in the design and production of Bailey bridges and the D-Day Mulberry Harbours, but also the design and construction of hundreds of the WD 2-8-0 and 2-10-0 locomotives. In 1943 he returned to the LMS as Chief Stores Superintendent and expected to be promoted to CME on the sudden death of Charles Fairburn in 1945. Instead George Ivatt received that appointment and Riddles got second-best as Vice-President.

With Nationalisation looming, Riddles was appointed Chief Mechanical & Electrical Engineer of the newly-formed Railway Executive in 1947. In this role he was responsible for the design and construction of 999 steam locomotives for British Railways – three classes of 4-6-2, two classes of 4-6-0, three classes of 2-6-0, two classes of 2-6-2T, one class of 2-6-4T and one class of 2-10-0. Probably the most successful of his designs, 251 of the latter type were built – in 1960 No 92220 *Evening Star* became the last steam locomotive to be built for British Railways.

Robert Riddles retired in 1953 and died on 18 June 1983.

The first of its class, British Railways Standard Class '9F' 2-10-0 No 92000 is seen at work on the Somerset & Dorset Joint Railway passing through Midsomer Norton station on 15 July 1961. A total of 251 of this class were built – 198 at Crewe and 53 at Swindon – between 1954 and 1960 with withdrawals taking place between 1964 and 1968.

The second Beeching Report

The little-known proposed destruction of Britain's railways

We have all heard of Dr Beeching's report 'The Reshaping of British Railways', which was published in March 1963, and we all know that one part of its recommendations, i.e. the wholesale closure of cross-country and branch lines, was eagerly implemented by both the outgoing Tory Government and the new double-crossing Labour Government under Harold Wilson. Although a few lines, such as the Far North of Scotland, Ayr to Stranraer, Settle & Carlisle, Cumbrian Coast, and Central Wales, eventually escaped the axe, over 4,000 miles were closed by 1966 leaving vast swathes of the country with no access to rail services. A further 2,000 miles had gone by the end of the decade even though Labour had made an election pledge in 1964 to halt the closures – their promises were like pie crusts.

What is less well-known is that Dr Beeching, the first chairman of the British Railways Board, also published a second report early in 1965 entitled 'The Development of the Major Railway Trunk Routes'. In this report he proposed investment in only nine mainlines serving only major centres of population and industry. By implication there would have been further swingeing closures of another 4,500 miles of railway but this time they weren't just branch lines or lightly used cross-country routes but, in many cases, major trunk routes. It seems inconceivable now that they would even have been considered but the following is a summary of the proposed closures:

Perth to Inverness
Aberdeen to Inverness
The ex-G&SWR line from Carlisle to Glasgow
All lines west and southwest of Glasgow
The ECML north of Newcastle
All lines to Scarborough
Leeds to Carnforth and Barrow
All railways in Wales apart from the main Newport, Cardiff
    and Swansea corridor
The Midland mainline
All lines in East Anglia apart from Liverpool St to Norwich
All lines in north Kent
London to Hastings and the South Coast route
    through Eastbourne

Bath to Southampton via Westbury
The ex-GWR route from Reading to Taunton via Westbury
The former L&SWR mainline west from Basingstoke to Exeter
All routes to Weymouth
All railway lines west of Plymouth

Even this was too much to stomach for the new Labour Government who promptly rejected the report. Three months after it was published Dr Beeching resigned as Chairman of the British Railways Board and returned to his old job with ICI – in fact it was rumoured that he was sacked by the then Minister of Transport, Tom Fraser. Needless to say Dr Beeching was still rewarded in the 1965 Birthday Honours and made a life peer!

RIGHT TOP: *These two maps from the 'Second Beeching Report' of 1965 show how Britain's railways would have been pruned even further if Beeching's recommendations had been implemented.*

RIGHT BOTTOM: *Angry demonstrations by rail workers over Dr Beeching and his cuts to the rail system and their subsequent loss of jobs.*

BELOW: *The 'Second Beeching Report' was published in early 1965.*

The development
of the major
railway trunk routes

BRITISH RAILWAYS BOARD
PRICE 15 SHILLINGS

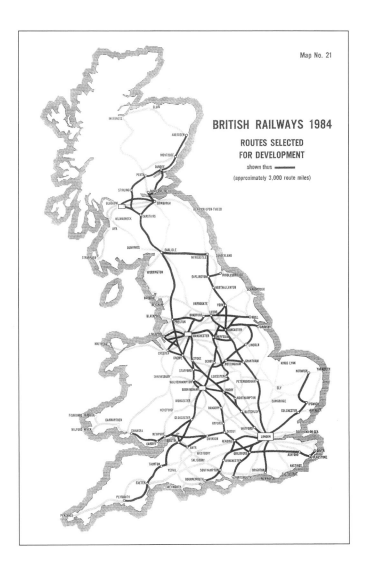

Map No. 21

BRITISH RAILWAYS 1984

ROUTES SELECTED
FOR DEVELOPMENT

shown thus ━━━━

(approximately 3,000 route miles)

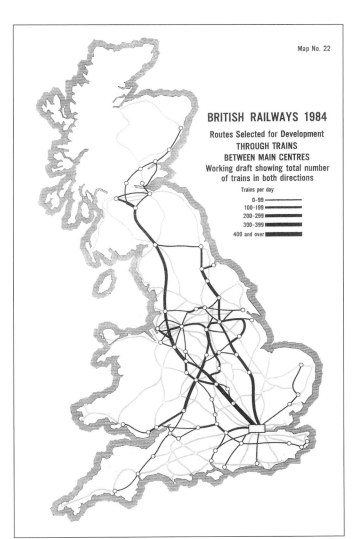

Map No. 22

BRITISH RAILWAYS 1984

Routes Selected for Development
THROUGH TRAINS
BETWEEN MAIN CENTRES
Working draft showing total number
of trains in both directions

Trains per day

0-99
100-199
200-299
300-399
400 and over

A bridge too far

The Tay Bridge Disaster

It was the night of Sunday 28 December 1879 and a Force 10 gale was blowing up the Firth of Tay. Having previously crossed the Firth of Forth by ferry on their journey from Edinburgh, the 75 passengers travelling on to Dundee joined their train at Burntisland and set off into the dark night. Pausing at St Fort for their tickets to be collected, the passengers settled down for the last leg of their journey across the newly-opened Tay Bridge. From the St Fort signal box, the signalman watched as the train's red tail light receded into the windswept darkness as it passed on to the bridge.

Built to shorten the railway journey between Edinburgh and Aberdeen, the Tay Bridge was officially opened by Queen Victoria on 1 June 1878. Taking nearly seven years to build, the 2¼ mile single-track bridge was an enormous feat of engineering and when completed it was the longest railway bridge in the world. Designed by Thomas Bouch, it was constructed of 85 cast-iron lattice-grid spans supported on cast-iron columns and strengthened with wrought-iron struts and ties. To allow shipping to pass under the bridge 13 spans, known as the High Girders, were built gradually higher than the rest of the bridge and were approached on each side up a gradient that varied between 1-in-74 and 1-in-130. During tests in 1878 a number of locomotives were coupled together and safely ran over the bridge at speeds of 40 mph. However, the effect of high winds on a train passing over such an exposed structure was unknown.

The 75 doomed passengers, including Thomas Bouch's son-in-law, travelling on the Burntisland to Dundee train never reached their destination. As it started to cross the High Girders the force of the gale force winds sweeping up the Tay Estuary brought about the collapse of the centre section of the spans and the train and its passengers plunged into the icy waters of the Tay. Confusion reigned at Dundee station when the train

didn't arrive and two railway workers volunteered to go along the bridge to ascertain the problem – crawling on all fours in a howling gale they found that a section of the bridge had disappeared and returned with the news that everyone was dreading.

At the official inquiry into the disaster it was concluded that the bridge collapsed due to a combination of bad design, construction and maintenance and that there were inherent weaknesses in the wrought-iron tie bars that secured the spans to the supporting columns – in short it was an accident waiting to happen. The blame fell squarely on the bridge's designer and engineer, Sir Thomas Bouch, and he died a broken man less than a year afterwards. The only survivor of the disaster was the North British Railway's 4-4-0 No 224 which was lifted from the riverbed, repaired and returned to service. A new double-track railway bridge was eventually opened in 1887 alongside the line of the original bridge and it remains in use today.

LEFT: *Steam launches and a diver's barge search for survivors of the Tay Bridge Disaster in December 1879. All 75 passengers and crew perished when the bridge collapsed into the icy waters of the Firth of Tay.*

BELOW: *Depicted in this 1957 British Railways' poster by renowned artist Terence Cuneo, the second Tay Bridge opened in 1887.*

TAY BRIDGE
SEE SCOTLAND BY TRAIN

Famous locomotive engineers 3

Sir Nigel Gresley (1876–1941)

The youngest of five children of the Reverend Nigel Gresley and his wife Joanna, Herbert Nigel Gresley was born in Edinburgh on 19 June 1876. He was brought up in the village of Netherseal in Derbyshire where his father was the rector. It was while the young Nigel Gresley was attending Marlborough College that he developed a love of railway engineering that was, in later life, to bring him accolades as one of Britain's finest locomotive engineers.

After leaving Marlborough the young Gresley began an apprenticeship at the London & North Western Railway's works at Crewe. To further his training Gresley moved to the Lancashire & Yorkshire railway's works at Horwich where he was taught by the famous engineer John Aspinall. After just three years as Assistant Superintendent in the Lancashire & Yorkshire's Carriage and Wagon Department at Newton Heath, Gresley was appointed Superintendent of the Carriage and Wagon Department of the Great Northern Railway in 1905. Six years later, at the age of 35, he succeeded H. A. Ivatt as the Locomotive Engineer of the Great Northern. In 1923 the Great Northern Railway became part of the newly-formed London & North Eastern Railway and Gresley was appointed Chief Mechanical Engineer, a position that he held at the company's Doncaster Railway Works until his death in 1941.

During his career, Gresley favoured three-cylinder locomotives with big boilers and a large fire grate and this policy led the LNER to become the first railway in Britain to build powerful 4-6-2 'Pacifics' in large numbers. During his tenure of office at both the GNR and LNER Gresley was responsible for 26 different locomotive designs including the 'A1' 4-6-2 in 1922, the 'U1' Garratt 2-8-0+0-8-2 in 1925, the 'A3' 4-6-2 in 1927 and the 'V2' 2-6-2 in 1936. However, his most famous locomotive must be the beautifully streamlined 'A4' 4-6-2 which first appeared in 1935. A locomotive of this class, No 4468 *Mallard*, still holds the world speed record for steam locomotives, a feat which was achieved in 1938 with a maximum speed of 126 mph.

Although mainly known for his locomotives, Gresley also introduced many innovative rolling stock designs including a five-car articulated dining car set, articulated suburban coaching stock and articulated sleeping cars. Sir Nigel Gresley died after a short illness on 5 April 1941 at his home in Watton-at-Stone near Hertford and is buried in Netherseal, Derbyshire.

LEFT: *Hauled by Nigel Gresley's Class 'A3' 4-6-2 No 4475 Flying Fox, 'The Flying Scotsman' makes its 10 a.m. departure from King's Cross station for Edinburgh, c.1930.*

BELOW: *With Gresley's Class 'A4' 4-6-2 No 4492 Dominion of New Zealand at its head, 'The Flying Scotsman' exits Potters Bar tunnel in 1937.*

Royal trains

From Victoria to Elizabeth

The first recorded train journey by royalty occurred on 14 November 1839 when Prince Albert travelled from Slough to Paddington on Brunel's recently-opened GWR broad-gauge line. Queen Adelaide, the widow of William IV who had died in 1837, travelled on the London & Birmingham Railway in 1840 and the company responded by building her own royal carriage, which can now be seen in the National Railway Museum in York.

The first reigning monarch to travel by train was Queen Victoria when she travelled back to London from Windsor Castle on 13 June 1842. Joining the train at Slough and accompanied by Isambard Kingdom Brunel, she travelled in a purpose-built four-wheeled carriage that had been supplied by the Great Western Railway.

The train, hauled by the GWR broad-gauge locomotive *Phlegethon*, took 25 minutes for the journey to Paddington. Following her acquisition of Osborne House in the Isle of Wight in 1843 and Balmoral in Scotland in 1848, Victoria soon became a regular long distance railway traveller and special trains were supplied for her use by the various railway companies involved. However, her trips were highly disruptive to normal traffic as Victoria disliked speed and her train journeys were limited to a maximum of 40 mph.

In later years Edward VII, who loved travelling at speed, had three new luxurious royal trains built at great expense to himself. The high cost of maintaining and running these trains was met by the royal household

which was even charged by the railway companies for the conveyance of royal pets! Many of the royal carriages built during Edward's reign were so comfortable that they continued to be used during the reigns of George V and George VI. Some of these historic vehicles can now be seen at the National Railway Museum in York. A new set of armour-plated royal carriages were built during World War II and these continued in use until a modern set was built to commemorate Elizabeth II's Silver Jubilee in 1977. The current royal train, consisting entirely of eight refurbished Mark III carriages, has been in use since 1986.

Railway companies often nominated specific locomotives for hauling royal trains but the most famous must be GWR 'Castle' Class 4-6-0 No 4082 *Windsor Castle*. Only a few weeks old, the locomotive hauled the royal train conveying King George V from Paddington for a visit to Swindon Works on 28 April 1924. After his visit the king drove *Windsor Castle* from the Works to Swindon Station. Commemorative plaques were mounted on the cab side in memory of this event and the locomotive was consequently used to haul all royal trains on the GWR, including George V's funeral train in 1936. When George VI died at Sandringham in 1952 *Windsor Castle* was undergoing repair at Swindon Works and locomotive No 7013 *Bristol Castle* (hastily renamed and renumbered as *Windsor Castle*) took over the role as royal engine to haul the funeral train from Paddington to Windsor on 15 February 1952. The engines never reverted to their original names and 7013 (aka 4082) was withdrawn from service in September 1964; 4082 (aka 7013) was withdrawn in February 1965.

In more recent times two Class 47 diesels, 47834 *Firefly* and 47835 *Windsor Castle,* were nominated to haul royal trains. They were later renumbered and renamed 47798 *Prince William* and 47799 *Prince Henry* but were replaced in 2003 by two EWS Class 67 freight locomotives, 67005 *Queen's Messenger* and 67006 *Royal Sovereign*. The cost of maintaining and using this train is paid out of the Grant-in-Aid that is voted by Parliament to the Royal Household each year.

In all its glory the LNER Royal Train heads through Potters Bar in Hertfordshire in the late 1930s. Hauling the train is 1923-built Class D16 (Claud Hamilton) 4-4-0 No 8783 which was kept in immaculate condition as a dedicated Royal loco for hauling the Royal Train from King's Cross to Wolferton, the nearest station for Sandringham House in Norfolk.

Small is beautiful 2

The world's smallest public railway

The world's smallest public railway, the Romney, Hythe & Dymchurch Railway, was conceived by two wealthy men, Captain 'Jack' Howey and Count Louis Zborowski, in the 1920s. Both men had a love of motor racing and miniature railways and were initially interested in buying the Ravenglass & Eskdale Railway in the Lake District where they planned to rebuild the narrow-gauge line as a 15in.-gauge line. This plan fell through but two one-third scale LNER steam engines, designed by Henry Greenly, had already been ordered from Davey, Paxman of Colchester. Meanwhile Count Zborowski was killed in a motor racing accident in the Italian Grand Prix at Monza and Howey teamed up with Greenly to look for a new location for the railway.

The pair finally chose Romney Marsh in Kent as the location for their miniature railway. No money was spared to produce an accurate one-third scale working miniature of a mainline railway. The line was double track and signalled, engines were replicas of LNER and Canadian express locomotives and passengers were carried in bogie

RIGHT: *Headed by 4-6-2* Black Prince, *'The Marshlander' nears the end of its journey to Dungeness in 1992. The loco was built in 1937 by Krupp of Essen, Germany.*

BELOW: *A late 1920s Romney, Hythe & Dymchurch Railway poster by artist N. Cramer Roberts depicting Greatstone station. The station opened in 1928 and closed in 1983. The footbridge shown in the poster was never built.*

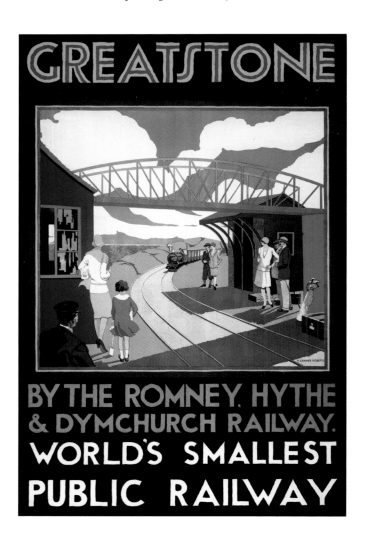

carriages. The first 8-mile section of the line, from Hythe to New Romney, was opened on 16 July 1927 and the then Duke of York, later to become King George VI, had the honour of driving the first train. A year later the line was extended a further 5½ miles westward to Dungeness lighthouse, where it makes a complete loop. Further steam locomotives were built and during the pre-war years the line became very popular with holidaymakers.

Located on the south coast of England, the railway also played its part in the defence of Britain during World War II. An armoured train was built complete with machine guns and the line also transported materials for Operation Pluto (Pipe Line Under The Ocean) in the days preceding the D-Day landings. The railway was completely reopened to the public in 1947 with Laurel and Hardy performing the opening ceremony. The period after the war brought mixed fortunes for the little railway and, with passenger numbers down, losses mounted after Howey's death in 1963 until the line was put up for sale in 1968. The new owners fared little better and it seemed that the line might well close until it was rescued in 1973 by a consortium headed by Sir William McAlpine. Since then the line has been restored to its former glory and now boasts 11 steam locomotives, including the two original 1925 locos, *Green Goddess* and *Northern Chief*, and two diesels which are used to operate a regular school train during term time. Rolling stock consists of over 65 assorted coaches including a unique buffet observation car and a royal saloon. The headquarters of the line is at New Romney where there is a large engine shed, turntable and workshop. The terminus at Hythe boasts an overall roof covering its three platforms and during peak periods trains run from here every 45 minutes, at speeds of up to 25 mph. Apart from January, services operate most weekends throughout the year with a full weekly service between April and October.

LNER famous trains

The Flying Scotsman

By 1860 services on the East Coast Main Line between London King's Cross and Edinburgh Waverley were under the control of the Great Northern Railway, the North Eastern Railway and the North British Railway. Through services between the two capitals were hindered by the lack of standard passenger carriages and in that year the three companies formed the East Coast Joint Stock to remedy this situation.

By 1862 new rolling stock for the first 'Special Scotch Express' was ready and the train became a regular feature departing each day at 10 a.m. from both King's Cross and Waverley stations. At that time the train took a leisurely 10½ hours to complete the 393 miles including passengers disembarking for lunch at York. This leisurely pace wasn't to last long and when Patrick Stirling, the GNR's Chief Mechanical Engineer, designed his famous 'Stirling

Single' locomotives in 1870 the East Coast route saw a rapid acceleration of schedules with a whole 2 hours soon being lopped off the King's Cross to Edinburgh journey.

By 1888 there had also developed a serious rivalry between the operators of the West Coast Main Line (L&NWR and CR) and the East Coast Main Line (GNR, NER, NBR) to achieve the fastest possible time between the two capitals. This resulted in what became known as the 'Race to the North' and on 20 August that year, with the surefooted help from the 'Stirling Singles' as far as York, the ECML between King's Cross and Edinburgh was covered in 6hr 19min at an average speed of 62.2 mph. The rivalry continued until 1896 when an Anglo-Scottish express, operated by the L&NWR, was derailed at Preston – safety limits had been flouted and a speed limit was imposed on the two rivals which stayed in place until 1932.

LNER 'A1' Class 4-6-2 No 4476 Royal Lancer *at speed on the East Coast Main Line with 'The Flying Scotsman' express, late 1920s. Built at Doncaster in 1923, this fine loco was rebuilt as an 'A3' in 1946 and withdrawn in late 1963.*

The beginning of the 20th century brought major improvements to the 'Special Scotch Express' with modern corridor carriages and dining cars. The heavier and longer trains were now headed by Ivatt's new 'Atlantics' as far as York but timings remained the same due to the 1896 speed restriction. The arrival of Nigel Gresley as Locomotive Engineer of the Great Northern Railway in 1911 led to the building of a series of groundbreaking 'Pacific' locomotive types. Two of his Class 'A1' were built at Doncaster in 1922 and 10 more had been ordered just before the 'Big Four Grouping' of 1923. As CME of the newly-formed LNER Gresley went on to develop this design into the 'A3' and later 'A4' streamlined Pacifics.

The 'Special Scotch Express' became officially known as the 'The Flying Scotsman' in 1924 and one of Gresley's 'A1' locos, No 4472, was also named in honour of the train. To reduce the journey time between King's Cross and Edinburgh some of the 'A1' locos were fitted with larger tenders not only containing more coal but also with a corridor linking the engine to the first coach of the train. The latter allowed a crew changeover halfway through the journey and so 'The Flying Scotsman' became a non-stop service in May 1928 – complete with a host of on-board facilities. The speed limitation agreement was abolished in 1932 and the gloves were off – by 1938 the journey time for the down 'The Flying Scotsman' had been reduced to 7hr 20min. The austerity measures of World War II soon brought an end to high-speed rail travel and it took some years before pre-war schedules were being attained. With the introduction of the record-breaking non-stop 'The Elizabethan' express in 1954 (taking only 6hr 30min to cover the 393 miles) 'The Flying Scotsman' had reverted to an intermediate stop at Newcastle – even though the journey time by 1961 had then come down to 7hr 2min with the introduction of the new 'Deltic' (Class 55) diesels.

The introduction of 100 mph running along many stretches of the ECML gave the 'Deltics' their racing ground and timings for 'The Flying Scotsman' continued to tumble. In turn, the 'Deltics' were replaced by HST sets between 1976 and 1981 and the opening of the Selby diversion improved matters further. Electrification was completed in 1990 and since then InterCity 225 sets with a maximum permissible speed of 125 mph have provided an even faster service. Currently the 10.00 a.m. departure from King's Cross takes only 4hr 23min to reach Edinburgh – progress indeed!

OVERLEAF: *34A's magnificent Class 'A4' 4-6-2 No 60013* Dominion of New Zealand *departs from King's Cross station at 10 a.m. with 'The Flying Scotsman' express to Edinburgh Waverley, 5 March 1960.*

BELOW: *Headed by 'Deltic' (Class 55) diesel D9018* Ballymoss *the up 'The Flying Scotsman' approaches Great Ponton at speed on 7 July 1962.*

120 into 4 = 'Big Four'

The creation of the 'Big Four' railway companies in 1923

By the outbreak of World War I there were 120 separate railway companies operating in Britain and, with a duplication of routes, many of them were competing directly with each other. Losses were mounting and the government of the day wanted to introduce a more efficient and economical working of the railway system. Nationalisation was considered by members of the fledgling Labour Party but there was not enough support for this at the time. After the war, during which the railways had come under state control, the coalition government under the premiership of David Lloyd George enacted the Railways Act of 1921 which amalgamated these 120 companies into four larger regional companies. Taking effect on 1 January 1923, the Act brought about the formation of the 'Big Four' as they soon became known.

The 'Big Four'
Great Western Railway (GWR)
London, Midland & Scottish Railway (LMS)
London & North Eastern Railway (LNER)
Southern Railway (SR)

Taff Vale Railway
Barry Railway
Rhymney Railway
Cardiff Railway
Alexandra Docks & Railway

Subsidiary companies within the newly-formed GWR included five that still continued to be independently worked (total mileage 169 miles), two that were semi-independent (total mileage 64 miles) and 19 that were originally leased to or worked by its constituent companies (total mileage 151¼ miles).

The GWR also operated one joint line (total mileage 41 miles) with the LNER, 15 joint lines with the LMS (total mileage 247¾ miles) and two lines with the SR (total mileage 9 miles).

Great Western Railway constituent companies (total mileage 3,566 miles):
Great Western Railway
Cambrian Railways

London, Midland & Scottish Railway constituent companies (total mileage 7,331 miles):
London & North Western Railway
Lancashire & Yorkshire Railway
Furness Railway
Midland Railway
North Staffordshire Railway
Caledonian Railway
Glasgow & South Western Railway
Highland Railway

Subsidiary companies within the newly-formed LMS included six that still continued to be independently worked (total mileage 170 miles) and 20 (total mileage 442 miles) that were originally leased to or worked by its constituent companies.

The LMS also absorbed three railways in Ireland:
Northern Counties Committee
Dundalk, Newry & Greenore Railway
Joint Midland & Great Northern Railway (Ireland)

The LMS also operated a total of 21 joint lines (total mileage 585¼ miles) with the LNER, 15 joint lines with the GWR (total mileage 247¾ miles), one joint line with the Southern Railway (the Somerset & Dorset Joint Railway – total mileage 105 miles) and one with the Metropolitan District Railway (total mileage 2 miles).

The LNER also operated a total of 21 joint lines (total mileage 585¼ miles) with the LMS, and one (total mileage 41 miles) with the GWR.

Southern Railway constituent companies (total mileage 2,115½ miles):
London & South Western Railway
South Eastern Railway
London, Chatham & Dover Railway
London, Brighton & South Coast Railway

Subsidiary companies within the newly-formed SR included four that still continued to be independently worked (total mileage 65½ miles) and 12 (total mileage 128¾ miles) that were originally leased to or worked by its constituent companies.

The SR also operated one joint line with the LMS (the Somerset & Dorset Joint Railway – total mileage 105 miles), two with the GWR (total mileage 9 miles), one with the LNER and the Metropolitan District Railway (total mileage 5 miles), and one with the GWR and LMS (total mileage 5¼ miles).

Railway companies not included in the 'Big Four'
Railways not included in the 'Big Four Grouping' of 1923 included the London Underground lines (total mileage 66 miles), the Liverpool Overhead Railway (6½ miles), the Mersey Railway (4¾ miles) and the Metropolitan Railway (65¾ miles). A total of 18 standard-gauge light railways (total mileage 206¾ miles), including those run and managed by Colonel Stephens (see pages 32–4), were excluded as were 15 narrow-gauge light railways (total mileage 101¾ miles).

London & North Eastern Railway constituent companies (total mileage 6,671¾ miles):
North Eastern Railway
North British Railway
Great Eastern Railway
Great Northern Railway
Great Central Railway
Great North of Scotland Railway
Hull & Barnsley Railway

Subsidiary companies within the newly-formed LNER included three that still continued to be independently worked (total mileage 48 miles) and 23 (total mileage 269 miles) that were originally leased to or worked by its constituent companies.

Brush strokes

Three notable railway poster artists

John Hassall (1868–1948)

John Hassall failed to enter the Royal Military Academy at Sandhurst so he emigrated to Canada in 1888 to farm with his brother. In 1890 he returned to London and had some of his drawings published in a magazine. He then went on to study art in Antwerp and Paris before returning to England in 1895 to begin work as an advertising artist for David Allen & Sons, the printing company that was to become famous for its London Transport posters. By 1900 Hassall had become a well established illustrator, cartoonist and poster designer, and his style of flat colours enclosed by black lines was also used in illustrations for children's books. His most

famous work is the 'Jolly Fisherman' depicted on the 1908 Great Northern Railway's poster, 'Skegness is So Bracing', for which he received a fee of 12 guineas. Strangely, he didn't visit the seaside resort until 1936 when he was given the 'freedom of the foreshore' and, despite his fame, he died penniless at the age of 80. Hassall's original Skegness masterpiece was presented to the town by British Railways in 1968 and now hangs in the Town Hall.

Norman Wilkinson (1878–1971)

Although he received an early training in music, Wilkinson went on to study at Southsea School of Art and became an accomplished maritime artist, illustrator, poster artist and inventor of wartime camouflage. His illustration career started in 1898 with work for the *Illustrated London News* and he went on to design shipping posters for companies such as Cunard and a vast number of railway posters, firstly for the London & North Western Railway and then for their successor, the LMS. During World War I he served with the Royal Naval Volunteer Reserve and hit upon the idea of camouflaging naval ships. His ideas were so successful that he led a team of camouflage artists in both World Wars and received an award for his invention of 'dazzle painting'.

As well as becoming one of the finest maritime painters of the 20th century (his painting *Plymouth Harbour* hung in the First Class smoking room of the *Titanic*), Wilkinson is famous for his large-format landscape railway posters that adorned stations up and down the country. He even persuaded 17 Royal Academicians to produce similar posters for the LMS in 1924. Recently seven of his original railway poster paintings were found behind a wardrobe in a North London house and were given reserve prices of up to £9,500 each! Even his printed railway posters can fetch £2,000 each.

LEFT: *John Hassall's famous Great Northern Railway poster of 1908 promoting Skegness as a resort.*

RIGHT: *Terence Cuneo's poster for British Railways, Southern Region, of 1962 depicts a whole host of locomotives and trains passing through Clapham Junction in London.*

Terence Cuneo (1907–96)

The doyen of post-war railway artists, Terence Cuneo studied at Chelsea Polytechnic and the Slade School of Art before going on to become a magazine and book illustrator. During World War II he worked as an artist for the *Illustrated London News* before being appointed as an official war artist, producing illustrations of aircraft factories and wartime events for the War Artists Advisory Committee and at the same time serving as a sapper. Following the end of the war Cuneo was commissioned to produce oil paintings of railway infrastructure and locomotives – he often took great risks when sketching on location, the highlight must have been him being lashed to the top of the Forth Bridge during a gale! His big break came when he was appointed the official artist for the Coronation of Queen Elizabeth II in 1953. Following this he was in great demand not only as an industrial and military artist but also as a railway poster artist, producing some widely acclaimed works for the British Transport Commission and British Railways. 'Clapham Junction' (produced for the Southern Region) and the 'Centenary of the Royal Albert Bridge' (produced for the Western Region) are just two of his fine works depicting life on British Railways during the late steam period. He went on to tackle the diesel and electric era, every painting having his tiny mouse trademark hidden away in the most unlikely place.

In addition to his railway paintings he is also well known for his vast number of paintings commissioned by British Army regiments illustrating battles of World War II, the Falklands War and the Gulf War. Original Cuneo paintings and even his British Railway's posters are much sought after – in recent years some of his original railway paintings have fetched up to £50,000. His paintings have appeared on British postage stamps, an InterCity train was named after him in 1990 and a statue to him has recently been unveiled at Waterloo station.

CLAPHAM JUNCTION
From the original oil painting by Terence Cuneo

Victorian blood, sweat and tears

The building of the Settle & Carlisle Railway

One of the major feats of Victorian engineering, the Settle & Carlisle route, beloved by steam enthusiasts across the world, was the last major mainline to be built in this country without the assistance of mechanical diggers. This heavily engineered route through wild terrain was born out of the Midland Railway's desire to reach Scotland by its own tracks. Receiving Parliamentary approval in 1866 the scheme nearly foundered before construction work had begun due to a financial crisis and a run on UK banks – apparently there's nothing new about this!

Engineered by John Sydney Crossley, work finally commenced on building the 72-mile line in 1870 – the statistics are staggering:

- Both the schedule for completion and final costs overran by at least 50%.
- An enormous workforce of around 6,000 navvies, housed in remote and rudimentary camps, caused mayhem with their drunken violence. Hundreds died through accidents and smallpox.
- The summit of the line, at Ais Gill, is 1,169ft above sea level.

- From the south the first 15 miles of line to Blea Moor were built at a ruling gradient of 1 in 100.
- 13 tunnels were built, of which the longest is Blea Moor with a length of around 1½ miles.
- 23 viaducts were built, of which the longest is at Ribblehead with 24 arches and a length of 440yds and the highest, at Smardale, is 131ft high.

The line was opened fully in 1876 and remained a vital Anglo-Scottish rail link until the 1960s when it was listed for closure in the 'Beeching Report'. Despite the ending of through trains and a rundown of services the S&C clung on to life until 1984 when it was announced that the line was to be finally closed. Following public outcry and a well-orchestrated national campaign the Government refused closure in 1989 – the rest is well known, with much-needed repairs of the bridges and tunnels and an upsurge in traffic along with regular steam-hauled specials, the Settle & Carlisle must rate as one of the most exciting railway journeys in Britain.

The railway navvy

Before the introduction of mechanical steam shovels (known as 'steam navvies') and other heavy excavating equipment in the late 19th century Britain's railways were carved out of the landscape by men using picks and shovels. The men at the 'coal face' were called navvies, an abbreviation of 'navigator' which was first applied to describe men engaged in the construction of works for inland navigation, or canals. When canals gave way to railways the name, not unnaturally, was used to describe the same class of men, whose employment was but little different under the new conditions. A 'nipper' was the generic term given to any boy employed in the construction of a railway. Often housed in remote temporary camps, life for the navvy was very hard and many died from accidents and disease.

The navvy was roughly classified under two headings – the navvy proper and the tramp navvy. The former was a respectable member of the community who enjoyed good health and was a good companion. In connection with his work he travelled all over the country and if he was industrious and reliable was usually promoted to a ganger.

The tramp navvy was a very different animal. He was considered to be a less desirable person, a poor unscrupulous specimen who was addicted to drink and was more often than not in need of a thoroughly good bath and disinfecting. Some of these individuals tramped the country, working in a gang for a day or so then living riotously for as many days as their wages would last – during the building of the Settle & Carlisle line in the 1870s, the Midland Railway even brought in Bible readers to try and curb drunken violence among these men. When they found themselves 'stoney-broke' tramp navvies would move on to the nearest job and repeat the same demoralising behaviour. So often were these men without any money that there was an unwritten law amongst them that if any out-of-work tramp found a former mate working in a gang, he was absolutely certain of receiving a shilling to help him on his way.

OVERLEAF: *Ex-LMS 'Princess' Class 4-6-2 No 6201* Princess Elizabeth *makes a fine sight as she heads along the Settle & Carlisle at Birkett Common with the 'Cumbrian Mountain Express' on 29 August 2009.*

BELOW: *On 14 October 2006, BR Standard Class '8P' 4-6-2 No 71000* Duke of Gloucester *heads a 'Cumbrian Mountain Express' railtour for Carlisle, crossing the impressive 24-arch Batty Moss Viaduct at Ribblehead, viewed from the rain-washed limestone escarpment on the eastern side.*

Goodbye Hazel, Doris, Audrey, Vera, Gwen and Mona

The 'Brighton Belle'

Farewell to the **BRIGHTON BELLE**

Sunday 30 April 1972

A free black and white print of this picture can be obtained by sending 3p stamp to the Public Relations & Publicity Officer (Dept RWR), British Rail, Southern Region, Waterloo Station, London, SE1.

Southern

Pullman cars were introduced by the London, Brighton & South Coast Railway in 1875. Six years later the company introduced the first all-Pullman train in the UK, the 'Pullman Limited' between London Victoria and Brighton. At the beginning of the 20th century the company changed the livery of all its coaches, including the Pullmans, to the now familiar brown umber and cream. This colour scheme was soon used on all Pullman coaches throughout the UK including the three new 35-ton 12-wheel vehicles introduced on the LBSCR service.

The LBSCR introduced a new Pullman train between Victoria and Brighton in 1908. Named the 'Southern Belle', this train made two returns each way on weekdays, taking exactly 60 minutes for the 50½-mile journey. It continued to operate as a steam-hauled service until 1933 when the London to Brighton line was electrified using third-rail pick-up. Three five-car all-Pullman electric multiple units then took over and the service was renamed the 'Brighton Belle' in 1934. In common with many other Pullman coaches the non-driving cars all received female names such as 'Hazel', 'Doris', Audrey', 'Vera', Gwen', and 'Mona'. The service was suspended during World War II but reinstated in 1946. By the early 1960s the train was operating three return journeys each weekday and two on Sundays but its age was beginning to show. Despite patronage by the great and the good the service was withdrawn by British Railways, amidst strong public protests, on 30 April 1972. Passengers travelling on the train on this last day were presented with a souvenir brochure and menu – the bar tariff makes interesting reading just one year after the introduction of decimalisation: ¼ bottle of champagne 75p; miniature Dubonnet 22p; miniature 'Royal Scot' whisky 37p; can of Guinness 15½p; can of Bulmer's Cider 12½p; small bottle ginger beer 8p. Those were the days!

LEFT: *A souvenir leaflet mourning the passing of the 'Brighton Belle' electric Pullman train on 30 April 1972. Apart from the Second World War the train had operated between London Victoria and Brighton since 1934.*

Fortunately this wasn't the end for the 'Brighton Belle's' Pullman coaches as nearly all of them were saved – some of them ending up in pub gardens, two on the Keith & Dufftown Railway while others were lovingly restored for use on the Venice Simplon Orient Express. Moves are now afoot to restore two of the driving cars and reunite them with their coaches so that the 'Brighton Belle' can run once again in the not-too-distant future.

BELOW: *Ex-Southern Railway 5-BEL unit No 3052 approaches Copyhold Junction, Haywards Heath with the 14.00 London Victoria to Brighton ('Brighton Belle') on 21 March 1972. This famous train was withdrawn just over a week later.*

GWR famous trains 2

The Bristolian

'The Bristolian' express was introduced in 1935 to mark the Centenary of the GWR. Travelling non-stop between Paddington and Bristol this lightweight train of only seven carriages was initially hauled by 'King' Class 4-6-0s and was timed to take 1hr 45min for the outward journey of 118¼ miles via Bath and for the return journey of 117½ miles via the Badminton cut-off. Before the Second World War, when the train was temporarily suspended, the up 'The Bristolian' left Paddington at 10 a.m. and the down train left Bristol at 4.30 p.m.

The service was reinstated in 1954 with an 8.45 a.m. departure from Paddington and a 4.30 p.m. return from Bristol, thus giving businessmen more time for their meetings in Bristol. Still normally 'King'-hauled, the timings were identical to pre-war days but the modification of some 'Castle' Class 4-6-0 locos soon brought some electrifying performances.

Built in 1949, 'Castle' Class No 7018 *Drysllwyn Castle* was the first of its class to be fitted with a double chimney and four-row superheater. Emerging from Swindon Works with its modifications in May 1956 the Bristol (Bath Road)-allocated loco was soon putting up electrifying 100 mph performances on the 'The Bristolian'. Soon other 'Castles' were similarly modified and the train occasionally completed the up journey via Badminton in under 94 minutes at an average speed of 75 mph. The sound of a 'Castle's' four-cylinder beat as it roared through Swindon at 80 mph was a thrilling experience for any young lad, the author included! The introduction of Swindon-built 'Warship' Class diesels in 1959 soon put an end to this steam spectacular – the last up steam-hauled train being hauled by No 5085 *Evesham Abbey* on 12 June.

The 'Warship' and later 'Western' Class diesel hydraulics were themselves replaced by HST 125s in 1976 and what purported to be 'The Bristolian' became just another anonymous train.

Flash forward to 2010 when restored 'Castle' Class 4-6-0 No 5043 *Earl of Mount Edgcumbe* hauled a commemorative 'The Bristolian' to mark the 175th anniversary of the GWR. Its return journey from Bristol to Paddington was completed in just under 1hr 50min, only 5 minutes slower than the 1950s schedule, arriving at its destination 45 minutes early – Messrs Churchward and Collett must have had smiles on their faces when looking down from GWR Heaven!

The first through trains between Paddington and Aberystwyth began on 14 July 1921 when a Luncheon and Tea Car Express was introduced by the GWR and Cambrian Railways. Leaving London at 10.15 a.m. the train changed engines on the Shrewsbury avoiding line where two Cambrian Railways 4-4-0s would take over for the rest of the journey to Aberystwyth, arriving at 4.20 p.m. Through carriages were also conveyed for Pwllheli, arriving at 5.45 p.m.

This train became officially known as the 'Cambrian Coast Express' in 1927 by which time the Cambrian Railways had become part of the GWR. Initially only running during the summer, the train ran officially 'non-stop' between Wolverhampton (Low Level) and Welshpool but actually stopped on the Shrewsbury avoiding line where two GWR 'Dukedog' 4-4-0s would take over for the rest of the journey. New 'Manor' Class 4-6-0s were introduced for this last leg of the journey after the Second World War and these continued in service until 1965 when BR Standard Class '4' 4-6-0s took over until 1967. By then the 'Castle' Class 4-6-0s had already been replaced for the Paddington to Shrewsbury leg of the journey by Brush Type 4 (Class 47) diesels with the train changing engines at Shrewsbury station.

Following the Second World War the 'CCE' was a Summer-Saturdays-only train until 1959 when it started operating on weekdays year-round. Regional boundary changes soon saw it transferred from Paddington to Euston and, following the end of steam on the Cambrian section in 1967, this final leg of the journey was taken over by BR Sulzer Type 2 (Class 25) diesels. The last train ran in 1991 using BR Class 37 diesels.

LEFT: *Headed by ex-GWR 'King' Class 4-6-0 No 6028* King George VI, *'The Bristolian', hurtles towards Twyford on 27 May 1959.*

BELOW: *The 'Cambrian Coast Express' prepares to leave Aberystwyth for its long journey to Paddington on 18 February 1961 behind Machynlleth shed's immaculate ex-GWR 'Manor' Class 4-6-0 No 7803* Barcote Manor.

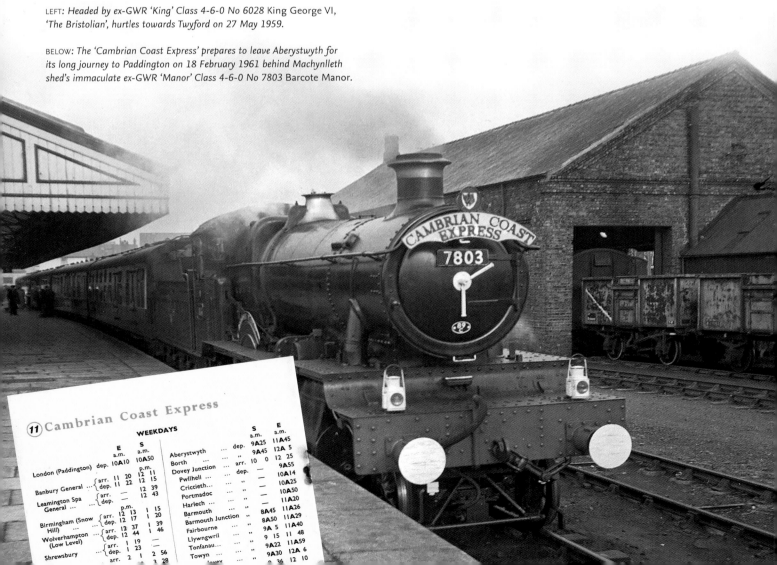

11 Cambrian Coast Express

						S	E
	WEEKDAYS					a.m.	a.m.
	E	S					
	a.m.	a.m.					
London (Paddington)	dep. 10A10	10A50	Aberystwyth	... dep.		9A25	11A45
		p.m.	Borth ...	... ,,		9A45	12A 5
Banbury General ...	{ arr. 11 20	12 11	Dovey Junction	... arr.		10 0	12 25
	{ dep. 11 22	12 15		... dep.		—	9A55
Leamington Spa General ...	{ arr. —	12 39	Pwllheli ...	... ,,		—	10A14
	{ dep. —	12 43	Criccieth...	... ,,		—	10A25
		p.m.	Portmadoc	... ,,		—	10A50
Birmingham (Snow Hill) ...	{ arr. 12 13	1 15	Harlech ...	... ,,		—	11A20
	{ dep. 12 17	1 20	Barmouth	... ,,		8A45	11A26
Wolverhampton (Low Level) ...	{ arr. 12 37	1 39	Barmouth Junction	... ,,		8A50	11A29
	{ dep. 12 44	1 46	Fairbourne	... ,,		9A 5	11A40
Shrewsbury ...	{ arr. 1 19		Llwyngwril	... ,,		9 15	11 48
	{ dep. 2 1	2 56	Tonfanau ...	... ,,		9A22	11A59
	arr.	3 28	Towyn ...	... ,,		9A30	12A 6
			Dovey	... ,,		9 36	12 10

Narrow-gauge Phoenix 1

A volunteer on the Ffestiniog Railway

It was coming towards the end of the long school summer holiday in 1966 and I had just returned from a steam safari in Scotland, the culmination of which was a ride on one of the last 'A4'-hauled Glasgow to Aberdeen 3-hour expresses. The last week of my holiday had already been booked some months before – my school chum, Richard, and I had volunteered our services to the Ffestiniog Railway in Porthmadog to assist them in tracklaying in their push towards reopening their narrow-gauge line up to Blaenau Ffestiniog.

For the journey to North Wales Richard had already purchased an old banger (either an old Austin or Morris) for the princely sum of £25. However it was prone to overheating so our journey from Gloucester had to be carried out over two days; the first leg on 2 September took us as far as Welshpool. Here we obtained a fairly cheap B&B for the night and went off to discover the delights of this lovely market town – first stop the station where I noted BR Standard Class 4 4-6-0 No 75012 hauling an up goods train. The evening was spent at a 'hop' in the Town Hall – you know, the kind where all the local girls congregate on one side of the dance hall and the young men gaze at them from the other.

ext day dawned bright and clear and, after a quick visit to the station where Stanier 'Black 5' 4-6-0 No 45145 was noted on a cement train, we set off in our jalopy once again heading for Snowdonia. A few miles out of Welshpool we stopped off at Llanfair Caereinion where the narrow-gauge Welshpool & Llanfair Light Railway was coming back to life again following closure by BR 10 years before. Complete with 'Swindonised' copper-capped chimney, one of the original W&L locos, 0-6-0T No 823 *Countess*, was about to depart with the 11.45 a.m. train to Castle Caereinion, the end of the line back then. We quickly hopped on board and thoroughly enjoyed our leisurely return journey along the Banwy Valley.

Back on the road again our journey through the Welsh mountains was punctuated by numerous stops to allow our trusty steed to cool down – quite often we had to pull over as steam erupted from beneath the bonnet.

At long last we reached our destination, a farmhouse B&B near Tan-y-Blwch, from where we would sally forth over the coming week to work on the Ffestiniog Railway's extension.

Supplied with a packed lunch and soft drinks Richard and I would drive down each day to the permanent way depot at Minffordd where we were met by the foreman in charge of tracklaying further up the line. From Minffordd we were conveyed in a stately style on board a Wickham speeder up through Tan-y-Bwlch and along the mountainside ledge to the site of Campbell's Platform where tracklaying was in progress.

A private halt, Campbell's Platform had just been established to serve the hostel of Plas Dduallt, and was named after its owner, Colonel Andrew Campbell. He was not only allowed to run his own train down the line to Tan-y-Bwlch but he was also instrumental in the building of the Dduallt spiral deviation further up the line. During the week that we worked there the pointwork and siding for the halt was being laid, a laborious manual job in this remote part of Snowdonia. During one lunchbreak we walked further up the overgrown line as far as the western portal of the old Moelwyn Tunnel, soon to disappear beneath a hydro-electric scheme and the reason for the later building of the Dduallt spiral and deviation.

At the end of each day we would return down to Minffordd in the speeder before taking a well-earned dinner in a local hostelry. We even found time to walk down the trackbed and through the rock-cut tunnels of the old Welsh Highland Railway through the Aberglaslyn Pass, little knowing that this long-closed narrow-gauge line would come back to life 45 years later. Returning to Gloucester on 10 September I noted Stanier '8F' 2-8-0 No 48339 on a down goods at Welshpool station – there was only six months to go before steam was eradicated on the Cambrian line.

LEFT: *Early preservation days on the Ffestiniog Railway when trains only ran as far as Tan-y-bwlch – Double-Fairlie 0-4-4-0T Merddin Emrys departs from Porthmadog Harbour station in the 1960s. This loco was built in 1879 at Boston Lodge Works.*

OVERLEAF: *Double-Fairlie David Lloyd George hauls a train toward Blaenau Ffestiniog past the site of Campbell's Platform on 1 November 2015. This loco was built at Boston Lodge Works in 1992.*

The Streakers

Britain's streamlined steam locomotives

During the 1930s, with increased competition from road and rail travel, railways in the USA and Europe were competing with each other for the title of the 'World's Fastest Train'. Between 1932 and 1935 the Great Western Railway was the undisputed champion with the 'Cheltenham Flyer' for its non-stop journey between Swindon and Paddington. However, the introduction of the high-speed streamlined 'Flying Hamburger' articulated diesel train in Germany and the US 'Burlington Zephyr' changed all this. Suddenly, streamlining was in vogue and, in Britain, both the LMS and the LNER developed powerful streamlined 4-6-2 Pacific locomotives that were built for speed. The GWR made a half-hearted attempt to streamline a couple of their locos while the Southern Railway belatedly arrived on the scene in 1941 with the introduction of its air-smoothed 'Merchant Navy' Class locomotives.

BELOW: *One of the LNER's 'Streakers', 'A4' Class 4-6-2 No 2511 Silver King was built in 1935 and withdrawn as BR No 60016 in March 1965.*

LNER streamlined locomotives

In Britain, the first streamlined locomotive to be built was the secretive 'W1' class 4-6-4 'Hush-Hush' high-pressure compound locomotive No 10000. Designed by Nigel Gresley for the LNER, the loco was introduced in 1929 but was never a great success and was rebuilt as a three-cylinder engine in 1937. The first major class of streamlined locomotives to be built in Britain were the Gresley Class 'A4' Pacifics. Their famous wedge-shaped design was inspired by a French Bugatti diesel railcar that Gresley had seen on a trip to France. After intensive testing of models in a wind tunnel the design was refined into the graceful locomotives that were introduced in 1935. Hauling a streamlined rake of seven articulated coaches, the first loco in service, No 2509 *Silver Link*, reached a speed of 112.5 mph on a test run in September 1935. First going into regular service on the new 'Silver Jubilee' express from King's Cross to Newcastle, these locomotives and their trains

provided the LNER with an enormous public relations coup. High speed services to Edinburgh and Leeds were soon introduced and the crowning glory came on 3 July 1938 when another locomotive of the 'A4' class, No 4468 *Mallard*, achieved a world record speed for a steam locomotive of 126 mph on a test run down Stoke Bank. This record still stands unbeaten today. Although the streamlined side skirts were removed in later years to assist easier maintenance, the entire class of 34 locomotives retained their streamlined casing until finally withdrawn in the 1960s. Buoyed by the success of the 'A4s', Gresley also added a similar streamlined casing to his Class 'P2' 2-8-2 locos in 1936. The first of these locos to be streamlined was No 2001 *Cock o' the North* but by 1944 all members of this class had been rebuilt as un-streamlined Class 'A2/2' 4-6-2s. Gresley's final experiment in streamlining came in 1937 when he added streamlined casings similar to the 'A4' Class to two members of the Class 'B17' 'Sandringham' 4-6-0 locomotives. The two locomotives treated were No 2859 *East Anglian* and No 2870 *City of London* which were used to haul expresses between London Liverpool Street and Norwich from September 1937. The streamlining was removed from these two locos in 1951.

LMS streamlined locomotives

Not to be outdone by the LNER's success with streamlined trains, the LMS introduced its streamlined 'Coronation' Class 4-6-2s in 1937. Designed by William Stanier to haul the crack 'Coronation Scot' express from London Euston to Glasgow, the first 10 members of this class were fitted with streamlined casings that had a rounded front-end complete with 'speed whiskers' which extended along the side of the loco and tender and continued along the sides of the matching carriages. On a test run on 27 June 1937, locomotive No 6220 *Coronation* broke the then British speed record for steam locomotives when it achieved a speed of 114 mph just south of Crewe – narrowly avoiding becoming derailed as it approached Crewe station at too high a speed! Two years later No 6229 *Duchess of Hamilton* (renumbered and renamed as No 6220 *Coronation*) visited the USA where it represented British railway achievement at the New York World's Fair. Unfortunately, World War II broke out while the loco and train were on a 3,000-mile tour around the USA and they were not repatriated back to England until 1943. To reduce maintenance costs the streamlined casing was removed from members of this class between 1946 and 1949.

The LMS's streamlined 'Coronation' Class 4-6-2 No 6222 Queen Mary hauling the 'Coronation Scot' in 1937.

Faced with the LNER's success the GWR undertook what can only be described as a rather pathetic attempt to streamline two of their locomotives. Fitted with a round bullet-shaped nose over the firebox door, streamlined casing over the outside cylinders, a continuous straight arch over the driving wheels, a V-shape to the front of the cab, a continuous roof linking the cab and tender and 'go-faster' fins behind the chimney and safety valves, 'Castle' Class 4-6-0 No 5005 *Manorbier Castle* and 'King'

Class 4-6-0 No 6014 *King Henry VII* appeared in service in 1935. The appearance of these graceful locomotives thus adorned was not the GWR's finest hour and, after a few years, the casings were removed and the experiment quietly forgotten!

BELOW: *The GWR's pathetic attempt at streamlining was applied to 'Castle' Class 4-6-0 No 5005* Manorbier Castle, *seen here heading the second portion of the 'Cornish Riviera Express in 1938.*

Last on the scene was the Southern Railway with the introduction of O. V. Bulleid's air-smoothed 'Merchant Navy' Class 4-6-2 locomotives in 1941. Though not fully streamlined, these innovative high-pressure locomotives first appeared with an air-smoothed casing which certainly gave the impression of speed. A total of 30 locomotives of this class were built between 1941 and 1949 but many of Bulleid's innovations proved costly to maintain and the locos were all rebuilt, minus their air-smoothed casings, between 1956 and 1960. Several members of the class remained in service until the end of steam on the Southern Region in 1967. Introduced in 1945, also with air-smoothed casings, 110 of Bulleid's 'West Country' and 'Battle of Britain' Class 4-6-2s were built. A lighter version of the 'Merchant Navies', they could operate on a wider range of Southern routes. Sixty of these locomotives were also rebuilt by British Railways between 1957 and 1961 while the remainder still carried their casing until withdrawn from service in the 1960s.

The Southern Railway's Bulleid Pacifics were more 'wind-cheating' than streamlined. Here is restored 'Battle of Britain' Class 4-6-2 No 34067 Tangmere speeding through Bradford-on-Avon station in Wiltshire.

Famous locomotive engineers 4

Sir William Stanier (1876–1965)

William Arthur Stanier was born in Swindon on 27 May 1876. His father was the Chief Clerk to William Dean, then Locomotive Superintendent of the Great Western Railway. After completing his education in 1892 the young William Stanier also joined the GWR where he started work as an apprentice draughtsman. He was promoted to Inspector of Materials in 1900 and became Assistant to the Divisional Locomotive Superintendent in Paddington four years later. Further promotions followed, first in 1912 when George J. Churchward, Chief Mechanical Engineer of the Great Western Railway, appointed him as Assistant Works Manager at Swindon Works, then in 1920 to Works Manager and finally in 1922 when he became principal assistant to the new Chief Mechanical Engineer of the GWR, Charles Collett. His time spent working under Churchward and Collett was to have a great influence on Stanier's later work for the LMS where he further developed many of the excellent features of GWR locomotive design.

Meanwhile, at the London Midland & Scottish Railway, Sir Henry Fowler was struggling with the development of both heavy freight and passenger locomotive designs for that company. On Fowler's retirement in 1932, William Stanier joined the LMS as their Chief Mechanical Engineer and set about reorganising and standardising the company's rather

LEFT: *Stanier's heavy freight locos were a great success, with 776 being built. Here Class '8F' 2-8-0 No 8314 is blowing off steam while the crew have a break.*

BELOW: *Two of Stanier's 'Lizzies' together at Euston station on 17 June 1960. On the left is No 46200* The Princess Royal *and on the right is No 46209* Princess Beatrice.

motley collection of locomotive designs. In the years between 1932 and 1947 over 2,000 Stanier-designed locomotives were built for the LMS incorporating well-tried GWR features such as the tapered boiler and superheating along with Stanier's own development of the Walschaerts valve gear. His designs included the famous 'Black Five' 4-6-0 of which 841 were built, the 'Jubilee' class 4-6-0 of which 190 were built and the '8F' 2-8-0 of which 776 were built. All of these locomotives provided the backbone of motive power for the LMS and its successor, British Railways (London Midland Region), until the end of steam traction in Britain in 1968. However, Stanier's most famous locomotive designs were the powerful 'Princess' and 'Coronation' class 4-6-2s which were the mainstay of the Euston to Glasgow passenger expresses for 30 years.

Although Stanier is most well known for his steam locomotive designs he also saw the future for diesel-electric power and was responsible for introducing the forerunner of the humble diesel shunter so favoured by British Railways. During World War II he was one of only three Scientific Advisors appointed by the Ministry of Production and was also President of the Institute of Mechanical Engineers. Stanier was knighted in 1943 and when he retired as CME of the LMS in 1944 was also elected a Fellow of the Royal Society. He died in Rickmansworth, Hertfordshire, on 27 September 1965.

BELOW: Stanier's 'Coronation' Class 4-6-2 No 46240 City of Coventry of Camden shed is set to depart from Glasgow Central with 'The Caledonian' express for London Euston on 21 July 1959.

The Slow & Dirty

The much-loved Somerset & Dorset Joint Railway

The delayed closure of the Somerset & Dorset Joint Railway on 7 March 1966 led to an outpouring of grief among railway enthusiasts and the loss of this much-loved institution, faithfully recorded from the early 1950s by the railway photographer and film-maker Ivo Peters and others, created a void in the lives of the people of Somerset and Dorset.

The S&D, as it became known, originated with the opening of the broad-gauge Somerset Central Railway from Glastonbury to Highbridge in 1854. This was extended to Burnham-on-Sea in 1858 and a branch from Glastonbury to Wells was opened the following year. To further their ambitions to reach the South Coast the SCR pushed eastwards to Cole in 1862 where it joined the standard-gauge Dorset Central Railway from Wimborne – this latter line was operated by the London & South Western Railway. In the same year the SCR and the DCR were amalgamated as the Somerset & Dorset Railway.

BELOW: Just before closure of the S&DJR in 1966 Ivatt Class '2' 2-6-2T No 41249 is about to depart from Highbridge with its two-coach train for Evercreech Junction.

To the north the mighty Midland Railway had reached Bath in 1869 and the Somerset & Dorset were quick to realise that an extension across the Mendips through the North Somerset coalfield to the city would be most advantageous. Involving considerable engineering works with steep gradients, tunnels and viaducts, the Bath extension from Evercreech Junction was opened in July 1874. At the southern end the line had just been extended to Bournemouth and soon through trains to that up-and-coming South Coast resort were running via the S&DR from the Midlands and the North. Although traffic over the S&DR increased rapidly the company was in a dire financial state caused by the heavy cost of building the extension. Unable to carry on, the S&DR agreed to lease

the railway jointly to the L&SWR and the Midland Railway and on 13 July 1876 it became the Somerset & Dorset Joint Railway. An improved direct connection to Bournemouth was opened in 1886 but trains still had to reverse up to the L&SWR station at Templecombe – this antiquated operation continued until closure in 1966. A branch from Edington Junction (on the Highbridge branch) to Bridgwater was opened in 1890.

Although the company's main workshop was at Highbridge, after joint ownership locomotives for the railway were built at the Midland Railway's workshops in Derby – these included the '2P' 4-4-0, '3F' 0-6-0 and 'Jinty' 0-6-0 tank. Derby also went on to build 10 powerful 2-8-0 tender locos specifically for use on the S&DJR and many of

these remained in service until the early 1960s. Towards the end of its life the line also saw BR Standard '9F' 2-10-0s, including No 92220 *Evening Star* hauling the 'Pines Express' and other through trains single-handedly over the Mendips. September 1962 saw the end of north–south through trains and from that date the S&DJR, or 'Slow & Dirty' as it was affectionately known, was doomed. Confirmed by the then double-crossing Labour Government in 1965, closure was finally scheduled for 3 January 1966. Railway enthusiasts from far and wide came to pay their last respects and special trains were run but a local bus operator had the last laugh when he withdrew his application to run an alternative bus service. For two more months the S&D struggled on with a skeleton service – passengers between Bath to Bournemouth had to wait at draughty Templecombe station where BR authorities had deliberately retimed trains so that there were no convenient connections. After a terrible lingering death brought about by the machinations of politicians and BR management the closure on 7 March 1966 came as a relief. Poor old S&D – you are still sadly missed.

BELOW: *S&DJR '7F' 2-8-0 No 53806 is seen here at Bath Green Park on 3 November 1960. This powerful loco was one of the second batch of this class built specifically to haul heavy trains over the Mendip Hills between Bath and Evercreech Junction. No 53806 was built by Robert Stephenson & Company in 1925 and withdrawn in in January 1964.*

Who was that man?

Some famous named steam engines and their namesakes

The practice of naming steam locomotives started in the early days of the railways but by the early 20th century it had started to take on a whole new meaning with companies such as the GWR leading the way. Soon whole classes of locomotives were being named after military leaders and heroes, regiments, football clubs, North Country hunts, saints, earls, poets, playwrights, Arthurian legends, royalty, warships, aircraft types, merchant shipping companies, locomotive designers, railway chief mechanical engineers, racehorses, seabirds, abbeys, lochs, glens, schools, cities, counties and baronial piles such as castles, halls, granges and manors. Even names of villages adorned the Isle of Wight's locomotives. The public loved it (they still do), the names adding to the romantic vision of railway travel to far-off places. However standardised, many of these names were quite often of famous men (not too many women apart from royalty and the odd *Boadicea*, *Lady Godiva* or a couple of Arthurian legend names ever appeared to adorn locomotives) that were dropped in at unexpected places. Many of these names were obviously railway officials but others are a bit harder to fathom out. Here are some examples of both (some obvious, some not so) as seen running during the British Railways era. Extremely obvious names such as *Isambard Kingdom Brunel*, *Sir Nigel Gresley* etc. have been omitted for space reasons!

FORMER GWR LOCOS
'Castle' Class 4-6-0

No 5066 *Sir Felix Pole* – (1877–1956) General Manager of the GWR, 1921–29

No 5070 *Sir Daniel Gooch* – (1816–89) first Locomotive Superintendent for GWR, 1837–64; Chairman, 1865–89

No 7000 *Viscount Portal* – (1885–1949) last Chairman of GWR, 1945–48

No 7001 *Sir James Milne* – (1883–1958) General Manager of GWR, 1929–47

FORMER SR LOCOS
'Battle of Britain' Class 4-6-2

No 34052 *Lord Dowding* – (1882–1970) Commander of RAF Fighter Command during the Battle of Britain

Named after the famous Worcestershire composer, the brass nameplate of ex-GWR 'Castle' Class 4-6-0 No 7005 Sir Edward Elgar. The loco was originally named Lamphey Castle but was renamed in 1957.

No 34053 *Sir Keith Park* – (1893–1975) a New Zealander, Air Chief Marshal of RAF during World War II

No 34054 *Lord Beaverbrook* (1879–1964) of Canadian origin, a wealthy newspaper owner and Minister of Aircraft Production and Minister of Supply during World War II

No 34058 *Sir Frederick Pile* – (1884–1976) General Officer commanding Anti-Aircraft Command during World War II

No 34059 *Sir Archibald Sinclair* – (1890–1970) Secretary of State for Air during World War II

No 34090 *Sir Eustace Missenden* – (1886–1973) last General Manager of the Southern Railway, 1941–48 and first Chairman of the Railway Executive, 1948–51

No 34109 *Sir Trafford Leigh-Mallory* – (1892–1944) Commander-in-Chief of Fighter Command, 1942; Commander-in-Chief of Allied Expeditionary Forces, 1943–44; killed in a plane crash in the French Alps

FORMER LMS LOCOS
'Patriot' Class 4-6-0

No 45530 *Sir Frank Ree* – General Manager of LNWR, 1909–14

No 45531 *Sir Frederick Harrison* – (1844–1914) General Manager of the London & North Western Railway, 1893–1909

No 45533 *Lord Rathmore* – (1838–1919) Irish-born politician and lawyer, Chairman of North London Railway and director of Central London Railway

RIGHT: *The nameplate of SR 'Battle of Britain' Class 4-6-2 No 34052 Lord Dowding. He was the Commander of RAF Fighter Command during the Battle of Britain.*

BELOW: *The nameplate of SR 'Battle of Britain' Class 4-6-2 No 34058 Sir Frederick Pile. He was the General Officer commanding Anti-Aircraft Command during the Second World War.*

No 45534 *E. Tootal Broadhurst* – (1855–1922) cotton manufacturer; High Sheriff of Lancashire, 1906; LNWR Director

No 45535 *Sir Herbert Walker K.C.B.* – (1868–1949) District Superintendent of LNWR (North Wales, 1893–1902, then Euston, 1902–12); General Manager of the London & South Western Railway, 1912–17; acting Chairman of Railway Executive Committee during latter stages of World War I; Director of Southern Railway, 1937–47

No 45536 *Private W. Wood. V.C.* – (1897–1982) born in Stockport, won V.C. in 1918 when, as a private in the 10th Battalion The Northumberland Fusiliers fighting near Casa Vana in Italy, he single-handedly destroyed a German machine-gun post and caused 140 men to surrender

No 45537 *Private E. Sykes V.C.* – (1885–1949) born in Mossley, Lancashire, worked for LNWR, served in France and Flanders with Tyneside Irish Brigade of the 27th Battalion of the Northumberland Fusiliers. Awarded V.C. in 1917 for 'most conspicuous bravery and devotion to duty near Arras on 19 April'

No 45539 *E.C. Trench* – LNWR Director

No 45540 Sir Robert Turnbull – General Manager of LNWR, 1914

FORMER LNER LOCOS
'A4' Class 4-6-2

No 60001 *Sir Ronald Matthews* (1885–1959) Chairman of the LNER; Chairman of Brush

No 60003 *Andrew K. McCosh* – (1880–1967) Minister of Supply, 1939–42; Director of LNER

No 60004 *William Whitelaw* – (1868–1948) Chairman of Highland Railway, 1902–12; Chairman North British Railway, 1912–23; Chairman of LNER, 1923–38; grandfather of William Whitelaw, Tory politician in Margaret Thatcher's government

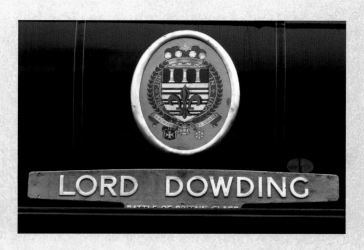

No 60005 *Sir Charles Newton* – (1882–1973) GWR 1897–1916; Great Eastern Railway 1916–23; Chief Accountant LNER, 1928; Chief General Manager of LNER, 1939–47

No 60006 *Sir Ralph Wedgwood* – (1874–1956) Chief Officer of LNER, 1923–39, Chairman of wartime Railway Executive Committee, 1939–41

No 60026 *Miles Beevor* – (1900–94) Chief legal advisor for the LNER, 1943–47; acting Chief General Manager of LNER, 1947; Chief Secretary and legal advisor for British Transport Commission, 1947–51; Managing Director of Brush, 1954–58

No 60034 *Lord Faringdon* – (1850–1934) railway financier and Chairman of Great Central Railway, 1889–1922

Peppercorn 'A1' Class 4-6-2

No 60114 *W.P. Allen* – (1888–1958) joined GNR as cleaner at Hornsey, later General Secretary of ASLEF

'A2/3' Class 4-6-2

No 60500 *Edward Thompson* – (1881–1954) mechanical engineer at Stratford Works, 1930–41; Chief Mechanical Engineer of LNER, 1941–46

'B1' Class 4-6-0

Seventeen of this class were named after LNER directors. Here are some of the more interesting ones:

No 61238 *Leslie Runciman* – (1900–89) shipping magnate (Walter Runciman & Co); first Director-General of British Overseas Airways Corporation, 1939–43; Deputy Chairman of Lloyds Bank, 1962–71; Director of LNER

No 61241 *Viscount Ridley* – (1902–64) British peer (3rd Viscount Ridley), the son of Matthew White Ridley (1874–1916, 2nd Viscount) who was MP for Stalybridge, 1900–04; Director of LNER

No 61243 *Sir Harold Mitchell* – (1900–83) born in Fife; MP for Brentford and Chiswick, 1931–45; Vice-Chairman of Conservative Party; British peer; many business interests around the world including coal mines, glass works and shipping; Director of LNER

No 61244 *Strang Steel* – (1882–1961) MP for Ashford, 1918–29; Lord Lieutenant of Selkirkshire, 1948–53; Director of LNER

No 61245 *Murray of Elibank* – (1877–1951) 2nd Viscount Elibank; served as diplomat in overseas territories, 1898–1917; MP for Glasgow St Rollox, 1918–22; Lord Lieutenant of Peeblesshire, 1939–45; Honorary Colonel of 8th Battalion The Royal Scots, 1939–45; Director of LNER

No 61246 *Lord Balfour of Burleigh* – (1883–1967) 7th Lord Balfour of Burleigh (of Burleigh Castle, Kinross); Scottish Representative Peer, 1922–63; Director of LNER; his father, the 6th Lord (1849–1921) served as Parliamentary Secretary to the Board of Trade, 1888–92; Secretary for Scotland, 1895–1903; Governor of Bank of Scotland, 1904–21

No 61250 *A. Harold Bibby* – (1889–1986) Liverpool shipping magnate; High Sheriff of Cheshire, 1934–35; Chairman of Bibby Line, 1932–69; Director of various maritime insurance companies, Governor of Rugby School, 1932–67; Director of Suez Canal Company, 1939–57; Director of LNER

No 61251 *Oliver Bury* – (1861–1946) English railway engineer with business interests in South America; Chief Mechanical Engineer on the Great Western Railway of Brazil; General Manager of Great Northern Railway, 1902–23; Director of LNER, 1923–45

BELOW: *The nameplate of 'A4' Class 4-6-2 No 60034 Lord Faringdon. He was a railway financier and Chairman of the Great Central Railway (1889–1922).*

The lap of luxury

The decline and fall of Pullman car services on BR

Providing a luxurious form of travel Pullman cars had run on Britain's railways since 1873. The first all-Pullman train began service on the London Brighton & South Coast Railway's London Victoria to Brighton route in 1881. Carriages for these services were built at the Pullman Car Company's works in Brighton and later by Metro-Cammell and the Birmingham Railway Carriage & Wagon Company. In exchange for a supplementary charge passengers enjoyed luxurious seating with stewards providing table-service refreshments and meals.

With their distinctive brown and cream livery Pullman trains continued to run on British Railways and by the 1960s still operated from London to many destinations. In their latter years the carriages were repainted with grey livery and blue window surrounds. The last Pullman service, the 'Manchester Pullman', was withdrawn in 1993.

OVERLEAF: *Soon to be replaced by the diesel 'Blue Pullman' ex-GWR 'Castle' Class 4-6-0 No 5055 Earl of Eldon heads through Brinkworth west of Swindon with 'The South Wales Pullman', c.1960.*

BELOW: *Seen here near Brentwood in 1930, the LNER's 'Eastern Belle' Pullman train headed by immaculate 'B12' Class 4-6-0 No 8552.*

Western Region

'The South Wales Pullman'
Paddington to Newport, Cardiff and Swansea; replaced by diesel 'Blue Pullman' (1960–73)

'Bristol Pullman'
Diesel 'Blue Pullman' from Paddington to Bath and Bristol (1960–73)

Other 'Blue Pullman' services
Paddington to Birmingham and Wolverhampton LL (1960–67)
Paddington to Oxford (1967–73)

Southern Region

'Golden Arrow'
London Victoria to Dover – for Calais and Paris (ended 1972)

'Brighton Belle'
Electric multiple units London Victoria to Brighton (ended 1972)

'Bournemouth Belle'
London Waterloo to Southampton and Bournemouth (ended 1967)

'Devon Belle'
    London Waterloo to Plymouth/Ilfracombe (1947–52/54)
'Thanet Belle'
    London Victoria to Ramsgate (1948–51); renamed
    'Kentish Belle' (1951–58)
'Ocean Liner Expresses'
    London Waterloo to Southampton Docks (ended 1970s)

London Midland Region

'The Midland Pullman'
    Diesel 'Blue Pullman' from London St Pancras to
    Manchester Central (1960–67)
'Manchester Pullman'
    London Euston to Manchester Piccadilly (1967–93)

Eastern/North Eastern Regions

'The Master Cutler'
    London King's Cross to Sheffield (1958–68)
'The Queen of Scots'
    London King's Cross to Leeds, Edinburgh and Glasgow
    Queen St (ended 1964)
'Harrogate Sunday Pullman'
    London King's Cross to Bradford/Harrogate (ended 1967)
'The White Rose'
    London King's Cross to Leeds and Bradford (ended 1967)
'Yorkshire Pullman'
    King's Cross to Harrogate/Bradford/Hull (Hull portion
    became separate train 1967/ended 1978)
'Hull Pullman'
    King's Cross to Hull (1967–78)
'Tees-Tyne Pullman'
    King's Cross to Newcastle (1948–76)

Night mail

The Travelling Post Office

Mail was first carried by train on the Liverpool & Manchester Railway in 1830. Soon, the vast increase in the amount of mail led to ways of devising a sorting system on board a moving train. A converted horse box with three mail sorters, the first Travelling Post Office (TPO) ran in January 1838 on the Grand Junction Railway between Birmingham and Warrington. This was so successful that it gave rise to the Railways (Conveyance of Mails) Act later that year in which all railway companies were required to carry mail.

The introduction of the Rowland Hill's uniform Penny Post system in 1840 led to a further upsurge in business and the growth in TPOs throughout the country. By 1852 there were 39 sorting clerks employed on services as far north as Perth and as far south as Exeter. The service was so successful that by 1885 specially dedicated mail trains, with no passenger accommodation, were introduced. At its height, by the outbreak of World War I, there were over 130 TPO services across the country although this number was never achieved again. Suspended during both World Wars, the TPO saw its routes much reduced until only 43 remained when services were reintroduced in 1945. From then on it was downhill all the way – by 1988 there were 35 TPOs and in 1994 there were only 24 – and on the night of 9/10 January 2004 the last remaining services made their final journey.

Lineside apparatus to pick up and out down mail while travelling at speed was first introduced in 1838 on the London & Birmingham Railway at Berkhampsted and Leighton Buzzard (site of the 1963 Great Train Robbery). An improved version with moveable nets fixed to the train and at the lineside came into operation in 1848 – this system remained in use until 1971.

'Night Mail'

*'This is the Night Mail crossing the border
Bringing the cheque and the postal order...'*

One of the most famous documentary films ever made, 'Night Mail' starred the West Coast Postal Special TPO, its crew and 'Royal Scot' Class 4-6-0 No 6115 *Scots Guardsman* on their overnight journey from London to Glasgow. Made by the GPO Film Unit in 1936 this classic short film features music by Benjamin Britten and verse by W. H. Auden.

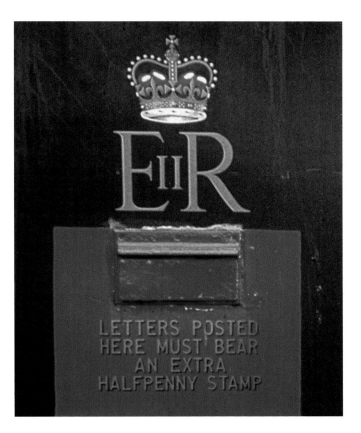

LEFT: *Ex-LNER Class 'A2/3' 4-6-2 No 60524* Herringbone *at the head of the 'West Coast Postal' TPO (Travelling Post Office) train at Carmont west of Stonehaven in September 1963. The loco was built in 1947 and withdrawn in early 1965. Carmont was the site of a fatal railway accident on 12 August 2020.*

RIGHT: *Post boxes for public use were positioned on the side of Travelling Post Office trains.*

BELOW: *As the Night Mail crossed the border at speed, mail sorters were kept busy throughout the night on Travelling Post Office trains.*

Keep fit!

A selection of walks along Britain's closed railways

Thousands of miles of railway lines were closed down following the implementation of the Beeching Report in the 1960s. Since then many ex-lines have been converted to footpaths and cycleways, the latter mainly by the charity Sustrans. Here are some of my favourites:

The West Country

The Camel Trail: Wadebridge to Padstow

The Tarka Trail: Barnstaple to Braunton; Barnstaple to Meeth

Dartmoor: Yelverton to Princetown

The Somerset & Dorset: Bath to Wellow and Glastonbury to Shapwick

The Isle of Portland

Southern England

Camber Tramway: Rye to Camber
Cole Green to Hertford
North London: Ally Pally branch
Three Bridges to East Grinstead
The Cuckoo Line: Polegate to Mayfield

Wales

Lon Eifion to Caernarfon to Brynkir
North Wales branches: Bethesda, Dyserth and Holywell
Upper Wye Valley through Rhayader and up the Elan Valley
Mawddach Trail: Barmouth Junction to Penmaenpool
Elan Valley Railway: Rhayader to Craig-Coch Dam
South Wales Mineral Railway: Briton Ferry to Glyncorrwg

Central England

Wye Valley: Tintern to Redbrook
Manifold Valley: Waterhouses to Hulme End
Monsal Trail: Topley Pike to Bakewell
North Staffs: Leek to Rushton Spencer
Wirral Way: Hooton to West Kirby
Kidsgrove to Etruria
Cromford & High Peak Trail: High Peak Junction to Dowlow
Tissington Trail: Ashbourne to Parsley Hay

*Winding around the Dartmoor tors is the trackbed of the
Yelverton to Princetown branch line which closed in 1956.
A walker passes under a granite cattle overbridge
beneath the transmitter mast on North Hessary Tor.*

Eastern England

Southwold Railway: Halesworth to Southwold

The Spa Trail: around Woodhall Spa and Horncastle

Lincoln to Fledborough

Sutton-on-Sea Branch Line Walkway

Water Rail Way: Washingboro to Woodhall Junction

Northern England

Border Country: around Kielder

Across the Fells: Keswick to Threlkeld

Yorkshire Coast: Scarborough to Whitby

Tees Valley: Middleton-on-Tees to Barnard Castle

Longdendale Trail/Trans-Pennine Trail: Hadfield to Penistone

Morecambe Promenade to Lancaster

The Mining Line: Battersby Junction to Rosedale

Hull to Hornsea

York to Selby

Low Moor to Dewsbury

Scotland

Glen Ogle: Callander to Killin Junction

The Great Glen: Gairlochy to Fort Augustus

The Waverley Route: Whitrope to Riccarton Junction

The Paddy: New Galloway to Gatehouse of Fleet

Morayshire Coast: Garmouth to Banff

The Fish Route: Dyce to Fraserburgh and Peterhead

Speyside Way: Nethy Bridge to Craigellachie

Fort William to Loch Treig

BELOW: *Lovingly restored Blacksboat station lies on the Speyside Way footpath and cycleway between Nethy Bridge and Craigellachie in Scotland.*

Southern Railway famous trains

Atlantic Coast Express

Until the GWR opened its shorter route from Paddington to Plymouth (via Westbury and Castle Cary) in 1904 there was immense competition between that company and the rival London & South Western Railway to provide the fastest service between the two cities. The latter's 11 a.m. departure from Waterloo to Plymouth was the forerunner of what became known as the 'Atlantic Coast Express' (ACE), which by 1927 under Southern Railway management contained through carriages to many destinations in Devon and North Cornwall – the name was selected in a competition organised by SR among its employees, the winner being a guard from Woking.

Trains between Waterloo and Exeter had always been forced to stop at Salisbury following a serious derailment at the station in 1906. It was here that locos were usually changed but with the introduction of the 'Lord Nelson' 4-6-0s in 1927 through running became the order of the day. However, due to the lack of water troughs on the SR, the Salisbury stop continued to be included until the end of steam to take on water and a crew change. By the outbreak of World War II the down 'ACE' consisted of through coaches to Sidmouth, Exmouth, Ilfracombe, Torrington, Bude, Padstow and Plymouth.

Southern Railway 'Lord Nelson' Class 4-6-0 No 862 Lord Collingwood departs from Salisbury with the up 'Atlantic Coast Express', c.1937.

Halted by World War II, the 'ACE' resumed service soon after the end of the war with Bulleid's new 'Merchant Navy' Pacifics in charge of the heavily loaded train as far as Exeter. Beyond this the various portions were taken on to their destinations behind his new 'Battle of Britain'/'West Country' Class Light Pacifics. By 1952 the train had become so popular with holidaymakers that it departed from Waterloo in two separate portions. During its peak in the late 1950s extra relief trains, headed by the rebuilt 'Merchant Navy' locos, were also added to cope with the amount of traffic. Timings were continually improved until 1961 when the 171¾-mile journey from Waterloo to Exeter Central was scheduled to take only 2hr 56min – this included stops at Salisbury and Sidmouth Junction.

Although increased car ownership in the early 1960s can partly be blamed on the downfall of the 'ACE' the other contributing factor came in 1963 when all lines west of Salisbury came under Western Region control. Anxious to stamp their authority on their erstwhile competitors, the end was swift and painful. The last 'ACE' ran on 5 September 1964 and soon downgraded 'Warship' diesel hydraulics took over services on what was to become a secondary route – much of the line west of Salisbury was singled and branch lines in Devon and North Cornwall, much loved by the poet John Betjeman, were closed.

'ACE' 1963 Summer Saturday timings from Waterloo

10.15 a.m. with through coaches to Ilfracombe
and Torrington

10.35 a.m. with through coaches to to Padstow and Bude

10.45 a.m. to Seaton with through coaches to Lyme Regis

11.00 a.m. with through coaches to Torrington
and Ilfracombe

11.15 a.m. with through coaches to Plymouth,
Padstow and Bude

'Merchant Navy' Class 4-6-2 No 35015 Rotterdam Lloyd *awaits departure from Salisbury with the 'Atlantic Coast Express', c.1962.*

During the late 19th century, years before the advent of air travel, the only way to travel between London and Paris was by boat train. Compared to the current Eurostar service through the Channel Tunnel, the journey was leisurely and involved a ferry journey between Dover or Folkestone and Calais. In 1906 the London Brighton & South Coast Railway (LB&SCR) introduced luxury Pullman cars and within a few years these were included in their boat trains from Victoria station. Soon after the formation of the Southern Railway in the 1923 Grouping an all-Pullman boat train was introduced and in 1929 it was officially named the 'Golden Arrow' – on the French side of the Channel the corresponding train between Calais and Paris was called 'Flêche d'Or'. In 1936 the SR built a luxury ferry, the *Canterbury*, for the sole use of its first-class passengers on the London to Paris route. The ship was also fitted with rails on the cargo deck which carried through coaches of the luxury 'Night Ferry' sleeper train between the two capitals.

The outbreak of World War II brought an end to the service, only returning again in April 1946. Bulleid's new air-smoothed 'Merchant Navy' and Light Pacific locomotives based at Stewart's Lane shed were now in charge of the train which, by 1951, had been augmented by the introduction of new Pullman cars and was temporarily renamed the 'Festival of Britain Golden Arrow'. Locomotives hauling the train were grandly adorned with a long golden arrow on each side and on the smokebox door. Two of the first batch of brand new BR Standard 'Britannia' Class '7' 4-6-2 locos, No 70004 *William Shakespeare* and No 70014 *Iron Duke*, were specifically allocated to Stewarts Lane in 1951 to haul the upgraded 'Golden Arrow', a job they continued to do until they were transferred to Longsight, Manchester, in 1958.

During the 1950s the popularity and speed of air travel between London and Paris spelt the end for this luxury train which was now made up of 1st-Class Pullman cars and standard 2nd-Class stock. Electric haulage by BR-built (Class 71) Bo-Bo locos (E5000–E5023) was introduced in June 1961 and continued until September 1972 when this famous train ceased to run.

BELOW: *Headed by Merchant Navy Class 4-6-2 No 35028* Clan Line, *the 'Golden Arrow' speeds below the white cliffs of Dover at Abbots Cliff, c.1957. This fine loco was rebuilt in 1959 and withdrawn in 1967 before being rescued from oblivion and restored to working condition.*

Return to Riccarton Junction

Britain's most remote railway community

The Border Union Railway (later known as the 'Waverley Route') between Edinburgh and Carlisle and the Border Counties Railway between Riccarton and Hexham both opened throughout on 1 July 1862. As part of the North British Railway's (NBR) empire the lines served a sparsely-populated hill-farming region on both sides of the Anglo-Scottish border. The junction between the two lines was at Riccarton, renamed Riccarton Junction in 1905, a remote and windswept spot in the Cheviot Hills that grew into Britain's most remote railway community.

As an important railway junction and interchange station the facilities at Riccarton included a two-road engine shed, turntable, coaling facilities, gas plant, smithy, two signal boxes, a carriage shed and extensive sidings for goods trains. With no road links to the junction the NBR built a railway village for its employees – drivers, firemen, shunters, cleaners, gangers, booking clerks and porters – and their families.

The railway village included the station master's house, 30 terraced houses for the workers and their families, a school and schoolmaster's house, a post office and grocery shop and a public house. At its height the population of Riccarton reached 120 people, all of whom were cut off from the outside world apart from their occasional forays by train to Hawick or Carlisle. The grocery shop, a branch of the Hawick Co-operative Society, was located on the island platform where a red telephone box was also later installed. Doctors had to travel to Riccarton by train from Hawick or Newcastleton and if hospital treatment was required the patient was sent by train to Carlisle.

Riccarton ceased to be a junction in October 1956 when the branch line to Hexham was closed and by 1963, when a forestry track was opened up to the village, the writing was on the wall for the 'Waverley Route'. In that year closure of the line was recommended in the 'Beeching Report' and with closure of the school the remaining children had to travel by train to schools in Newcastleton or Hawick. The end finally came on 6 January 1969 when trains ceased to run over the line and Riccarton Junction closed for good.

The large site at Riccarton Junction has since been overtaken by nature and most of the buildings are long gone. To the north is Whitrope, now the headquarters of the Waverley Route Heritage Association. The Association plan to eventually lay track to Riccarton Junction. From the car park at Whitrope it is possible to walk south along the trackbed for 2 miles through forestry plantations to deserted Riccarton Junction. Still inaccessible by road, Riccarton Junction is one railway pilgrimage worth making. Here the island platform has been partially restored with station nameboard and (disconnected) red telephone box. A few ruined railway buildings, including the former NBR schoolhouse, still remain and are eerily silent. To the south the trackbed leads through more forestry plantations to Steele Road where the former station building is now a private residence.

ABOVE: *The author at lonely Riccarton Junction in 2011.*

Waiting patiently to be reconnected to the national rail network and miles from anywhere, the sad remains of what was once Riccarton Junction station and its remote railway village.

Narrow-gauge Phoenix 2

The rebirth of the Welsh Highland Railway

What must be one of the most complicated stories of the life of a railway was completed in 2011 with the reopening throughout of the Welsh Highland Railway between Caernarfon and Porthmadog in North Wales.

In the beginning was the North Wales Narrow Gauge Railways Company's 1ft-11½in.-gauge line which opened between Dinas Junction, south of Caernarfon, and slate quarries at Bryngwyn in 1877. A branch to Rhyd-Ddu, on the lower western slopes of Snowdon, was opened in 1881. Despite financial problems the NWNGR acquired a Light Railway Order in 1900 to extend southwards from Rhyd-Ddu to Beddgelert, but this was never built. Another company, the long-winded Porthmadog, Beddgelert & South Snowdon Railway (PBSSR), started construction of

a line northwards from Croesor Junction, on the antiquated Croesor Tramway, to link with the NWNGR's southern terminus via Beddgelert but, although some earthworks were built, the project was soon abandoned. Some of the earthworks and a road bridge near Beddgelert can still be seen today.

The next twist in this tale came in 1921 when, with financial backing from the Government and local authorities, the Welsh Highland Railway was formed by taking over the NWNGR and what remained of the PBSSR. The missing link between Rhyd-Ddu and Croesor Junction and the relaid Croesor Tramway to Porthmadog was opened in 1923. With borrowed locomotives and rolling stock from the Ffestiniog Railway the new company struggled on until 1934 when the Ffestiniog agreed to lease the line. Despite the latter's efforts to make the line a success this was shortlived and all trains ceased to run in 1937. The line was finally lifted in 1941 and the trackbed, owned by Caernarvonshire County Council, slowly reverted to nature.

Fast forward to 2011, following 45 years of legal wrangling, volunteer effort and major funding from the Millennium Commission, European Regional Development Board, the Welsh Assembly and the Wales Tourist Board, the Welsh Highland Railway has risen like a phoenix from the ashes. Hauled by narrow-gauge Beyer-Garratt locos rescued from South Africa, trains now run from Caernarfon along the route of the closed standard-gauge line to Dinas and then south to Porthmadog via Beddgelert and the beautiful Aberglaslyn Pass, a distance of 25 miles. At Porthmadog passengers can continue their journey to Blaenau Ffestiniog on the Ffestiniog Railway, making the 40-mile journey from Caernarfon the longest narrow-gauge ride in Britain.

TOP LEFT: *Meeting at Beddgelert – Hunslet 2-6-2T* Russell, *built in 1906, and Baldwin 4-6-0T No 590, built in 1917, with their respective trains for Dinas Junction and Porthmadog, c.1925.*

LEFT: *Former South African Railways 2-6-2+2-6-2 Garratts No 87 and No 138 double head a demonstration goods train at Ynys-Fach on the Welsh Highland Railway on 3 November 2013.*

It sometimes rains in North Wales! Welsh Highland Railway trains passing at Ryhd-Ddu station on 3 November 2013. On the right ex-South African Railways Garratt 2-6-2+2-6-2s No 87 and No 138 trundle through with a demonstration goods train.

BODYSGALLEN

4 into 1 = BR

The creation of British Railways in 1948

The idea of nationalising Britain's railways dates back to the early days of the Labour Party. However, although Private Members' Bills were put forward as early as 1906, it wasn't until the Labour Party had a big enough majority in Parliament after World War II that this dream became a reality. For strategic reasons Britain's railways came under government control during World War I and in 1920 the then Minister of Transport, Sir Eric Geddes, first put forward a serious proposal to nationalise the railways. However, this plan came at the time of a post-war coalition government and sufficient support within Parliament was not forthcoming. Instead, the 1921 Railways Act created four large railway companies out of a previous total of 120 and the 'Big Four' – the GWR, LMS, LNER and SR – were created (see pages 190–91). Despite most freight and passenger traffic still being carried by rail, the grouping was not a total success and by the beginning of World War II many parts of the system were suffering from lack of investment. The railways again came under government control during World War II and when the Labour Party were elected with a landslide majority in 1945 they seized the opportunity to create their Socialist dream and nationalise Britain's run-down railways. When it was finally given the green light by Parliament the 1947 Transport Act created the British Transport Commission (BTC) to oversee the modernisation and integration of all of Britain's public transport systems. This not only included all but a few minor railways, but also all public road, canal and air transport etc. From 1 January 1948 the railways were run by a body called the Railway Executive which was, in principle, answerable to the BTC. So British Railways was born.

From the outset British Railways had one hand tied behind its back. Even before World War II railway companies were forced by the Government to carry goods at a rate set by a Parliamentary Tribunal. This Common Carrier status was continued after Nationalisation but no similar price fixing was applied to road transport which was free to undercut the railway's charges. British Railways, legal liability as a Common Carrier was not ended until 1956 by which time it was too late as road transport had by then creamed off much of the freight business.

On formation, British Railways was faced with the enormous task of not only repairing about 20,000 miles of worn-out track and associated infrastructure but also of modernising and standardising its fleet of over 20,000 steam locomotives, over 1 million goods wagons and over 55,000 passenger carriages. With a payroll of over half a million workers, the new British Railways soon placed an enormous burden on the British taxpayer. Standardisation of locomotive types soon went ahead, with 11 classes of successful standard locomotives built between 1951 and 1960, enabling BR to scrap many non-standard and ageing steam locomotives. New standardised passenger carriages and freight wagons were also introduced.

When formed, British Railways was divided into six geographical regions similar to the make-up of the old

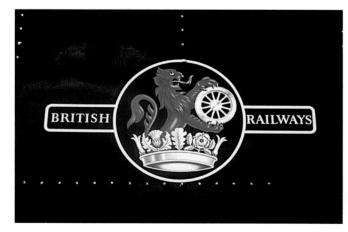

'Big Four' railway companies. Although there was some central control these regions still possessed a large amount of autonomy – a situation which did not lend itself to an integrated rail system or standardisation of equipment. Many of the old practices of the previous 'Big Four' railway companies still held sway and when the 1955 Modernisation Plan was announced some regions, in particular the Western Region, went their own way with disastrous results in later years.

FAR LEFT: *The original British Railways 'Cycling Lion' logo as used from 1948 to 1956.*

LEFT: *BR's second corporate logo as used between 1956 and 1965.*

BELOW: *BR's corporate design for station totems known as the 'sausage' or 'hot dog'. The older and rarer ones can fetch over £2,000 at railwayana auctions.*

The Muddle & Get Nowhere Railway

The long-lamented Midland & Great Northern Joint Railway

Formed in 1862, the mighty Great Eastern Railway had a virtual stranglehold on railways in East Anglia which lasted another 31 years until the formation of the Midland & Great Northern Joint Railway in 1893. As its name suggests the railway was jointly owned by the Great Northern Railway and the Midland Railway – the latter, eager to extend its sphere of influence to the towns and ports of Norfolk, saw an opportunity when the Eastern & Midlands Railway, serving King's Lynn, Fakenham, Norwich, Cromer and Yarmouth and a railway works at Melton Constable, fell on hard times in 1889.

Together with two other constituent companies, the Bourne & Lynn Railway and the Peterborough, Lynn & Sutton Bridge Railway the newly-formed M&GNJR had a route mileage (mainly single-track) of 183 miles, making it the largest joint railway operation in Britain. The company owned an assortment of locomotives but the stars of the show were certainly the 15 handsome 4-4-0s built by Beyer, Peacock between 1881 and 1888 for the former Lynn & Fakenham Railway and the later Eastern & Midlands Railway. The M&GN's locomotive livery was an attractive yellow ochre until 1922 when a new dark brown livery was introduced; passenger carriages were finished in a teak

colour. In 1936 the LNER took over the running of the railway and introduced Class 'K2' 2-6-0s and ex-GER 'Claud Hamilton' 4-4-0s to replace the ageing Beyer, Peacocks. Under British Railways the fairly new Ivatt '4MT' 2-6-0s (nicknamed 'Doodlebugs') became the mainstay of motive power on the system until closure in 1959.

As a cross-country railway the M&GNJR provided a vital connection between the Midlands and the North and East Anglia. Goods traffic in both directions was heavy, so was holiday traffic from the Midlands and the North to the seaside resorts of Norfolk during Summer Saturdays. With its long single-track sections speed was never one of the railway's main attributes and, following World War II, competition from road transport and the changing habits of holidaymakers led to a dramatic drop in traffic. In 1958, years before Dr Beeching

arrived on the scene, the British Railways Committee, looking to reduce its mounting losses, recommended complete closure of the system. Despite an outcry from local supporters the 'Muddle & Get Nowhere Railway' closed on 28 February 1959 and its loss has been mourned ever since. The only part of the system to escape was the 11½-mile Sheringham to Melton Constable section but even this succumbed to the Beeching 'axe' in 1964. Fortunately, in more recent years, the line between Sheringham and Holt has been reopened as the steam-operated North Norfolk Railway.

LEFT: *Ex-LNER Class 'D16/3' 4-4-0 No 62567 seen here at Wisbech in 1957.*

BELOW: *Ex-LNER Class 'D16/3' 4-4-0 No 62517 at Caister-on-Sea with a train full of holidaymakers returning home to Derby after a week at Yarmouth, July 1957.*

Faster and faster

Mallard's epic record-breaking run

During the 1920s and 1930s, fierce competition between publicity-seeking railway companies at home and abroad led to a rash of speed record attempts. In Britain, there was intense rivalry between the London Midland & Scottish Railway (LMS) and the London & North Eastern Railway (LNER), both of whom had competing routes between London and Scotland. Wind-cheating streamlined casings were *de rigueur* on the powerful 'Pacific' locomotives and by 1935 the LNER 'A4' Class 'Pacific' *Silver Link* had attained 112.5 mph. Not to be outdone, the LMS 'Pacific' *Coronation* achieved 114 mph just south of Crewe station on a test run of the 'Coronation Scot' express in 1937. However, the all-time world record for steam locomotives was finally achieved by the LNER on 3 July 1938 by Sir Nigel Gresley's 'A4' Class 'Pacific' No 4468 *Mallard*.

Designed for running regularly at over 100 mph, the three-cylinder design and 6ft-8in. driving wheels of Gresley's streamlined 'A4' Class 'Pacifics' were ideally suited for this record-breaking attempt. Crewed by driver Joseph Duddington and fireman Thomas Bray, the 165-ton *Mallard* together with seven coaches including a dynamometer car together weighing a further 240 tons accelerated to a speed of 126 mph on a downhill stretch of Stoke Bank between Little Bytham and Essendine. Sadly, during the speed-record attempt *Mallard* suffered from an overheated middle big end bearing and was forced to struggle back to Doncaster Works for repair.

Later claims by American railroads that they had exceeded *Mallard*'s officially recorded speed were never substantiated so the British locomotive still retains its place as the fastest steam locomotive in the world. *Mallard* continued to haul express trains on the East Coast Main Line between Kings Cross and Edinburgh until 1963 when she was withdrawn from service. She can be seen today at the National Railway Museum in York.

BELOW: *Unbeaten holder of the world speed record for steam traction set in 1938, Class 'A4' 4-6-2 No 60022 Mallard at rest at Grantham station in 1962. Fortunately this famous loco was preserved and is now part of the National Collection at the National Railway Museum in York.*

British rail speed records

Date	Locomotive	Location	Railway Company	Speed (mph)	Traction type
8 October 1829	*Rocket*	Rainhill	Liverpool & Manchester	29.1	steam
15 September 1830	*Northumbrian*	Between Parkside and Eccles	Liverpool & Manchester	36	steam
13 November 1839	*Lucifer*	Madeley Bank	Grand Junction	56.7	steam
1 June 1846	*Great Western*	Nr Wootton Bassett	Great Western	74.5	steam
11 May 1848	*Great Britain*	Nr Wootton Bassett	Great Western	78	steam
June 1854	No 41	Wellington Bank	Bristol & Exeter	81.8	steam
March 1897	No 117	Between Melton Mowbray and Nottingham	Midland	90	steam
9 May 1904	*City of Truro*	Wellington Bank	Great Western	100	steam
5 March 1935	*Papyrus*	Stoke Bank	London & North Eastern	108	steam
27 September 1935	*Silver Link*	Stoke Bank	London & North Eastern	112.5	steam
27 June 1937	*Coronation*	South of Crewe	London, Midland & Scottish	114	steam
3 July 1938	*Mallard*	Stoke Bank	London & North Eastern	126	steam
12 June 1973	Prototype HST	Between Northallerton and Thirsk	British Rail	143.2	diesel
20 December 1979	APT-P	Between Beattock and Gretna	British Rail	162.2	electric
1 November 1987	HST	Between Darlington and York	British Rail	148.4	diesel
17 September 1989	Class 91 No 91010	Stoke Bank	British Rail	162	electric
30 July 2003	Class 373 set 3313/14	Channel Tunnel Rail Link section 1	Eurostar	208	electric

The Clockwork Orange

The Glasgow Subway

Although not Glasgow's first underground railway (that distinction belongs to a 3-mile section of the Glasgow City & District Railway which opened in 1863), the Glasgow Subway is the third-oldest underground metro system in the world.

With its ornate red sandstone headquarters at St Enoch the Glasgow District Subway Corporation opened for business on 14 December 1896. It was unusual to say the least as it was built to a gauge of 4ft and trains on the 6½-mile double-track orbital railway were powered by a clutch and cable system. The two lines, burrowing under the River Clyde twice, were known as the Outer Circle and the Inner Circle and served 15 stations. Trains ran clockwise and anticlockwise respectively taking 24 minutes for a complete circuit but each line ran in a separate tunnel and the continuously moving cables were driven from a steam-powered winding station located south of the river near Shields Road station.

Until modernisation in 1977 there was no direct connection with the railway's workshops at Govan so trains requiring servicing had to be lifted off the running lines by a crane.

The original 'gripper' carriages that were used on the line were supplied by the Oldbury Railway Carriage & Wagon Company with 'non-gripper' trailer carriages supplied by Hurst, Nelson of Motherwell. The subway was taken over by Glasgow Corporation in 1923 which went on to electrify the lines in 1935 and converted the original 'gripper' carriages to operate on 600V DC collected via a third rail. Another Subway oddity was that power for train lighting came from conductor rails located on the sides of the tunnels, a system that had been installed earlier when the line was still cable powered. Amazingly these late-19th-century vehicles, some retaining their original lattice gates, remained in service until 1977 when the whole system was closed down for modernisation. Many

Glaswegians have fond memories of these old carriages as the backs of the seats were attached to the sides of the carriages while the seat itself was attached to an independently moving floor! Even members of staff wore uniforms that had been introduced in 1901.

Modernisation of this by now antiquated transport system was well overdue when the subway was closed down in 1977. Three years later it was reopened with refurbished stations and new carriages supplied by Metro-Cammell. Each train was made up of three carriages initially painted in a bright orange livery – hence the nickname 'The Clockwork Orange'. The depot at Broomloan was also refurbished and for the first time connected to the main system by rail. Nearly the entire contents of Merkland Street station were used to build a replica station in the former Glasgow Museum of Transport (now at the Riverside Museum).

Surprisingly, the Glasgow Subway system has never been expanded although there are proposals for extending the Subway to the south and west, in places using existing disused railway tunnels.

The Modern Subway Challenge: Is it possible to get off a clockwise Subway train at Buchanan Street station and get on the same train at St Enoch station? The train takes 55 seconds to travel between the two stations! Apparently someone has achieved this remarkable feat.

LEFT: *An Inner Circle train enters Partick Cross station on the Glasgow Subway, 1930s. Note the moving cables between the tracks.*

BELOW: *Nearing the end of its 80-year life before modernisation – an interior view of a passenger car on the Glasgow Subway, 16 September 1976.*

All amenities

Britain's railway hotels

The provision of hotels by railway companies in the UK dates back to the very early days of rail travel – the first was built at Euston by the London & Birmingham Railway in 1839. During the 19th century over 100 railway hotels were built, many actually adjoining the station they served such as the famous Royal Station Hotel in Hull, the Caledonian Hotel at Princes Street station in Edinburgh and the largest, the Great Western Royal Hotel at Paddington. Hotels were also opened at railway connected ports such as Dover, Newhaven, Fishguard and Holyhead, at seaside resorts such as St Ives, Morecambe, Hunstanton and Ayr and at golfing centres such as Gleneagles, Dornoch and Turnberry. The GWR's Manor House Hotel at Moretonhampstead, Devon, and the LMS's Welcombe Hotel at Stratford-upon-Avon were the height of luxury when opened in 1929 and 1931 respectively, while the Art-Deco Midland Hotel at Morecambe, designed by Oliver Hill with sculpture by Eric Gill, became an architectural icon after it was reopened in 1930.

Perhaps one of the most famous railway hotels was the Midland Hotel in Manchester which was built next to MR's Central station and opened in 1903. Regularly used by American cotton traders, within a year the hotel had a staff of 380 and paid £24,000 per annum in wages, serving 400 meals each day in the grill room and 500 meals in the French Restaurant. The famous American Bar served 450 people each day with refreshments – half of these being American 'temperance' drinks. During its first year the German Restaurant sold 80,000 special German dishes and 500,000 portions of lager beer. The Turkish Bath was visited by 180 people per week and the barber's shop by 500 customers. The hotel's bakers made 3,000 separate portions of bread each day; the laundry handled 1.5 million articles of clothes in a year. The hotel had a sub-post office which, in its first year, dispatched 50,000 telegrams and 1 million telephone messages. The building was lit by 7,200 electric lights at a cost of £6,500 per year.

By 1948 the number of railway-owned hotels had shrunk to around 35 and many of these were in a run-down state after the privations of World War II. Following Nationalisation the hotels were run at various times by the British Transport Commission, British Transport Hotels and the British Railways Board until they were individually sold off in the early 1980s. Albeit with different names, for example the Caledonian Hilton in Edinburgh, the Hilton London Paddington and the Landmark London in Marylebone, many have since been refurbished and restored to their old glory. One of the most famous, the Midland Hotel at Morecambe, has reopened its doors following years of neglect and a subsequent major refurbishment.

LEFT: *A welcome sight for passengers from East Anglia – the Great Eastern Hotel at Liverpool Street station on 8 September 1975.*

BELOW: *Waiters laying the tables in the restaurant of the North British Hotel, adjacent to Edinburgh Waverley station, c.1930.*

Gobblers, Knick Knacks and Spam Cans

Steam locomotive nicknames

In the early days of steam locomotives each was given a name, a practice derived from their rivals, the stage coaches. Then there were seldom two locomotives alike, but later, when four or five or more similar locos were built, they were referred to collectively by the name given to the first of the class, such as 'Precursor', or according to the main theme of names, for example, 'City' Class.

While the names of steam locomotives is a fascinating subject in itself the nicknames they were given is probably more interesting. One perfect example is the class of 2-4-2 tank locomotives designed by T. W. Wordsell for the Great Eastern Railway in 1883. These locos had an enormous appetite for coal and were duly nicknamed 'The Gobblers'. The 0-6-0 passenger tanks of the Great Eastern were called 'Jubilees' because they made their first appearance in 1897, the year of Queen Victoria's diamond jubilee.

Also on the Great Eastern section, the 999 class of 0-6-0 goods engines were known as 'Waterburys' because when running with steam shut off the motion made a noise which resembled the sound of a ticking clock – the Waterbury Clock Company had been making fine clocks in Waterbury, Connecticut, since 1857. Locos of a larger class of the same type on the Great Northern section were called 'Knick Knacks' for a similar reason, while the corresponding class on the old Great Central were called 'Pom Poms', from the sound of their exhaust beat.

The Great Central 'Atlantics' built at the beginning of the 20th century were considered so graceful that they were referred to as the 'Jersey Lilies', after the celebrated actress Lily Langtry. Also on the Great Central, what became the standard R.O.D. (Railway Operating Department) 2-8-0 during World War I, Robinson's Class 8K were so large in comparison to other locos of that period that they became affectionately known as 'Tiny'.

Nicknames could also vary widely between engine shed locations, loco crews and railway enthusiasts. The Southern Railway along with its constituent companies had its fair share of locomotive nicknames, not all of them complimentary! Stroudley's diminutive 'A1' and 'A1X' 0-6-0 tanks were known widely as 'Terriers'; Marsh's 'C2x' 0-6-0s were known as 'Dromedaries'; Drummond's C14 2-2-0 tanks were 'Potato Cans'; Stroudley's 'E1' 0-6-0 tanks were 'Sea Sick Tanks'; many classes of Marsh's 4-4-2 tanks were '*ankers'; Bulleid's unrebuilt 'Pacifics' were appropriately named 'Spam Cans' and his austerity 'Q1' 0-6-0s had various names such as 'Biscuit Tins', 'Coffee Pots' and 'Frankensteins' while his innovative 'Leader' class were called 'Chinese Laundries'.

There were, of course, numerous other nicknames or abbreviations given to steam locomotives. Classic examples known to railway enthusiasts of the 1950s and '60s include 'Brits', '9Fs', 'Black Fives', 'Dub Dees', 'Crabs', 'Jubes', 'Pats', 'Semis', 'Lizzies', 'Streaks' etc., etc. The diesel era ushered in even more nicknames, most of them unmentionable, but we will draw a veil over that!

One of the most common locomotives on the London Midland and Scottish regions of British Railways were Stanier's Class '5' 4-6-0s, nicknamed 'Black Fives'. Here No 44707 heads a long goods train through Newton Stewart station on the 'Port Road' between Dumfries and Stranraer, 17 April 1965. This remote and scenic line closed less than two months later.

The 'Tiddley Dyke'

The Midland & South Western Junction Railway

Affectionately known as the 'Tiddley Dyke' (although the reason for this is lost in the mists of time), the Midland & South Western Junction Railway was formed in 1884 by the amalgamation of two existing railway companies – the Swindon, Marlborough & Andover Railway and the Swindon & Cheltenham Extension Railway.

However, nearly 40 years previously, a proposal for the grandly named Manchester & Southampton Railway had been put before Parliament by the London & Birmingham Railway. With its chief engineer Robert Stephenson, the L&BR saw this new railway as an important north–south artery leaving the Midland Railway's Bristol to Birmingham mainline at Cheltenham Lansdown and joining the London & South Western Railway at Romsey. Despite the backing of the Midland Railway and the London & Birmingham Railway and progressing through two sessions of Parliament the proposal was eventually thrown out in 1848.

Another 36 years elapsed before the southern section of what later became the M&SWJR opened for business. This was the single-track Swindon, Marlborough & Andover Railway (SM&AR) which opened throughout (apart from Grafton to Marlborough) between Red Posts Junction at Andover and Rushey Platt at Swindon in 1884. However, there was a little difficulty at Marlborough as the missing link between Grafton and the town failed to be built due to a shortage of funds. Until 1898 trains had to travel via a short link with the GWR's branch from Savernake which had already opened in 1862 – the GWR insisted that passengers wanting to change at Savernake had to use GWR trains from Marlborough!

To the north of Swindon the single-track Swindon & Cheltenham Extension Railway was authorised in 1881. However only the section from Rushey Platt to Cirencester Watermoor had been completed by 1883 when the company ran into financial difficulties. A year later the company amalgamated with the SM&AR to form the Midland & South Western Junction Railway – the missing link northwards from Cirencester to Andoversford was completed in 1891. At the northern end the M&SWJR had obtained running rights over the GWR's Cheltenham to Kingham line between Andoversford and Banbury Line Junction at Cheltenham. Here their trains terminated at the Midland Railway's Lansdown station.

Now more or less complete but nearly bankrupt and in the hands of a receiver, the M&SWJR was saved from oblivion when Sam Fay, seconded by the London & South Western Railway, was appointed Secretary and General Manager in 1892. During his seven-year tenure Fay turned the ailing M&SWJR into a thriving concern, opening a locomotive, carriage and wagon repair works at Cirencester, completing the missing link between Grafton and Marlborough and obtaining running powers over the LSWR's 'Sprat & Winkle Line' between Andover and

Midland and South Western Junction Railway.

GENERAL MANAGER'S OFFICE,
SWINDON, WILTS,

August 22nd, 1911.

RAILWAY STRIKE.

As there has been no occasion to resort to a ... this Railway, and as the differences

In consideration of which the Directors have pleasure in granting time-and-a-half to the Station, Running and Permanent Way Departments for Friday and Saturday last.

The employes may rest assured that the Commission of Inquiry shall be carefully followed with a view to protecting their interests in regard to any recommendations which the Commission may make affecting the conditions of service of railway employes.

JOHN DAVIES,
General Manager.

Redbridge. By the time Fay had left in 1899 (soon to become General Manager of the Great Central Railway) trains could travel from the North and Midlands over Midland Railway metals to Cheltenham then via the M&SWJR and the LSWR to Southampton – one weekday train which carried through carriages between Liverpool Lime Street and Southampton travelled via the M&SWJR, although the total journey time of 7hrs 10min via this meandering north–south route must have been tedious for passengers.

Providing a link between military centres such as Tidworth and Ludgershall on Salisbury Plain and Southampton Docks, the M&SWJR naturally saw heavy use during the South African Wars and World War I. Racehorse traffic in the Marlborough area, milk traffic north of Swindon and pigeon trains from the North were also important in the railway's early years. However, at the 'Big Four Grouping' of 1923, the M&SWJR became part of the Great Western Railway. The company's 29 locomotives, products of Dübs, Sharp, Stewart and Beyer, Peacock, were 'Swindonised', three 2-4-0s even surviving into the British Railways era. By the 1950s services had become very reduced with only one through train each weekday running between Cheltenham Lansdown and Southampton Central, the 94½-mile journey taking around 4 hours to complete. In 1958 this train was diverted to run into Cheltenham (St James) station

(the option for changing trains at Lansdown was now lost) and the regular but unusual sight of a SR 'Mogul' and its short train of SR green carriages at the station can be well remembered by the author. By then the writing was on the wall for this delightful rural line and it closed on 10 September 1961.

Survivors

Despite closure 50 years ago parts of the M&SWJR live on:

- The Swindon & Cricklade Railway now operates steam trains along a mile of track each side of Blunsdon station, north of Swindon.
- Much of the trackbed between Cricklade and Marlborough is now a footpath and cycleway forming part of National Cycle Network Route 45.
- The section of line between Red Posts Junction at Andover and Ludgershall remained open for military traffic to Tidworth Camp until 2015.

LEFT: *The leaflet given to the employees of the Midland & South Western Junction Railway offering time-a-half pay to them during the railway strike of 1911.*

BELOW: *Built by Dübs & Co in 1894, 2-4-0 loco No 1336 was the sole survivor of three ex-M&SWJR locos that passed into British Railways' ownership. It is seen here in all its 'Swindonised' glory at Reading shed shortly before withdrawal in 1954.*

War service

Foreign service for Britain's railways in the First World War

The Railway Operating Division (ROD) of the Royal Engineers was formed in 1915 to operate both standard-gauge and narrow-gauge railways in theatres of conflict during World War I.

War Department Light Railways

By 1915 both sides in the bloody 'Great War' had ground to a halt, digging in with a trench system that stretched from the English Channel to the Swiss border.

Supplying the front line from the nearest standard-gauge railhead was fraught with difficulties with early lorries proving useless in the mud-soaked and shell-blasted landscape. Horses, used in their hundreds of thousands, were the only answer for pulling artillery, ambulances and supply wagons. However, at the beginning of the war they were in short supply and nearly a million had to be bought from overseas for service with the British Army.

Prior to the war both the Germans and French had developed lightweight 60cm-gauge light railways that could quickly be laid and provide a flow of equipment and stores to the front line. On the British side the Royal Engineers had decided in their wisdom that motor

Built for service in France during the First World War, Baldwin Class '10-12-D' 4-6-0PT No 608 was repatriated from India, restored, and can now be found at work on the Ffestiniog Railway.

lorries would be more effective – how wrong they were and it wasn't until 1916 that the Minister of Munitions recommended the use of tactical light railways.

By 1917 the War Department Light Railways were using narrow-gauge 4-6-0 tank locomotives, supplied mainly by Hunslet, Kerr, Stuart, ALCO and the US company Baldwin. These were successfully used in rear areas moving supplies from standard-gauge railheads to marshalling yards nearer the front. From here supplies were moved to the front line by small and unobtrusive 0-4-0 petrol tractors mainly supplied by the Motor Rail & Tramcar Company – around 1,000 Simplex tractors, some of them armoured, saw active service during the war.

Following the end of the war some Baldwin 4-6-0 locomotives saw service on four British narrow-gauge railways – Ashover Light Railway, Glyn Valley Tramway, Welsh Highland Railway and Snailbeach District Railway. An example that once served in India has been preserved on the Leighton Buzzard Narrow Gauge Railway.

Railway Operating Division of the Royal Engineers

As the two opposing sides in the war ground to a bloody halt the French standard-gauge railway system became increasingly incapable of handling the vast amounts of ammunition and supplies needed to sustain the Allied front line. By 1916 the ROD had already started to requisition locomotives and rolling stock from British railway companies for use, not only in France but also further afield in Mesopotamia, Greece, Palestine, the Balkans and Italy. Around 600 locos (mainly 0-6-0 goods locos) and thousands of wagons were sent abroad from the South Eastern & Chatham Railway, London, Brighton & South Coast Railway, London & South Western Railway, Great Western Railway, London & North Western Railway, Midland Railway, Lancashire & Yorkshire Railway, Caledonian Railway, North Eastern Railway, Great Central Railway, Great Northern Railway, Great Eastern Railway, and North British Railway. It must have been a strange sight for soldiers seeing GWR 'Deans Goods' or 'Moguls' working freight trains in Northern France. Despite a few being lost at sea most of these locos survived the war and were either sold to the host nation or returned home.

As the war dragged on the demand for heavy freight locos outstripped supply so the ROD adopted the Great Central Railway's Class '8K' 2-8-0 as its standard freight locomotive. Designed by John Robinson, the 521 locos were built in various batches by the GCR, North British Locomotive Company, Robert Stephenson, Nasmyth, Wilson and Kitson.

These powerful freight locos were so successful that when they returned home after the war many were bought by the GWR (100), LNER (273) and LMS (105). A few even went to Australia where three of them have since been preserved.

Many of the ROD 2-8-0s were called up again during the Second World War, seeing active service in Egypt, Palestine, Syria and Iraq. Many British examples survived into the BR era with the last being withdrawn in 1966. Only one, No 63601, has been preserved.

BELOW: *Midland Railway double-framed 0-6-0s worked in France and Italy during the First World War. They were eventually returned to Derby where ROD 2727 is seen in the early 1920s.*

Index

Acknowledgements

t = top; b = bottom; l = left; r = right; m = middle

Photo credits
Alamy: 4/5 (Lewis Grimwood); 64 (John Henshall);
    162 (KGPA Ltd); 177b (Islandstock); 209 (Chris Cole);
    230/231 (Ian Rutherford)
Ben Ashworth: 6/7b
Mike Ashworth Collection: 176
Henry Casserley: 242; 249; 251
Colour-Rail: 8 (R Tibbits); 9 (K Nuttall); 10 (T Owen); 11; 13; (T Owen);
    14; 18; 19 (T Owen); 22; 23 (E Russell); 24; 26 (D Forsyth): 27 (M Chapman);
    30 (D Ovenden); 32; 35; 36 (A Price); 38 (T J Edginton); 39 (P Wells);
    41 (T Owen), 46; 47; 49tr (P J Chancellor); 49br; 51; 52/53 (T Owen);
    54; 59 (National Railway Museum); 60 (David A Lawrence); 61 (G H Hunt);
    65 (T Owen); 66; 67 (M Chapman); 69 (D Forsyth; 70 (D Preston);
    72 (R Patterson); 73 (T Owen); 79; 80; 81mr (A Price); 81b; 82 (T Owen);
    84b (P Lubliner); 86; 87 (G H Hunt); 89 (T Owen); 90 (Tony Cooke);
    91 (R Patterson); 93; 97 (T Owen); 101; 102 (T Owen); 103; 106 (P Moffatt);
    107 (C Hogg); 108 (T Owen); 109b; 110 (T Owen); 111; 115 (D Preston);
    118; 124 (T Owen); 125; 127; 130 (R Patterson); 136 (P Hughes);
    137; 138/139; 141; 142; 145 (D L Dott); 146 (David A Lawrence);
    147t; 147b (D Ovenden); 148; 149; 151b (N Browne); 154;
    158/159b (D Preston); 159t (K Fairey); 161; 168 (C C Herbert); 170; 171b (P Hughes);
    175 (B Swain); 176/177; 186; 188/189 (Tony Cooke); 200 (T Owen);
    202/203; 206; 210 (P Hughes); 211 (M J Reade); 213; 214/215 (M J Reade);
    216 (C Leigh-Jones); 217bl (T Owen); 217br (T Owen);
    218 (S P Sutton); 219; 220/221 (G Warnes); 222 (D Hepburne Scott);
    223tr (Stephenson Locomotive Society); 227; 228; 229 (G H Hunt);
    236bl; 236br; 237 (David A Lawrence); 238; 239 (E Alger);
    240 (C Banks Collection); 243; 244 (D L Dott); 246/247 (R Tibbits);
    250 (Max Birchenough)

Terence Cuneo/Science Museum Group: 179; 193
Gordon Edgar: 134/135; 160; 194/195; 196/197; 204/205; 232/233b; 234/235
Mike Esau: 167
John Goss: 78; 166; 199; 201
Julian Holland: back cover; 7tr; 16/17; 20; 25; 26br; 27bl; 31; 44br; 50; 52b; 53b; 54tl;
    55; 58; 74/75; 98; 99; 109tr; 112; 116/117; 119tr; 119bl; 119br; 123tr; 123br; 128;
    129tr; 129b; 132tl; 140; 145bl; 150br; 155; 171tr; 198; 201bl; 224/225; 226;
    231tr; 248
Gavin Morrison: 156/157; 184/185; 187; 212
Rob Rowland: front cover
Science Museum Group: 28; 29; 37; 42/43; 44bl; 45; 48; 56; 57; 62; 63; 76; 84t;
    94/95; 96; 104/105; 113; 114bl; 114br; 120/121; 121tl; 121tr; 126; 131bl; 131br;
    132/133; 143; 150; 151tr; 152bl; 152br; 153; 165; 169; 172; 178; 180; 181;
    182/183; 184bl; 190bl; 190br; 191l; 191tr; 192; 207; 208; 245
Unknown: 21; 71; 77; 83; 100; 144; 177tl; 177tr; 223b; 232t

Every effort has been made to trace the copyright holders; if any have been
overlooked, please contact us at the address on page 2.

With thanks for research assistance and advice to:
Gordon Edgar

Front cover:
Brief Encounter at *Severn Bridge*, by Rob Rowland. In this late 1950s' scene
ex-GWR 'Castle' Class 4-6-0 No 4085 *Berkeley Castle* passes under the arches
of the Severn Railway Bridge with a late afternoon train heading north on the
South Wales mainline from Cardiff to Gloucester. High above an ex-GWR '1400'
Class 0-4-2T passes sedately over the viaduct with a local train from Berkeley
Road to Lydney.